P9-AQV-408

The Aging Network

Programs and Services

Fifth Edition

Donald E. Gelfand, PhD

Springer Publishing Company

LIBRARY
UNIVERSITY OF ST. FRANCIS
JOLIET, ILLINOIS

Copyright © 1999 by Springer Publishing Company, Inc.

All rights reserved

No part of this publication may be reproduced, stored in a retrieval system, or transmitted in any form or by any means, electronic, mechanical, photocopying, recording, or otherwise, without the prior permission of Springer Publishing Company, Inc.

Springer Publishing Company, Inc.
536 Broadway
New York, NY 10012-3955

Cover design by Janet Joachim
Acquisitions Editor: Bill Tucker
Production Editor: Jeanne Libby

99 00 01 02 03 / 6 5 4 3

Library of Congress Cataloging-in-Publication Data

Gelfand, Donald E.
    The aging network : programs and services / by Donald E. Gelfand.
— 5th ed.
        p.   cm.
    Includes bibliographical references and index.
    ISBN 0-8261-3058-5 (hardcover); 0-8261-3057-7 (softcover)
    1. Aged—Services for—United States.   I. Title.
HV1461.G44   1998
362.6'0973—dc21   98-28249
                                                                                    CIP

Printed in the United States of America

362.6
G314
5ed

Contents

Preface to the Fifth Edition   *vii*

Introduction   *ix*

PART I. The American Elderly and Programs

1 The Older American   3

2 Legislative Bases for Programs and Services   11

PART II. Income Maintenance Programs

3 Age, Employment, and Income Maintenance   29
   Jules Berman and Donald E. Gelfand

4 Illness, Medical Care, and Income Maintenance   45
   Jules Berman and Donald E. Gelfand

PART III. Programs for the Aged

5 Information and Assistance   61

6 Health and Mental Health   69

7 Transportation   82

8 Crime and Legal Assistance Programs   91

9 Employment, Volunteer, and Educational Programs   111

10 Nutrition Programs   123

PART IV. Services for the Aged

11 Multipurpose Senior Centers   139

12 Housing   154

13 In-Home Services   179

14 Adult Day Care   192

15 Long-Term Care Residences   204

16 Challenges for the Aging Network   224

Appendix: National Nonprofit Resources Groups in Aging   233

Index   *239*

Preface to the Fifth Edition

There has been no fundamental change in the configuration of aging services in the United States during the 1990s. Instead, service providers and researchers in the field have been preoccupied with clarifying the balance between services provided by agencies and the enormous quantity of services provided by families and friends of older Americans. In addition, the field of aging has had to struggle to maintain funding for services. This is particularly true of health services provided through Medicare.

The Older Americans Act authorization expired in 1995, but reauthorization ran into the press of other issues considered more important by Congress. As of January 1998, Congress has not reauthorized the Act. Whenever this reauthorization occurs, it is clear that it will not provide for any innovative approaches but only for refinements in existing programs.

As in previous editions this volume provides information on regulations of such programs as Medicare and Medicaid, but no effort is made to cover every aspect of every program and service. My intent is to highlight the primary components of specific programs and services and to emphasize the most recent and important changes. Although positive or negative aspects of existing programs and services are mentioned, a comprehensive evaluation of all income maintenance, health, and aging network programs is beyond the scope of this volume.

The last authorization of the Older Americans Act forms the basis of most of the discussion. Many of the publications available from the organizations listed in Appendix A provide additional details about programs at the federal, state, and local levels.

I am grateful to the staff of Springer Publishing Company for their support in the development of this volume. I am particularly grateful to my wife, Katharine, for her patience during the process of preparing this edition.

Detroit, 1999

Introduction

The problems facing practitioners working in the field of aging are numerous. First, they have to constantly confront their own attitudes about aging. Second, they have to acquire skills in a field that is by nature complex and interdisciplinary. Third, unlike practitioners and students in the 1950s or 1960s, they have to gain an understanding of what seems to be a myriad of programs and services; many of which seem to crosscut each other. Similar efforts often appear to be available under different governmental or private auspices. This complexity is related to the primary organization of the American federal system along functional lines such as education, employment, housing, and transportation. Agencies dedicated to population groups, such as children or the aged, are both smaller and very recent in organization.

The experiences of the 1970s and 1980s reinforce the sociological axiom that there are unanticipated consequences to every policy initiative. In the field of aging, one of the consequences has been the development not of a seemingly clear-cut continuum of programs and services, but rather what can be drawn almost as a maze.

The last half of the 1980s appeared dedicated to simplifying the complexity of obtaining access to these programs for older persons. There still remain problems of fragmentation and lack of coordination, or even communication, among various service providers. The most important effort of the 1980s was probably the development of mechanisms that "channel" individuals into services that best meet their needs by having a central intake system at the local level, or the development of a case management approach. This approach has continued into the 1990s with an emphasis on relating formal services to informal services, particularly in relation to caregiving for impaired older persons. With this emphasis, it is necessary for providers and students to have a clear understanding of existing programs and services and how they can intermesh and operate more efficiently.

Throughout this volume the reader will find an effort to clarify the goals, target populations, and important components of specific programs and services. Each chapter also outlines the background, past and present funding, and variations in these programs and services as they are delivered to older populations across the country.

ORGANIZATION OF THE BOOK

Part I focuses on the present status of older Americans and the general thrust of programs and services in aging. After a brief glimpse at the characteristics of older adults in Chapter 1, Chapter 2 moves into an extensive examination of federal legislation authorizing programs and services for the aged. The major emphasis is on the provisions of the Older Americans Act.

In Part II, the complex but crucial topic of income maintenance programs is explored, including both the burgeoning private pension plans and major public programs such as Social Security, Supplemental Security Income, Medicare, and Medicaid.

Part III provides readers with details on major programs in aging, ranging from information and referral efforts to crime prevention programs throughout the United States.

Part IV moves on to a discussion of the enlarging service delivery systems for the elderly, including senior centers, the growing in-home services, and adult day care centers. This part concludes with an examination of the always controversial but important nursing homes.

Having discussed the myriad efforts that fall under each of these headings, Chapter 16 provides an opportunity to reflect on the factors that have allowed for such rapid development of these programs and services and their probable future.

Part I

The American Elderly and Programs

The end of the 1980s probably saw an end to any rapid expansion of programs and services for the American older population. Rather than being stereotyped as sick and unable to care for themselves, the older population was being portrayed as stereotyped "greedy geezers." Obviously, neither stereotype is completely valid. By examining relevant statistical data, Chapter 1 reviews the current status of the aged in the United States in a perspective helpful to the planning and development of programs.

The groundwork having been laid, Chapter 2 plunges into an in-depth examination of the programs and services for the aged. The focus is on program authorizations and funds emanating from the Older Americans Act and on related programs stemming from a variety of federal and state legislation. The complexity of existing legislation will be quickly evident to the reader, but an understanding of the titles and acts discussed is imperative for the student and practitioner planning to work in the field of aging.

1

The Older American

THE ELDERLY POPULATION

Before we examine any programs, some attention must be paid to the number and characteristics of older Americans. This foundation should enable the reader to assess critically the specific programs and services discussed in the remaining chapters of this book. Rather than viewing characteristics statically, the focus will be on the changing status of the elderly during the 20th century.

Size of the Population

Few people are surprised to learn that the number of Americans is growing, but the rapid growth even exceeds 1988 projections by the U.S. Census Bureau. The American population of 255 million is now expected to reach 275 million by the year 2000 and 383 million by 2050, a 50% increase over 60 years (Pear, 1992). From a population of 33.5 million in 1995, the population over the age of 65 is expected to increase to 39.4 million individuals by the year 2010. The biggest increase will be visible between 2010 and 2030, when the proportion of older persons in the United States will grow to 69 million, a 75% increase (Siegel, 1996). In 2030, Americans over the age of 65 will account for 20% of the population.

Men born in 1995 could expect to live 73.2 years and women 79 years. The longer life expectancy of women than men is expected to last into the 21st century. These life expectancy figures hide some important intergroup differences. Minority elderly still have lower life expectancy rates than White elderly: Black males born in 1995 have a life expectancy 9 years shorter than White males born that year, and Black females have a

3

6 years shorter life expectancy than their White counterparts. Hispanic males and females born in 1995 have a longer life expectancy than White males (74.9 years vs. 72.5 years for men, 82.2 years vs. 79.3 for women). The shortest life expectancy is found among American Indians. A 1997 Centers for Disease Control and Prevention report contained positive news. Life expectancy for Black males born in 1996 increased to a record of 66.1 years, for Black women to 74 years, and for White males to 73.8 years. These figures also represent a reduction in the gap in life expectancy between Whites and Blacks (Centers for Disease Control and Prevention, 1997).

As could be expected from the increasing life expectancy figures, the median age of the population will also be rising. In the year 2000, the median age in the United States will be 35.5 years. The "youngest" group will be Latinos with a median age of 27 years. Asians/Pacific Islanders will have a median age of 31.4 years; American Indians, Eskimos, and Aleuts, 27.6 years; and African Americans, 29.9 years. Whites will be the "oldest" group, with a median age of 36.6 years (U.S. Bureau of the Census, 1996). These differences in median age are related to differentials in birth rates among the various ethnic populations, as well as the impact of immigration on American population growth. Immigration accounted for one-third of population growth in the United States in 1995 (Day, 1995)

Perhaps more important than life expectancy at birth is the life expectancy of individuals who reach the age of 65 and 85. In 1995, men who reached the age of 65 had an average life expectancy of 15.5 more years, and women 19.2 years. At age 85, the average life expectancy for men was 5.2 years and for women 6.8 years (Siegel, 1996). By the year 2050, the life expectancy for men at age 65 will be 20.3 years, and for women, 22.4 years. The life expectancy at age 85 will be 6.8 and 9.4 years for men and women, respectively. Based on these figures, the growth of the population in their 70s and 80s is not surprising. Some scientists, however, argue that age 85 is the upper limit for life expectancy (Olshansky, Carnes, & Cassel, 1990).

There were already 12 million persons over the age of 75 in the mid-1980s. The over-85 population will increase from approximately 3.6 million individuals in 1995 to 5.7 million in 2010 and 8.5 million by 2030. The result of this increase is that the population over the age of 85 will have grown from 1.4% of the population in 1995 to 4.65% of the population in 2050 (Siegel, 1996).

The proportion of African American and Latino elderly in the American population will continue to grow in the next century. By 2050, African American elderly will comprise 14% of the older population, as opposed to 8% in 1990. Assessing the growth of elders from minority backgrounds, Siegel (1996) estimates that between 1995 and 2010 the numbers of

African American elderly will grow by 26.2%, but the number of Latino elderly will grow by 89.2%. Although Latino elderly were only 4% of the older population in 1990, their numbers will increase to 14% of this age segment by 2050. The population of Asian/Pacific Islanders, Native Americans, Eskimos, and Aleuts will grow by 103%, but their actual numbers are much smaller than those of African Americans and Latinos. All of these sharp increases are in contrast to the expected 14% growth rate among Whites during these 50 years.

Health Status

The major problems of older persons are not acute illnesses, but chronic conditions that affect their functioning. Problems in functioning are usually assessed on the basis of the relative inability of the individual to carry out basic Activities of Daily Living (ADLs: bathing, dressing, feeding oneself, reaching and using the toilet, and transferring between bed and chair). The Instrumental Activities of Daily Living (IADLs) include the ability to perform household tasks such as meal preparation, housecleaning, money management, shopping, getting around in the community, and using the telephone. The proportion of older persons who cannot perform the ADLs is not increasing. Researchers at Duke University have thus estimated that the number of seriously disabled older adults increased by only 800,000 between 1992 and 1994, and could drop by 100,000 individuals by 2004 (Koretz, 1997). Siegel (1996), however, focuses on the ratio of disabled elderly in the overall population. Based on the current ratio of older adults with some disability, he projects that the number of disabled older persons will triple by 2040 (Siegel, 1996). In 1995, 23% of Americans over age 65 had some difficulty with ADLs and 28% with the IADLs.

A large proportion of problems in functioning among older persons stems from chronic conditions, the most common of which are arthritis (32/100 persons), hypertension (34/100 persons) heart disease (32 /100 persons), hearing impairments (29/100 persons), cataracts (17/100 persons) orthopedic impairments (16/100 persons), sinusitis (15/100 persons), and diabetes (10/100 persons) (American Association of Retired Persons, 1996).Beyond the pain associated with a condition such as arthritis, the impact on older persons may include difficulty in feeding themselves, cooking, taking medicines, or even walking. The other conditions listed above can also have a major impact on the daily lives and activities of older people. As the American population continues to age, the prevalence of other diseases may dramatically increase. One example of this change is the 17% increase in diabetes between 1980 and 1987, a change explained in large part by the increase in the number of older persons.

TABLE 1.1 The Living Arrangements of Americans Age 60 or Older by Race and Ethnicity *(Percent)*

Ethnic Group	Living Alone	Living With Spouse Only	Living With Spouse, & Kin	Living With No Spouse, Kin Present	Living With Non-kin	Institution-alized
Total	24.5	45.7	12.3	11.8	2.6	3.2
White	24.9	48.8	10.8	9.8	2.3	3.3
Black	26.7	21.6	17.9	25.9	4.8	3.1
Hispanic	16.2	27.3	26.3	24.3	4.3	1.6
Asian	10.0	25.9	33.8	25.5	3.6	1.2
Native American	23.9	30.2	19.2	20.7	3.6	2.3

Source: 1990 U.S. Census of Population.

LIVING PATTERNS

There are now 1.5 million nursing home beds in the United States, but the over-65 population in nursing homes still represents less than 6% of the total number of older American adults. The vast majority of older Americans want, and will continue to maintain, their residence in the community (American Association of Retired Persons, 1996).

One of the most striking statistics of recent years is the increasing proportion of older individuals who are maintaining their own households. Among older individuals over the age of 60, one quarter were living alone in 1990, and 46% were living only with a spouse. Table 1.1 provides an indication of the differences in living arrangements among major ethnic groups in the United States

The data in Table 1.1 indicate differences in the percentage of Latino and Asian elderly living alone compared to White and Black elderly. Minority elderly are also much more likely to live with a spouse and with a relative. While longevity accounts for the overall percentage of older persons living alone, living alone also requires reasonably stable financial resources. In part, these resources can be provided by a combination of Social Security benefits, Supplemental Security Income (SSI), or private pensions. The number of elderly living alone also reflects the dispersal of families over a wide area. Poorer families consistently live closer to their elderly relatives. It has also been shown that family income is positively related to the use of long-term care residences for elderly parents. Poorer families who cannot afford nursing home care are thus more likely to have an older family member living with them.

During the 1970s and 1980s, rural states, such as Iowa, Arkansas, and Missouri, had high proportions of elderly. In these states, younger families have moved to more urbanized regions and have not been replaced by any significant numbers of new residents. Although a proportion of the elderly have joined in the migration to the suburbs, many suburban residents have grown old in their neighborhoods. Thus, 40% of the White elderly in metropolitan areas were living in the suburbs in the 1980s as compared to one third in 1960 (U.S. Senate, 1982). As research continues to show, older people tend to remain in communities where they have lived for a long period of time. Between 1982 and 1983, only 4.9% of older persons moved, compared with 16.6% of all age groups (U.S. Senate, 1986). This "aging in place" phenomenon has produced a new situation. There are now more older people living in suburban communities (46%) than in central cities (30%) (American Association of Retired Persons, 1996).

Cultural Backgrounds

Although many senior advocacy groups speak out against stereotyping, there is a continued tendency to discuss the elderly as a homogeneous group whose values and beliefs are defined by their age. In reality, the cultural backgrounds among the present generation of individuals over 60 are enormously varied. In 1960, 4.2 million of the American elderly had been born overseas. This group had declined to 3.7 million in 1970, comprising approximately one seventh of the population over 60 (Fowles 1978).

It is difficult to obtain accurate tallies of older individuals born overseas because the United States now has many illegal as well as legal immigrants. A 1995 estimate was that there were one million legal immigrants over the age of 65 in the United States (Friedland & Pankaj, 1997). More important than the absolute numbers is the increased diversity resulting from the entry into the United States of substantial numbers of Latinos from Central and South America and Asians from Korea, China, Cambodia, India, Laos, and Vietnam, as well as Haitians and Caribbean Islanders. Although Latinos and Asians tend to have a relatively young median age, demographic data indicate an increase in the proportion of elderly among each of these groups. Differences in cultural attitudes toward aging and utilization of services, as well as a lack of fluency in English among foreign-born elderly, may create problems for providers attempting to implement aging programs.

Education

The minimal educational background of many present-day elderly also creates problems for service providers, who must understand that many present-day older adults possess limited verbal, writing, and reading skills. Programs that involve extensive reading and discussion may thus not be practical for many elderly. At a more basic level, many elderly will have difficulty understanding and following instructions on medication, and may utilize their medication improperly. As the differentials in educational background between the elderly and the general population become less distinct, these problems will abate. The improvement in educational background is already evident if data for the period from 1970 to 1994 are examined. During this period the percentage of persons over the age of 65 who had completed high school rose from 28% to 62%. There are still substantial differences in the educational backgrounds of White and minority elderly. Among older Whites, 65% had graduated from high school in 1994, while only 37% of African American elderly and 30% of Latinos had high school diplomas (American Association of Retired Persons, 1996).

Employment and Income

Recent changes in American work patterns have not been of major benefit to many American and foreign-born elderly. The inability of these older adults to obtain higher education during the early 1900s relegated them to careers as blue-collar workers. Men and women whose work has centered around low-paying jobs have meager financial resources for their old age. Low wages have meant low Social Security benefits and inadequate or nonexistent pensions. Part-time and intermittent work has prevented many women from accumulating enough "quarters" to qualify for Social Security.

Many of the elderly being served by present-day programs are individuals with limited ability to pay for costly programs. Income maintenance programs such as Supplemental Security Income (SSI), Medicare, food stamps, and housing subsidies have helped to raise the income floor of the elderly. In 1995, only 10.5% of individuals over age 65 fell below the federal poverty level, but this figure does not adequately convey the income problems faced by minority elderly. Among older Blacks, 25% were living below the federal poverty level, as were 24% of older Hispanics. These figures contrast with the 9% of White elderly who are below the official poverty level (American Association of Retired Persons, 1996). In 1997, the federal poverty level was $7,890 for one person; $10,610 for two persons; $13,330 for three people, and $16,050 for four people. A study of households with one member over the age of 70 found that minority households have much less "wealth" than

Whites: "For every dollar of wealth an older White household has, Black households have 26 cents, and Hispanic households have a third as much wealth as their White counterparts" (Smith, 1997, p. 77).

Although their status has been improved on many fronts, the elderly still suffer from a variety of deficits which require the assistance of formal and informal interventions. After examining the existing programs and services, I will return in Chapter 16 to a discussion of the challenges faced by the aging network attempting to provide these programs and services.

REFERENCES

American Association of Retired Persons (1996). *A profile of older Americans*, Washington, DC: Author.

American Society on Aging. (1991). *Serving elders of color: Challenges to providers and the aging network*. San Francisco: Author.

Cantor, M. (1991). Family and community: Changing roles in an aging society. *The Gerontologist, 31*, 337–346.

Centers for Disease Control and Prevention. (1997). *Births and deaths, U.S., 1996*. Hyattsville, MD: National Center for Health Statistics.

Day, J. (1995) *Sixty-five plus in the United States*. Washington, DC: U.S. Department of Commerce, Economics and Statistics Administration.

Fowles, D. (1978). *Some prospects for the future elderly population*. Washington, DC: Administration on Aging.

Friedland, R., & Pankaj, V. (1997). *Welfare reform and elderly legal immigrants*. Menlo Park, CA: Henry J. Kaiser Family Foundation

Leon, J., & Lair, T. (1990). *Functional status of the noninstitutionalized elderly: Estimates of the ADL and IADL difficulties*. Rockville, MD: Agency for Health Care Policy and Research.

Himes, C., Hogan,D., & Eggebeen, D. (1996). Living arrangements of minority elderly. *Journals of Gerontology, 51B*, S42–S48.

Koretz, G. (1997, July 17). Growing old gracefully. *Business Week*.

Logan, J., & Spitze, G. (1988). Suburbanization and public services for the aging. *The Gerontologist, 28*, 644–652.

Olshansky, S., Carnes, B., & Cassel, C. (1990). In search of Methuselah: Estimating the upper limits to human longevity. *Science, 250*, 634–650.

Pear, R. (1992, December 4). New look at the U.S. in 2050: Bigger, older and less white. *New York Times*, pp. A1, 10.

Siegel, J. (1996). *Aging in the 21st century*. Washington, DC: National Aging Information Center.

Smith, J. (1997). Wealth inequality among older Americans. *Journals of Gerontology, 52B*, 74–81.

Soldo, B., & Agree, E. (1988). America's elderly. *Population Bulletin, 43*(3) (entire issue).

Stone, L., & Fletcher, S. (1988). Demographic variations in North America. In E. Rathbone-McCuan & B. Havens (Eds.), *North American elders* (pp. 9–34). Westport, CT: Greenwood.

U.S. Bureau of the Census (1990). *The need for personal assistance with everyday activities: Recipients and caregivers.* Washington, DC: U.S. Government Printing Office.

U.S. Bureau of the Census, (1996). *Current Population Reports: Population projections of the U.S. by age, sex, race and Hispanic origin: 1995 to 2050.* Washington, DC: U.S. Government Printing Office.

U.S. Senate, Special Committee on Aging (1982). *Developments in aging, 1981: Part I.* Washington, DC: U.S. Government Printing Office.

U.S. Senate, Special Committee on Aging. (1986). *Developments in aging, 1985: Part III.* Washington, DC: U.S. Government Printing Office.

U.S. Senate, Special Committee on Aging, American Association of Retired Persons, Federal Council on the Aging, & U.S. Administration on Aging. (1991). *Aging America: trends and projections.* Washington, DC: Author.

2

Legislative Bases for Programs and Services

The present generation of elderly benefits from the "categorical" programs, designed to serve all individuals who fall into a specifically defined group (in this case older adults) and from generic programs that benefit all age groups. In this chapter, we will intensively review the legislation underlying existing aging programs. After highlighting the important legislation, we will examine other sources of programs and services for the aged and the major funding mechanisms underlying these services. Our attention will focus on the legislative initiatives and programs formulated at the federal level and implemented by state and local governmental units.

The major influence on programs for older adults has been the Older Americans Act (OAA) initially passed by Congress in 1965. Many of the features of the Act were influenced by the 1961 White House Conference on Aging. The Act has been amended 11 times; the eleventh amending of the Older Americans Act was signed into law by President Bush and reauthorized the OAA through fiscal 1995.

The 1992 amendments added a large number of possible initiatives to the activities of the Administration on Aging. There is also an increased specificity throughout the amendments on the need of state and local providers to target their efforts toward the most "needy" older individuals, including needy minority elderly. It is important to note that a unique element of the Older Americans Act has been that all authorized programs and services are offered free of charge to the client. During the late 1980s, there was sentiment on the part of many provider agencies for initiation of "cost-sharing" on the part of clients based on their incomes. The agencies assert that cost-sharing would increase their income and allow them to expand more programs and services. Other groups believe that cost-sharing would

11

stigmatize OAA programs and reduce the participation of many elderly, particularly minority elderly (Gelfand & Bechill, 1991). This chapter will examine the basic thrust of each of the titles of the OAA and compare important changes in the 1992 amendments with previous versions of the Act. The specifics of individual programs and services are provided in subsequent chapters.

THE OLDER AMERICANS ACT

Purpose of the Act

The basic purpose of the Older Americans Act is to "help older persons" by providing funds to the states for services, training, and research. All three of these activities are to be coordinated through the Administration on Aging (AoA). As part of a reorganization plan, the Office of Human Development Services was abolished in 1991. The Administration on Aging was a major component of this Office. As a result of the reorganization, the AoA became an independent agency that reports directly to the Secretary of the Department of Health and Human Services.

TITLE I: OBJECTIVES

In 1965, the goals of the OAA were couched in sweeping language which encompassed 10 difficult but laudable objectives:

1. An adequate income
2. The best possible physical and mental health
3. Suitable housing
4. Full restorative services
5. Opportunity for employment without age discrimination
6. Retirement in health, honor, and dignity
7. Pursuit of meaningful dignity
8. Efficient community services when needed
9. Immediate benefit from proven research knowledge
10. Freedom, independence, and the free exercise of individual initiative (Butler, 1975, p. 329)

In 1978, a new stress was placed on the provision of community services that enabled the older person to make a choice among a variety of subsidized living arrangements. In 1987, objective 7 was altered to emphasize the participation of older persons in "meaningful activities" and objective 10 was expanded to guarantee "protection against abuse, neglect and exploitation." The 1992 amendments expanded objective 4 to not only include impaired elderly, but also to support services for the caregivers of impaired elderly.

The target population of the OAA was originally individuals over the age of 65. In 1973, this was changed to the age of 60 without extensive opposition in Congress. Part of the logic in the reduction of the eligible age was that the programs and services developed under the Act's provisions would assist older individuals in preretirement planning. A review of the Act's history and titles reveals that the Administration on Aging has become responsible for the operation of an extensive service delivery program for older people (Gelfand & Bechill, 1991).

TITLE II: ADMINISTRATION ON AGING

A direct outcome of the enactment of the OAA was the organization of the Administration on Aging. Directed by the Assistant Secretary of Aging, AoA is charged with carrying out the provisions of the OAA. The Assistant Secretary is appointed by the President and confirmed by the U.S. Senate.

As can be seen by even a quick perusal of the OAA, the responsibilities of the AoA are extensive. They range from providing information on problems of the aging to planning, gathering statistics, setting policies, and coordinating ongoing efforts in aging at federal and local levels with private and public organizations. The data-gathering responsibilities of the AoA were increased by the 1987 OAA amendments. These responsibilities include gathering information on services funded, individuals served, and the extensiveness of support by the Area Agencies on Aging for elderly with the greatest economic and social needs, particularly low-income minority elderly, low-income elderly in general, and frail older persons. This latter group would include individuals with mental as well as physical handicaps.

The 1978 OAA amendments outlined a role for the AoA as an advocate of aging programs throughout the federal government (Sec. 202a). Sections 202 and 203 also stressed the importance of the Assistant Secretary's intervention in a variety of planning, regulatory, and coordinating activities.

Recent reauthorizations of the OAA stress the Assistant Secretary's role and responsibility to consult with other federal agencies concerned with programs that have an impact on the elderly. The 1992 amendments establish an Office of Long-Term Care Ombudsman Programs within the Administration on Aging. The mandate of this office is to recommend policies regarding ombudsman programs. One staff person is also to be designated by the Assistant Secretary as a Nutrition Officer responsible for the administration of all nutrition programs funded through the OAA. In addition, the

Act authorizes the establishment of a National Center on Elder Abuse and a National Aging Information Center.

TITLE III: GRANTS FOR STATE AND COMMUNITY PROGRAMS IN AGING

Title III is the most important component of the Older Americans Act. This title outlines the types of services that should be provided at the local level in order to develop "comprehensive and coordinated services" enabling older adults to maintain "maximum independence" (Sec. 301). The basic foundation for providing these services is an agency designated by the governor of each state with responsibility for aging services. In many states, this agency has been a newly formed Office on Aging. State offices on aging are not always provided with a mandate to oversee all aging programs; some remain within already established departments. In 28 states, the Office on Aging is part of a human services department, while in another 21 states the Office on Aging is independent.

The agency designated by the governor is responsible for the development of a 3-year statewide plan for serving the elderly. Geographic service areas must be designated by the agency, and local Area Agencies on Aging (AAAs) must be established. Within each of these areas, the state agency has latitude in outlining geographic service areas. In many states, these areas have coincided with health and mental health planning units.

The AAA develops its own 3-year service plan, which must be submitted for approval by the state agency. An area agency can be a unit of county, city, or town government or even a private nonprofit agency. Preference must be given to an already established Office on Aging. In 1990 approximately 680 AAAs were already in existence across the country. In 13 states, the state agency is also the AAA.

Since its original passage, the categories of services that need to be addressed in an AAA service plan have grown. The 1987 amendments added disorders related to Alzheimer's Disease, the 1992 amendments add case management as an appropriate service. The State and AAA plan must set "specific objectives" [306a(5)(A)(I)] to identify a variety of older individuals who need services, rural elderly; older individuals with greatest economic need; older individuals with greatest social need, with a particular emphasis on low-income minority elderly; severely disabled elderly; elderly whose ability in English is limited; and older persons suffering from Alzheimer's and related disorders. The area plan must demonstrate coordination of services provided through the AAA and services provided through other agencies, including community action agencies.

In the 1975 amendments, four priority areas were noted: transportation, in-home services, legal services, and home repair and renovation programs. In 1978, the three priority areas were access services (transportation, outreach, information, and referral); "in-home services" (homemakers, home health aides, visiting, and telephone reassurance efforts); and legal services. In 1987, the OAA required that the area plan demonstrate coordination of in-home, access, and legal services with ongoing activities of other community organizations working with Alzheimer's Disease patients and their families. In 1992, case management was classified as an access service.

Supportive Services

Supportive services as defined in the Act include a wide range of programs, ranging from health care efforts to transportation, housing assistance, residential repairs, and an ombudsman program designed to "investigate and resolve complaints by older individuals who are residents of long-term care facilities" (Sec. 307). The 1981 amendments also authorized a number of new initiatives, including efforts formerly undertaken by other federal agencies. These efforts include crime-prevention and victim-assistance programs, the installation of security devices, job counseling programs, and the Senior Opportunities and Services Program (formerly operated by the Community Services Administration), which focused attention on the poor elderly.

The 1992 amendments added a number of supportive services to the already substantial list. These include translation services for non-English speaking elderly, representation in guardianship cases, counseling for older individuals who provide care to adult children, expanded types of therapies, expanded counseling in regard to various types of insurance, "lifestyle changes, relocation, legal matters, leisure time, and other appropriate matters," support services for family members caring for older individuals needing long-term care, services for individuals who are currently, or may become, guardians, and services that will "encourage and facilitate interaction between school-age children and older individuals. . ." [Sec. 313]. If the need for funds is less for supportive services than for nutrition, states could transfer 30% of supportive service funds to nutrition programs in FY 1993. This figure was reduced to 25% for FY 1994 and 1995 although the AoA Assistant Secretary can approve additional transfers of 5%.

In 1981, the Senate introduced an amendment to the OAA requiring specific state programs for geographically concentrated groups of non-English speaking elderly. A full-time AAA employee was to be assigned to provide counseling, as well as information and referral, to non-English speaking older persons. This staff member would also have the responsibility of ensuring that local service providers are "aware of cultural sensitivities and

. . . take into account effectively linguistic and cultural differences" [Sec. 307(a)(20)].

Nutrition Programs

Until 1978, nutrition programs comprised Title VII of the Older Americans Act. In 1978, Title VII was deleted and reclassified as Section C of Title III. While in 1978 the Act stressed the provision of congregate meals, the 1981 amendments asked for increased flexibility only, noting that primary consideration be given to congregate meals settings but allowing an AAA to award a grant to an organization that provided only home-delivered meals. Another major change was the restriction by Congress on the diversion of funds earmarked for nutrition to supportive services such as recreation, information, and assistance or counseling. The ability to use funds for supportive services that was part of the 1978 amendments was important in allowing nutrition programs to expand their efforts. Congregate programs accept donations, and home-delivered meals programs are permitted to charge for their services based on income levels in the community. The funds obtained by these charges can be used for supportive services and to facilitate access of the older person to the meal sites. The 1992 amendments include a new initiative to offer school-based meals for older persons who volunteer in schools, and fund intergenerational, social, and recreational programs for older volunteers [Sec. 316]. OAA funds can be used to pay 85% of the costs of these meals or for intergenerational activities that involve older people and students. Under the 1992 OAA amendments, 30% of the nutrition funds could be transferred between congregate and home-delivered meals. Waivers for limited additional transfers can be approved by the Assistant Secretary.

Senior Centers

In 1981, Title V dealing with multipurpose senior centers (first included in the 1973 amendments) also became part of Title III. The 1981 amendments again recognize that the multipurpose senior center is not a separate service entity, but rather a "community facility" for organizing and providing the gamut of social and nutritional services authorized by the OAA. In 1978, the House-Senate conferees were unwilling to authorized separate funding for multipurpose senior centers. This unwillingness represents the viewpoint that centers are part of the social services delivery network of the state and its AAAs (U.S. House of Representatives, 1978). In fact, Title III stresses that "where feasible, a focal point for comprehensive service delivery" should be created with "special consideration" given to "designating multipurpose senior centers as such focal point" [Sec. 306(a)(3)]. The AoA is authorized to make grants to the states for construction, acquisition, and renovation of buildings usable as senior centers. Mortgages for these centers can be insured by HHS, and social services funds can be used for the centers' operating costs.

Although the exact amount of funds expended for each of these Title III activities will vary from state to state, the 1987 amendments required that the state plans specify a minimum percentage of funds that each AAA must spend on each service and program. In addition, documentation is now required from AAAs on how service providers will meet the needs of low-income minority aged. In this effort, service providers must attempt to provide services to low-income minority elderly in proportion to their representation in the population of older adults in the area. Thus, if low-income minority elderly are 10% of the elderly population in an area, 10% of the services providers' funds should be targeted to their needs.

Additional Programs and Services

Besides the supportive and nutrition services already mentioned, a number of new elements were added in 1987 to Title III. These include in-home services for frail elderly and their families [Sec. 341], funds for services such as transportation designed to meet the "special needs" of older individuals [Sec. 351], and disease-prevention and health-promotion services [Sec. 361]. The 1992 amendments include an extensive list of 12-disease prevention and health-promotion services that range from health assessments and screening through nutritional counseling, physical fitness and dance, music, and art therapy. Supportive activities for caregivers of frail elderly are a new component of the 1992 OAA amendments, but reflect the increased focus on families as well as older individuals. These activities involve training, technical assistance, and information.

TITLE IV: TRAINING, RESEARCH, DISCRETIONARY PROJECTS AND PROGRAMS

Title IV has been a mainstay of training and research efforts in the field of aging. This includes efforts of state and local governments as well as a variety of public and private organizations. Under Title IV-A, diverse training projects have been funded, including short-term training courses, in-service institutes, and seminars and conferences. Concern about a shortage of trained personnel to serve the aging is growing in Congress, and the 1978 amendments encouraged a coordinated approach to expanded training activities, especially training directed at serving minority elderly.

Since 1965, Title IV-B research priorities have reflected changing concerns in the field of aging. In recent years, the research priorities have reflected the government's interest in problems faced by family caregivers as well as in dissemination of information about programs for older persons. Increased emphasis has also been placed on the funding of projects conducted by AAAs and state units of aging.

As was true of previous enactments, the 1992 amendments authorize a substantial number of demonstration and research efforts. Among them are special programs in long-term care, demonstration projects of multigenerational programs, supportive services in federally assisted housing, transportation demonstrations that improve the mobility of older persons, demonstration programs for older persons who have developmental disabilities, ombudsman programs in publicly assisted housing, demonstrations that provide information and counseling about retirement and pension benefits, and demonstrations on how increased resources from non-federal funds can be obtained for aging programs. An interesting innovation is the "Neighborhood Senior Care Program," which aims to increase the number of professionals who volunteer their time to older local residents who are at risk of being placed in hospitals or nursing homes.

TITLE V: COMMUNITY SERVICE EMPLOYMENT

Title V of the 1981 OAA was formerly Title IX, originally added to the OAA in 1973. The stress in Title V is on coordination of projects underway in a variety of state, federal, and private agencies. The title also attempts to delineate the role of groups that contract to provide community service employment for older adults. As in the past, the priority recipients of community employment services are individuals over 55 who are unemployed or whose prospects for employment are limited. Individuals with an income equal to or less than the intermediate budget for retired couples developed by the Bureau of Labor Statistics are eligible for Title V programs. The OAA also stresses second-career training in "growth industries and in jobs reflecting new technological skills" [Sec. 502(e)(2)].

TITLE VI: GRANTS FOR NATIVE AMERICANS

This title authorizes funds for Indian tribes to develop social and nutritional services for the aged if Title III programs are not already providing adequate services. The enactment of a separate title on Indian elderly represents an enlargement of the 1975 amendments to the OAA, which encourage states to directly fund Indian tribes interested in providing services to the elderly if these services are not already available. In 1987, OAA amendments explicitly recognized the needs of older Alaskan natives and Native Hawaiians as well as programs and services needed by older Native Americans. The amendments also strengthened the role of native tribal organizations in the provision of services and provided guidelines for application for and use of Title VI funds (Sec. 614). A similar section (Sec. 623) relates to funding for Native Hawaiians.

TITLE VII: VULNERABLE ELDER RIGHTS PROTECTION ACTIVITIES

This new Title VII was adopted in 1992, but some of its components were formerly included in Title III. Title VII has four major components: The "State Long-Term Care Ombudsman Program" [Sec. 712]; "Programs for Prevention of Elder Abuse, Neglect and Exploitation" [Sec. 721]; "State Elder Rights and Legal Assistance Development" [Sec. 731]; and "State Outreach, Counseling and Assistance Program for Insurance and Public Benefits" [Sec. 741]. These sections reflect concern that older people do not receive the benefits to which they are entitled, as is certainly the case with the Supplemental Security Income program. The title thus aims to "expand State responsibility for the development, coordination, and management of statewide programs and services directed toward ensuring that older individuals have access to, and assistance in securing and maintaining, benefits and rights" (Congressional Record, 1992, p. 8989). In addition to the funds authorized for the different parts of this title, $5 million for fiscal 1992 and "such sums as necessary" are authorized for organizations involved in protecting the rights of vulnerable Native American elderly [Sec. 751].

In the effort to assist AAAs and other state agencies in understanding issues related to the rights of older people, the state has to appoint a focal point for state-level policy review, analysis, and advocacy on these issues. Personnel who will be involved with these issues must be designated, including a "State legal assistance developer." The State Outreach, Counseling and Assistance Program will help older individuals compare available Medicare supplemental policies and obtain those benefits to which they are entitled. The program will also help older people compare life insurance, other insurance, and pension plans. When needed, the program will help the individual obtain benefits and refer the older client to legal assistance when appropriate.

FUNDING OF AGING PROGRAMS

Prior to 1973, funding for aging programs and services was minimal. Gold (1974) has characterized the programs and services supported in the 1960s as community demonstrations. The passage of the Nutrition Services Act in 1972 was thus a major breakthrough in its focus on large-scale direct services for the elderly. Until 1981, Congressional appropriations for activities under the OAA had increased dramatically, enabling the implementation of a wide range of programs and services.

During the 1980s, federal funds appropriated for Title III-B programs increased by only 10%. In FY 1990, Congress appropriated only 74% of the funding authorized by Congress (Kutza, 1991). This funding gap has forced states and localities to increase their financial support for many programs and services authorized through the Older Americans Act. Table 2.1 shows the appropriations for OAA programs in fiscal 1997.

Geographic Funds

A crucial element in the development of aging programs and services is the formula used by individual states to distribute funds they receive from the federal government. The percentage of minority elderly, poor elderly, and individuals over age 75 have all been common elements in intrastate formulas. As a United States General Accounting Office study (1990) noted, the Administration on Aging did not officially approve or disapprove particular state formulas, and there was a large diversity of formulas. These formulas came under scrutiny when a Florida court ruled that the state's formula was discriminatory. The 1992 OAA amendments require that intrastate formulas be developed in consultation with Area Agencies on Aging and in accordance with guidelines set by the AoA Assistant Secretary. AoA must also approve all intrastate formulas.

The formulas must take into account the distribution of older people in the state, as well as the geographic distribution of older persons with "the greatest economic need and older individuals with greatest social need, with particular attention to low-income minority old individuals" [Sec. 305(a)(2)]. Each state must specify how it will meet the needs of low-income minority elderly in each local area.

"Economic" and "social" need are more precisely defined in the 1992 amendments than they had been in earlier OAA authorizations. "Economic need" is defined as an income below the federal poverty line. "Social need" can be caused by a variety of factors that include

(a) physical and mental disabilities; (b) language barriers; and (c) cultural, social, or geographical isolation, including isolation caused by racial or

TABLE 2.1 Older Americans Act Appropriations: Fiscal 1997 (Dollars in Thousands)

OAA Title	Activity	$ Amount
III-B	Supportive Services & Centers	300,556
	Nutrition Services:	
III-C-1	Congregate Meals	365,535
III-C-2	Home-Delivered Meals	105,339
III-D	In-home Services—Frail Elderly	9,623
III-F	Preventive Health Services	15,623
IV	Research/Training Demonstration	4,000
V	Senior Community Service/Employment	463,000
VI	Grants to Indian Tribes	16,057
VII	Grants to States for Protection of:	[See Note 1 below]
	— Ombudsman Services	0
	— Prevention of Elder Abuse	0
	— Insurance and Benefits Counseling	0
	— Federal Council on Aging	0
	Program Direction	14,975
	Total, AoA (excludes Title V)[2]	**830,168**

[1] Title III-B-1 includes earmarks of $4,4449 million for Ombudsman and $4,732 million for Elder Abuse.
[2] Title V is administered by the Department of Labor.

ethnic status that (i) restricts the ability of an individual to perform normal daily tasks; or (ii) threatens the capacity of the individual to live independently. [Sec. 102]

Local Area Agencies on Aging must indicate the extent to which they have been able to serve older persons who fit these criteria.

Block Grants

Funds to support programs for the elderly are available through many federal agencies besides the Department of Health and Human Services. A large proportion of these funds are not specifically targeted for elderly groups, but allow the elderly to be considered as an eligible population.

Decisions on allocation of these funds increasingly are made at the local level. This is characteristic of General Revenue Sharing, Community Development, and the new block grants enacted in fiscal 1982. As opposed to categorical grants, block grants distribute funds directly to the state. States are allowed to utilize these funds for specific broad areas, but with little federal regulation and reporting. Among the initial block grants enacted in FY 1982 were the Alcohol/Drug Abuse and Mental Health block grant, the Social Services block grant, the Energy Assistance block grant, and the Community Services block grant. These contained funds that could be used to support programs for older persons. The Reagan Administration expressed a strong interest in including other programs within the block grant framework.

In 1981–82, federal regulations for block grants specified only that a public hearing be held concerning the allocation of block grant funds, and that a report be sent to the federal government explaining how the block grant funds would be targeted on the basis of need. No specific evaluation on the effectiveness of distributed funds was planned. In specific programs, some "strings" were attached to the block grants by Congress. In the Alcohol/Drug Abuse and Mental Health block grant, states were expected in FY 1982 to continue to fund mental health centers at a "reasonable" level, and the funds could not be shifted among the three programs of this block grant until 1982. The block grants thus offered the states and local communities increased flexibility to determine program and population priorities; that is, whether the elderly are a group requiring special attention and funding.

The Social Services block grant is a replacement for Title XX of the Social Security Act. In 1974, Title XX was included in the Social Service Amendments to the Social Security Act, replacing Titles IVA and VI. Title XX funds were distributed according to the size of the state's population. The state was required to design a package of services and define the eligible population. Among the services for the aging that received funding in various states under Title XX were adult day care, foster care, homemaker services, nutrition programs, senior centers, protective services, services in long-term care residences, and funds for comprehensive community mental health centers.

Despite the seeming comprehensiveness of this list, the number of programs and services for the elderly funded under Title XX was limited. This limitation resulted from federal requirements that states fund at least a specific group of "mandated services" and a ceiling that Congress placed on Title XX allocation.

Federal mandated services included adoption, day care for children, early periodic screening, diagnosis, and treatment of chronic and potential illnesses, employment counseling, family planning, foster care for children, information and referral, protective services for abused and neglected spouses and children, and services to the disabled, elderly, and blind. These required services were deleted from the block grant, but there is still a strong feeling in many states that Title XX was originally designed to provide services to children because of its origins in Titles IVA and VI of the Social Security Act.

Title XX had five goals:

1. To help people become or remain economically self-supporting
2. To help people become or remain self-sufficient
3. To protect children and adults who cannot protect themselves
4. To prevent and reduce inappropriate institutionalization
5. To arrange for appropriate placement and services in an institution when this is in an individual's best interest (State of Maryland, 1978)

In order to avoid rancor in distribution of block grant funds, many states have chosen to maintain these goals. Funds to help older people pay home energy bills are available through the Low Income Energy Assistance Program. Individuals are eligible if their income does not exceed 150% of the federal poverty level of 60% of the median income of the state. In 1997 the federal poverty level was $7,890 for one person, $10,610 for a two-person household, $13,330 for three people and $16,050 for a four-person household.

The Community Services block grant replaces the programs formerly operated under categorical grants by the Community Services Administration and allows the states to allocate funds to Community Action Programs in local areas or fund other agencies for poverty programs. Congress appropriated $490 million for the Community Services Block Grant (CSBG) in FY 1997. The CSBG can provide education, employment and housing assistance, and emergency food assistance for individuals, including low-income older persons.

Community Development Block Grants (CDBG) are earmarked for improvement of substandard physical facilities and housing and expanded economic opportunities for low- and middle-income individuals. Of these funds, 75% must be spent by the local community in low- or moderate-income deteriorated areas. Priorities of CDBG include the elimination of slums and blight and the meeting of urgent community development needs. In FY 1995 CDBG funding was $4.6 billion. In Montgomery County, Maryland, CDBG funds are used in public-private partnerships through which private agencies or businesses receive funds to deliver important services to eligible individuals.

The additional services in Title III, and the Title IV demonstrations, reflect the burgeoning number of issues currently under discussion in the field of aging, particularly caregiving issues, legal rights, and elder abuse. One important change is the perceived need to not only provide services to older people, but also to the individuals who assist them. The increased specificity about greatest needs, and the requirement that the Assistant Secretary of Aging approve the intrastate funding formula, indicate a concern that programs and services are not equitable in their distribution. Whether the new specificity will guarantee more equitable distribution of funds and services is a task for the evaluation of the 1992 amendments.

The implementation of the Older Americans Act, through a variety of existing and new programs and services, is what is now termed the "aging network." The structure of this informal network (Figure 2.1) includes both federal, state, and local organizations that provide important programs and services for older people.

REFERENCES

Butler, R. (1975). *Why survive: Being old in America*. New York: Harper and Row.
Congressional Record. (1992). H.R.2967, 102 Congress, 2nd session, 138 Congressional Record, No 130, Part II.
Gelfand, D., & Bechill, W. (1991). Older Americans Act: A 25 year review of legislative changes. *Generations, 15*, 19–22.
Gold, B. (1974). The role of the federal government in the provision of social services to older persons. In F. Eisele (Ed.), *Political consequences of aging Annals, 415*, 55–69.
Kutza, E. (1991). The Older Americans Act of 2000: What should it be? *Generations, 15*, 65–68.
State of Maryland, Department of Human Resources. (1978). *Proposed FY 1979 Title XX Comprehensive Annual Services Plan*. Annapolis, MD: Author.
United States General Accounting Office. (1990). *Older Americans Act: Administration on Aging does not approve intrastate funding formulas*. Washington, DC: U.S. Government Printing Office.
United States House of Representatives. (1978). *Conference report No. 95–1618: Comprehensive Older Americans Act Amendments of 1978*. Washington, DC: U.S. Government Printing Office.

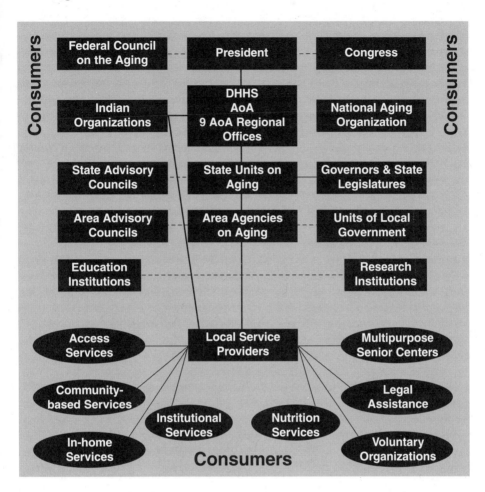

FIGURE 2.1 National aging services network.
Source: Administration on Aging, (n.d.).

LIBRARY
UNIVERSITY OF ST. FRANCIS
JOLIET, ILLINOIS

Part II

Income Maintenance Programs

The system of income maintenance in the United States is a complex, fragmented one. Responsibility is divided among all the units of government and the private sector. The system, if it can be called one, was created step by step over a period of many years. Programs were created or modified, and occasionally abandoned, as circumstances arose or changed. A prime example of incrementalism, the system is an illustration of block-by-block building to meet recognized need, often without careful consideration of the impact of the new developments upon existing programs.

The present system of income maintenance is characterized by program distinctions made on the basis of:

- *Governmental responsibility.* Some programs are federally operated, others are operated by the states, and some are operated privately.
- *Financing.* Appropriations from the general revenues of government, both federal and state, finance some programs. Others are financed out of reserve funds created by insurance premiums.
- *Relationship to the work force.* Some programs are limited to those who have an attachment to the work force, while others are available without such connection.
- *Eligibility.* There are some universal programs with no means test. Others are limited to those who pass a means test, with the test varying from program to program.

- *Participant contribution.* Some income maintenance programs are financed in part from contributions or taxes imposed upon the individual. Others are financed by payments made by the employer or from governmental tax revenues.

The consequences of the interplay of these factors are not only confusion in grasping what the system includes, but also revelation of the weaknesses in the system. There is some duplication of coverage, and there are also gaps and omissions. There are serious variations in the level of adequacy of payments among the programs. Although some elements in the overall system are well financed, others are less secure. A number of programs operate in obscurity, thus limiting their utilization by many potential clients.

Elements in the U.S. income maintenance system will be reviewed here from the point of view of the resources available to help older people. The programs will be considered in terms of governmental response to the risks to which people are exposed, which include:

- Growing old without adequate income
- Being unemployed and without income
- Being ill and unable to work in order to support oneself and one's dependents
- Being ill and unable to pay for medical care

Chapter 3 will focus on the risks of inadequate income for the elderly. The role of income maintenance programs in periods of illness and existing medical care coverage programs will be the focus of Chapter 4.

3

Age, Employment, and Income Maintenance*

GROWING OLD WITHOUT ADEQUATE INCOME

The risk of becoming old and being unable to work is one of the most serious situations that people face. While many older people retire from employment voluntarily, the tendency is for people to remain employed for as long as possible. Older workers who become unemployed because of obsolete skills, or because companies go out of business or consolidate, very often do not find another job. These workers are thus less able to plan their entry into retirement than are those who have been steadily employed.

Historically, the aged have been recognized as in need of help, as evidenced very early by the enactment of poor laws. In the 1920s, the impact of the rigorous poor law was eased by the introduction of the Old-Age Pension, a means-tested program of aid usually available at age 70. These programs were liberalized and incorporated into the Social Security Act (SSA) of 1935 in the form of grants to the states for old-age assistance. The SSA also established the Old-Age Benefit Program. Since it was apparent that it would be several years before that program would actually provide benefits, the means-tested program was the major source of income for the elderly.

Progressive liberalizations in the retirement provisions of the Social Security Act have resulted in that being a primary source of income for many aged since 1951. The old-age assistance program gradually diminished in size, to the point that it provided assistance for only a small

* This chapter and Chapter 4 were written for the 1st and 2nd edition of The Aging Network by Jules Berman, Professor Emeritus, School of Social Work, University of Maryland.

proportion of the aged. In 1974, the old-age assistance program was federalized and merged with similar programs for the blind and disabled as part of the Supplemental Security Income (SSI) program.

A succession of favorable actions by the Congress, combined with the growing interest of industry, have resulted in an enormous growth in private pensions. Today they play a significant part in the retirement plans of a large number of people.

Before these programs are examined in greater depth, it is important to view them in relationship to each other. The old-age benefit program under the Social Security Act is generally considered the basic program. Not only is the program broad in its coverage, but the rights that are accumulated under the program are "portable;" that is, the rights are cumulative throughout one's lifetime and are carried from one employer to another. Social Security has become the cornerstone of protection in old age. Although benefits are increasing in adequacy and will assure future beneficiaries of about 44% of their preretirement income, the amount will inevitably fall short of what many people will need or want in their retirement years. It is at this point that the private pension system enters the picture.

The government has acted to encourage the growth of private pensions with a view toward provision of income in addition to Social Security benefits. Social Security was never intended to provide benefits which were measurable against a specific standard of adequacy. The adequacy of Social Security income is obviously improved when combined with private pensions. Employers are now encouraged to establish private pension programs. Workers are given an opportunity to negotiate with employers in the establishment of such plans. Indeed, under rulings of the National Labor Relations Board, employers are required to bargain in good faith with their employees, not only over hours and wages, but also in regard to their pension plan.

In recent years, further steps have been taken by the Congress to encourage the growth of private pensions. The self-employed have been able, since the 1950s, to establish their own retirement plans, the so-called Keogh plans. Even persons working for others have been able to set up their own Individual Retirement Accounts (IRAs) to supplement Social Security benefits in retirement. The tax reform legislation of 1981 made it possible for any person, to set up an IRA whether or not that person is included in a private pension plan of an employer.

With the establishment of the SSI program, the federal government has finally tackled the difficult problem of minimum adequacy. In 1997 the federal government assured the aged of $484 income per month ($726 for a couple living together). This amount could consist of an SSI supplement to Social Security or other income, or it could all be the SSI payment. The figures given above are indexed to the cost of living and are adjusted annually, as are basic Social Security benefits.

Old-Age Benefits

The entire Social Security program is work-related. Individuals are eligible for benefits only if they have been in employment (or self-employment) or are dependent upon one who has been so employed. Specific requirements concerning the length of employment and the kind of work must be met in order to qualify for benefits. The basic requirements for Social Security are the same for all programs—old-age benefits, survivor's benefits, and disability benefits—and are only slightly modified for medical benefits. The basic requirement involves 40 quarters, or 10 years, of work in "covered employment." In 1992, $570 income earned an employee a quarter's credit Social Security. Employers must still identify the quarters in which the work occurred. This makes it slightly more difficult to obtain credit for work performed at low wages.

The 40 quarters that are needed in order to be eligible for Social Security can be accumulated over a period of a lifetime. "Covered employment" has been broadly defined to include all work performed as an employee in commerce or industry or in self-employment. Work in certain government operations or nonprofit organizations is also included, if a particular agreement has been made between the federal government and these other levels of government or nonprofit employers.

Workers covered by Social Security pay a tax on their earnings, and employers add a like amount. The size of the ultimate benefit is based on a calculation which takes into account the total of such taxable earnings. When the system was first initiated in 1936, the maximum earnings subject to tax were $3,000 a year. Over the years, this amount has gradually been increased. In 1979, the taxable earnings base was $22,900. The ceiling on earnings subject to tax was $65,400 in 1997. People whose annual incomes are in excess of these amounts pay taxes only on that portion of their annual earnings as specified in the law for that year. When the taxable base is increased, it affects only those workers who have been earning more than the previous year's taxable base.

The tax rate is also fixed by law. In 1997, the tax rate was 7.65% of the first $68,400 of an individual's earnings. Of this amount, 6.2% is allotted for Social Security and disability insurance; the remainder is for Medicare. The tax rate for the self-employed is now equivalent to that paid by the salaried worker and employer. This change, however, did not come fully into effect until 1990. Self-employed persons pay their Social Security tax each year at the same time they pay their federal income tax (U.S. House of Representatives, 1991). There is no maximum taxable earnings for Medicare.

Veterans receive gratuitous credit for military service between September 1940 and December 1957. When veterans apply for benefits, it is assumed that they earned $160 per month during their years of military service. After

1957, servicemen paid the Social Security tax on their military earnings and therefore are eligible for benefits the same as any other employed person.

The size of the benefits reflects the level of earnings during the wage earner's working years. Upon application for benefits, lifetime earnings, that is, earnings from age 21 until the time of application, are totaled. The five lowest years of earnings are excluded, and the number of months—less the excluded five years—is divided into the total earnings. The resulting amount—the Average Monthly Earnings—is then plotted against a table provided in the law to determine the monthly benefit which will be received. The table of benefits reflects some favorable treatment for low-paid workers, in that they receive more in benefits as a proportion of previous earnings than do higher-paid workers.

In 1979, the law also incorporated a new principle: the adjustment of previous earnings to upgrade them to more nearly reflect current wage levels. Wages paid 25 or 30 years ago seem completely unrealistic by today's scale; yet their small amounts depress the Average Monthly Earnings figure, which is crucial to the size of the benefit to be paid. Included in the law has been the goal of having benefits replace, for average earners, about 44% of previous earnings which had been subject to the Social Security tax. This provision has the effect of increasing the size of some benefits, while keeping new awards from exceeding this level of replacement.

Benefits are automatically adjusted annually, without any action by the Congress, to reflect changes in the cost of living. Inasmuch as Social Security benefits are only partially subject to income tax, this adjustment enables beneficiaries to maintain their purchasing power under the pressures of upward movement of prices (inflation). Until this procedure became automatic, an act of Congress was necessary to adjust benefits. The average monthly Social Security benefit in 1997 was $749 and the maximum benefit was $1,326.

A minimum benefit of $122 per month had been provided under the law for wage earners whose lifetime earnings, which were covered by Social Security, were low. The $122 was provided no matter what the formula would yield in benefits. The minimum benefit was discontinued by Congress in 1981 except for beneficiaries already on the rolls. There is still a one-time death benefit for survivors of $255.

There is another form of minimum benefits which helps persons who have worked many years in covered employment, yet at wages so low that they will enter retirement with very small benefits. The law now provides that long-term low-paid workers will receive benefits larger than they would under the normal formula incorporated in the law. This provision was added to the law in 1972 because the minimum benefit discussed earlier was found to be aiding many persons who were not long-term workers but who had been in other retirement systems, and for whom the Social

Security benefits were only supplementary. Even so, those workers who were in real need of some protection against a low benefit were not being sufficiently aided by the old minimum benefit.

Until the year 2000, the normal age for retirement is 65. Workers who have the required number of quarters of coverage can retire at an age as low as 62. The benefits for these earners are reduced on an actuarial basis so that their early retirement does not cost the system any money. This reduction is 20% for those retiring at age 62, proportionately less, as the individual is nearer age 65 when applying for benefits. More than half of current applications for retirement benefits are being made by persons who are below 65 years of age. The age at which an individual can collect full benefits will gradually rise over the next 30 years. In 2027, the age for full benefits will be 67 for individuals born in 1960 or after. The current full benefit retirement age of 65 will thus be considered an age for reduced benefits.

The benefits of a retired wage earner may be increased if his or her spouse is of the appropriate age. This provision was added to the law in 1939 at a time when the pattern of family living was for the husband to be in gainful employment to support his spouse and children. The 50% increase in the wage earner's benefits was on behalf of the wife who had not been employed outside the home. That addendum is paid in the instances of spouses who have no earning records of their own, or in cases where a spouse's earning record would yield a benefit of a lesser amount than she (or he) would receive as a dependent spouse. The Social Security Administration will make a comparison at the time of application for benefits and award the larger of the two amounts. While the addendum is added to the wage earner's monthly check, the wife can receive a separate check if she requests it. An addendum is also allowable if the retired wage earner has dependent children living at home. In this instance, benefits are payable on behalf of such children up to the age of 18, unless the children are full-time elementary or secondary students.

The addendum covering the spouse of a retired worker is available for both a husband and wife. That is, the wife can be the wage earner, to whom a 50% increase will be granted on behalf of her husband, if the husband had no wage earning record or if his wage record will yield benefits smaller than 50% of his wife's. The law provides, however, that if the husband or wife who is claiming benefits on the basis of the earnings of the other is also receiving benefits from any governmental program, the spouse's benefits will be reduced by the amount of the additional benefit being received. The purpose of this provision is to disallow the Social Security benefits claimed by a spouse who is covered by the U.S. Civil Service retirement system or a comparable state system and who consequently is not in any way dependent upon the spouse who is covered by Social Security.

Benefits are payable to retired wage earners if they meet the retirement test as stated in the law. The test of retirement is put in terms of annual earnings. Individuals receiving Social Security benefits but also earning an annual amount higher than the amount stated in the law may lose part or, if the earnings are sufficiently large, all of their benefit. In 1996, Congress voted to raise the earnings limit. This raise began at $12,500 in 1996 for retirees between the ages of 65 and 69, and will reach $17,000 by the year 2000 and $30,000 by 2002. This means that in the year 2002 individuals can earn $30,000 without losing any of their Social Security benefits. Income other than earnings is not counted for a retirement test, which means that individuals may have unlimited income from investments, rents, and the like without any impact on their benefits. Earnings above the amounts stated reduce the monthly benefits on the basis of a $1 reduction for every $3 earned.

The earnings test is the most unpopular provision in the Social Security Act. It has been criticized as a discouragement to work and a denial of essential supplementary income to people whose basic benefits are insufficient. Counter to this are the arguments that Social Security is not designed as a pension, but as a wage replacement benefit, and that the elimination of the earnings or retirement test would increase the cost of the system, with the additional money going to people who are the least needy.

A common problem experienced by older people involves the death of a spouse and the remarriage of the surviving spouse who receives Social Security benefits. Often, the remarriage is to a person who also receives benefits. A spouse who receives survivor's benefits could lose them upon remarriage. As a result of amendments to the law which became effective in 1979, the remarriage of a surviving spouse after age 60 will not reduce the amount of benefits.

Another problem occurs in the breakup of a marriage which leaves a divorced mate without any marriage ties to a retired worker and thus unable to claim the spouse's 50% addendum. Other recent changes in the law state that a divorced spouse who was married for 10 years may claim benefits based on the former spouse's earning record at the time of retirement. The fact that the wage earner may have remarried does not affect the benefits to the divorced spouse. Prior to 1983, the divorced spouse was in a difficult position if he or she did not have an earning record and the former spouse chose to continue working. Under the 1983 amendments to the Act, the divorced spouse can now collect Social Security benefits at age 62, regardless of whether or not the former spouse applies for his or her own benefits.

FINANCING SOCIAL SECURITY

The financial integrity of the Social Security system is of crucial importance to its 34 million beneficiaries. All costs of the program, including the cost of administering it, come from a tax imposed on employers and employees. This tax money is identified separately in the United States Treasury and is available for appropriation to pay benefits and the cost of administration. Although most wage earners believe the Social Security tax is a single figure, it is actually a series of smaller tax sums designed to reflect the cost of the various elements of the system. These include the retirement program, disability, survivors, and health insurance. In recent years, it has become apparent that some of these so-called trust funds for individual program purposes were running short and soon would be in deficit. The 1983 amendments, which increased both the tax base and the tax rate, rescued the Social Security system from imminent deficit. The amendments increased the flow of money into the Treasury from wage earners and employers and thus gave assurance that, for at least a time, the income was equal to the outgo.

Since the Social Security system is financed solely by the tax on employers and employees, there is no other money from the Treasury going into the basic system. Unless the nation should decide to allocate some general revenue funds to pay at least part of the costs, the benefits will continue to be paid for by the payroll tax.

The problems of Social Security are both short-range and long-range. In the short range, sluggish economic activity (reduces the number of employee contributors as a consequence of unemployment) and inflation (which requires an upward adjustment in benefits) can put a strain on the money needed for payments to beneficiaries. In the long run, the growing number of aged in the population and the reduction in the working-age population means that a reduced proportion of younger people will be supporting an increasing proportion of older people.

Under the pressures of keeping the Social Security system solvent, a bipartisan commission developed proposals in 1983 that were signed into law. As already noted, the 1983 amendments set new tax rates and salary bases. These increases are designed to bring additional money into the system and offset the increasing number of beneficiaries and the cost-of-living adjustments to which they are now entitled.

Besides requiring individuals already paying Social Security taxes to pay more, the 1983 amendments also tried to use two other strategies to shore up the Social Security trust fund: (1) increase the number of individuals paying the taxes; and (2) encourage people to retire later and thus continue to pay into the system for a longer period.

For the first strategy, the 1983 amendments required all new federal workers to pay Social Security taxes. This change added a significant pool of new taxpayers who formerly paid into a separate federal civil service system. Any local and state governments currently covered by the Social Security system were now forbidden to withdraw from the system in order to set up their own retirement plan.

One element of the strategy to encourage people to work longer was the already discussed liberalization of the retirement test that took place in 1990. Even more important is the raise in the age of retirement with full benefits, from 65 to 66 in 2009 and to 67 in 2027. This means that individuals who retire at age 65 in 2009 will receive only 93% of the benefits to which they are entitled. In 2027, when the age of retirement for full benefits is 67, individuals who retire at 65 will receive only 86.7% of their benefits. In contrast, individuals who do not retire at 67 but continue to work will receive 8% more benefits for each year they work (e.g., 108% at age 68, 116% at age 69) (Cohen, 1983).

Social Security beneficiaries are now also guaranteed to receive increased benefits even in periods of low inflation. In 1986, Congress abolished the requirement that the yearly rate of inflation must be at least 3% before any cost-of-living adjustment is triggered. At least one group of beneficiaries, however, has found that the 1983 amendments did not necessarily provide them with any increase in their total income. Half of Social Security benefits are now counted as taxable income for individuals whose gross income combined with Social Security benefits exceeds $25,000 ($32,000 for a married couple). For single individuals with income over $34,000 ($44,000 for a married couple), 85% of their benefits are taxable. The counting of Social Security benefits as taxable income is a major departure from past practices. Importantly, the funds derived from these taxes are contributed to the Social Security trust funds as a means of further ensuring its solvency.

SURVIVOR'S INSURANCE

Benefits for survivors of deceased wage earners under the Social Security system are available to the survivors (wife or husband and young children) of a prematurely deceased wage earner. These benefits are also available to the surviving spouse (age 60 or older and younger children if any) of a wage earner who was either retired or had been eligible for retirement. For purposes of this chapter, only the latter group of survivors—the older people—will be discussed.

As explained earlier, an addendum will be added to the benefit of a spouse if he or she is at least 60 years of age. This benefit is paid not only on behalf of spouses who have had no employment record of their own that would qualify them, but also to those who have a record of work in covered employment but for whom the earned benefit is less than 50% of the wage earner's Primary Insurance Amount (PIA). The survivor's benefit will be 100% of the wage earner's PIA. Thus it is possible that a woman whose earned benefit was less than 50% of her husband's will, upon the death of her husband, receive a larger benefit—her husband's PIA—and this is not an uncommon occurrence.

A benefit of the same size will also be paid to the widow or widower of a wage earner who had been eligible for a retirement benefit but who had not claimed it because of continuing employment, that is, assuming the survivor meets the usual age requirement. In the event the aged survivor also has responsibility for young children of the deceased, the benefit will be 75% of the PIA plus a payment made on behalf of each child equal to 75% of the PIA. Benefits are also payable to dependent parents of deceased wage earners.

Beneficiaries of survivor's benefits are subject to the same earnings test as are retired people. Therefore, if a widower or widow is employed and receiving an income, the survivor's benefit might be reduced or even eliminated, depending on the amount of the survivor's earnings.

SUPPLEMENTARY SECURITY INCOME

The SSI program was established in 1974 on the basis of legislation enacted in 1972. It provides for federalizing the former grants-in-aid programs of old-age assistance, aid to the blind, and aid to the permanently and totally disabled. Except for the disability component, these programs had been administered by the states since 1935, with states administering grants for the disabled since 1950. Under the 1972 legislation, the federal government provides assistance to the aged, blind, and disabled who qualify under the specific provisions of the law. National standards are used both for eligibility and for payment.

There are several major differences between the SSI program and the comparable old-age and disability programs in the Social Security system. Unlike Social Security, the SSI program is means-tested. Funds for the SSI program come from the general revenue of the Treasury, while Social Security is financed by a payroll tax on employers and employees. The SSI program is available to anyone who meets the qualifications of age, blindness, and disability, without regard to their participation in the work force. The Social Security program is directly related to employment, either by the beneficiary or by his or her dependents. Although both Social Security and SSI are administered by the Social Security Administration, a distinction is maintained between the two programs.

National eligibility requirements for SSI are:

- No one is eligible who is an inmate of a public institution.
- If an otherwise eligible person is in a medical institution such as a nursing home, the payment to that individual is reduced to $30 per month.

- No one is to receive an SSI payment if she or he is eligible for, but has not applied for, another kind of benefit payment, such as worker's compensation or Social Security.
- Anyone who is otherwise eligible, but who has been medically established to be a drug addict or an alcoholic, will receive payment only if undergoing appropriate treatment for the condition at an institution approved by the Secretary of the Department of Health and Human Services and if she or he demonstrates compliance with the outlined treatment.
- Payment to eligible persons under SSI will not be made if those persons are outside the continental United States. If such persons are out of the country and later return, they are required to wait 30 days before being reinstated for SSI payment.
- A disabled person under the age of 65 must accept a referral to the state vocational rehabilitation agency for a study of their condition and must accept a proposed plan of treatment in order to continue eligibility for SSI.
- Applicants must be either citizens or legally admitted aliens in order to be eligible for SSI.
- Persons who are age 65, or blind, or disabled are eligible. If the eligibility is blindness or disability, the individual must meet the test used in the Social Security program of disability insurance.
- The resources of an eligible individual must not exceed $2,000 for an individual and $3,000 for a couple.

The system promises a certain level of income, which consists of SSI alone, if the individual has no other income, or a combination of SSI and other income to reach the established payment level. In determining the amount an individual or a couple will receive, some modifications are made in the treatment of income:

- Only net income from employment is counted. Income includes earnings, cash, checks, and in-kind income such as food and shelter.
- The first $240 per year of income such as from Social Security is not counted, but all income paid on the basis of need is fully counted.
- Earned income of eligible persons up to $780 per year is not counted.
- Casual and inconsequential income not to exceed $60 in a quarter is not counted.
- If the eligible individual is living in another person's household and is receiving support or maintenance in kind, the SSI payment is reduced by one-third.

A state may establish a higher payment level at its own expense but may not add eligibility requirements. The federal government will administer that payment at no administrative cost to the state. Many states have chosen to provide a state supplement, with some states administering it themselves. This means that the payment level varies around the country, as individual states decide whether to add to the federal payment, how much to add, and to what extent these supplements should be increased as living costs rise. In FY 1998, there were 1,019,000 individuals receiving SSI on the basis of age out of a total of 6,111,000 recipients ("Maximum federal SSI benefit," 1997).

STATE GENERAL ASSISTANCE PROGRAMS

Most states have a program of general assistance that is the direct linear descendant of the old poor law relief programs. Like these earlier programs, they are largely local in character. Some states, however, help finance the program and may even set state standards. The primary eligibility provision is need, which often is severely tested.

This program is available to persons who do not qualify for other programs such as Social Security and SSI. A likely candidate, for example, is a needy person aged 60. Unless such persons are disabled or blind, they would not be eligible for Social Security or SSI and could very well be in need. Inasmuch as there is no federal financial help in the state programs, the availability of benefits depends upon state eligibility requirements and often some local requirements. During the early 1990s, General Assistance programs in many states suffered major cuts as the recession reduced state revenues, in some states they have been eliminated completely.

PRIVATE PENSION PLANS

Private pensions are becoming an increasingly large part of the national income support system. As noted earlier, the federal government has encouraged and facilitated their development. Although the government has looked favorably on these programs, it is difficult for the federal government to impose effective controls over them. The reason is that, fundamentally, these are private programs, and the federal government cannot readily make demands about what industry and commerce do with their private programs.

By 1974, however, several situations had developed in private pension plans which forced the federal government to take action. Evidence was accumulating that there was gross inequity in the benefits being paid. There were indications of corruption by managers of the plans. Plans were being set up which were poorly funded and which, in all probability, would not be able to pay benefits. Meanwhile, workers were making retirement plans under the expectation of receiving benefits from their private pension plans to supplement what they knew would be inadequate Social Security benefits.

The private sector has a choice of whether or not it wants to provide a pension plan; and it retains the choice of discontinuing a plan, once one is set up. The benefit rights of an individual are only rarely transferable when the worker moves from one employer to another. Social Security remains the only income support insurance program with that feature.

The main objective of the federal legislation was to assure the receipt of benefits upon retirement after a period of service for an employer. A further assurance was provided by setting up a reinsurance fund, similar to the Federal Deposit Insurance Corporation, which insures bank deposits. The reinsurance fund collects a small fee from all pension funds and maintains a reserve to pay off accumulated obligations to beneficiaries of any bankrupt fund.

The standards imposed by federal law on the private pensions operate separately for funds in which the employee has contributed as compared to those in which the employer makes all the contributions. There are more severe requirements for vesting (the rights to a benefit) for the former than for the latter. For the employer-financed funds, vesting the benefits takes place following 5 years of service. After that time, the size of the benefit payment to which the employee is entitled grows in size as the number of years employed, when added to the employee's age, becomes larger. Conceivably, an employee could work for several companies, working the minimum number of years for each, in order to have vested rights and, upon retirement, receive several benefit checks, although each would be a small one.

Vesting can be accomplished in two ways. Under "cliff vesting" funds are 100% vested after 10 years. This is reduced to 5 years for individuals hired after 1989. Under "graded vesting" 25% of the funds are vested after 5 years. The percentage of the contributions vested increases until 100% is vested after 15 years. As is true of "cliff vesting," graded vesting for employees hired after 1989 begins at 3 years (25% vested) and is completed after 7 years.

There are several important characteristics of the private pension system:

- The payments are growing in adequacy, although they do not equal those of Social Security. An exception is benefits to high-level executives, who often have a generous pension plan built into their remuneration.
- Benefits are payable to survivors of deceased plan members in a small but slowly growing number of plans.

- Few plans provide for adjustment to the cost of living, and if they do, it is not usually the full increase.
- The plans tend to favor the long-term employee, who, by virtue of continuous employment by one employer, can become eligible for a more significant payment.
- In a few instances, an employee may carry over benefit rights to another employer in the same industry. An example is the trucker's pension fund, which operates across the industry.

Private pension funds share the same problem of nearly all retirement plans in the United States: they are marginally secure financially. The insurance fund accumulates reserves very slowly and could be wiped out by a few large claims made simultaneously. The actuarially determined obligation for pension payments on some corporations, even large corporations, is excessive. One issue which will gradually have to be faced is the extent of the corporate obligation for payment under terms of the plan versus the shareholders' rights to the assets of the company. As corporations encounter difficult economic times, such as the recession of the early 1990s, they may also reconsider their involvement in an extensive pension effort.

The Insurance and Public Benefits section of the 1992 Older Americans Act amendments (Title VII) is supposed to help older workers evaluate the pension plans in which they are enrolled or for which they are eligible. The aim of this state-run program is to help older individuals understand the ability of these pensions to meet their post-retirement needs and the relationship of these pensions to other public benefits and insurance plans. While it is likely that this issue will be resolved without reaching a crunch, it does suggest that the private pension system has to face the reality of financing troubles.

Individual Retirement Accounts (IRAs) are one alternative for individuals who do not have private pension plans available. The interest on these accounts in banks, mutual funds, or insurance companies is not taxable until the individual withdraws the funds between the ages of 59 1/2 and 70. Earlier withdrawal is subject to major penalties on the interest. Under the Tax Relief Act of 1997, individuals with an adjusted gross income of $30,000, and couples with an adjusted gross income of $50,000, can contribute $2000 worth of deductible income into an IRA each year. Individuals with an adjusted gross income of $95,000 ($150,000 for couples) can contribute $2000 after-tax income to an IRA. These funds must stay in the IRA for at least 5 years and are not taxed when they are withdrawn from the IRA.

Although pension reform has been extensive, there is no indication that these legislative efforts have reduced the gap between minority and non-minority workers in pension coverage. In fact, this gap appears to be growing. In 1979, 50% of White workers, 45% of African American workers, and 38% of Latino workers had pension coverage. By 1993, 45% of White workers, 34% of African American workers, and 25% of Latino workers were covered by pensions (Chen & Leavitt, 1997). These changes probably represent some loss of opportunities for minority workers to obtain jobs where pension coverage is offered as well as the increase in voluntary salary reduction plans. Among workers offered these voluntary plans, White workers have a higher rate of participation. The effect of these differences in pension coverage rates will mean that more minority older persons than before will have to rely on Social Security to meet their financial needs after they retire.

UNEMPLOYMENT AND INADEQUATE INCOME

The distinction between unemployment of an older person and retirement is often a thin one. An older person who loses his or her job may be vigorously looking for another one, yet, since he or she needs income, may be forced to apply for and accept some income transfer benefits. Before moving on to the Social Security program, the person may wish to exhaust his or her unemployment compensation rights. Many older persons receive unemployment compensation, either before moving on to Social Security or simultaneously. It is possible for a person to receive both unemployment compensation and old-age benefits at the same time.

Unemployment compensation is a program of benefits for persons who were employed in specified fields of work but who have, not of their own choosing, left their jobs. The program is administered by the states, who have considerable latitude in establishing eligibility standards, including the amount of the weekly benefit. Unemployment compensation is financed by a federally imposed tax, most of which is returned to the states by the federal government to pay the cost of the benefits granted and the cost of administering the program, which includes the operation of an employment service. States may add to the amount of the tax, making more funds available to support more generous benefits. States may also increase the duration of benefits, and pay the cost of less onerous provisions for eligibility. Many states do this.

The number of workers covered by unemployment compensation has been increasing in recent years, until most workers in commerce and industry and many people in public employment and in teaching professions are now covered. Some progress has been made in incorporating casual employment, such as domestic and farm work, into the system. Even so, most people engaged in these kinds of jobs are still not covered, nor are self-employed persons. Benefits are payable only after a worker has been in employment for a specified period of time set by the states and therefore varying from state to state, with 26 weeks emerging as the most common length of time.

The trend has been for Congress to provide extended benefits in the course of an economic recession. The receipt of benefits has extended for as long as 15 months in recent years, but a duration of more than 9 months is no longer likely. Many people question the wisdom of these extensions on the grounds that the availability of benefits tends to discourage diligent search for work. Such a long period of unemployment also strongly indicates that a work program is needed rather than an income transfer program. If benefits are to be extended, many observers contend, the recipients of such benefits ought to be means-tested, which they are not now. Some unemployment benefits are subject to income tax. Some states include an addendum for dependents, but generally benefits are awarded to the worker without regard for family circumstances.

Eligibility for benefits hinges upon the unemployed individual being ready, willing, and able to work. Presumably, illness or disability should exclude a worker, although in practice the unavailability of the worker for a job often is not known to the state. An unemployed person is not expected to take the first job that materializes without regard to experience or training; the system allows the worker to hold off accepting employment until a job becomes available that uses their skills. As time passes, however, the unemployed worker is expected to lower his or her job expectations and accept less ideal work. Workers are not expected to take strike-breaking jobs, nor ones that offer below the usual wages.

Workers who wish to receive unemployment compensation are required to register for work with the employment service. If that office is successful in finding a job for the recipient of unemployment compensation, the unemployed person is expected to accept it, unless he or she can show good cause for not doing so. Inasmuch as the employment service has few job openings for older workers, it is unlikely that an older person's willingness to work will be put to a test. Even if the employment office should refer the unemployment compensation beneficiary to a job, the employer may reject him or her, and this would not affect continued eligibility for benefits.

It has been a practice for older persons to apply for unemployment compensation as a prelude to retirement. Since the likelihood is very slight that they will be faced with a decision of whether or not to accept suitable employment which may be found by the employment service, the unemployment compensation program offers some additional tax-free income for the almost-retired person. While this appears to be legal, it is not within the spirit of the law and there have been discussions about making such persons ineligible for unemployment benefits.

The basic program of unemployment compensation benefits is sometimes supplemented by private funds created as a consequence of labor-management agreements. In the automobile, steel, and some other highly organized industries, management contributes toward a fund used to supplement the basic unemployment compensation program whenever needed. This supplement can take the form of continuing benefits after the regular program ends or, more likely, can supplement the size of the basic benefit. These funds are relatively new, having been established only in recent years. When put to a test, they were proven to be insufficient to last the duration of the unemployment period in the industries, although they were helpful to the workers who received them. These supplementary funds tend to provide more help to those with the greatest job seniority.

REFERENCES

Cohen, W. (1983). *Social Security: The compromise and beyond.* Washington, DC: SOS Education Fund.

Chen, Y., & Leavitt, D. (1997). The widening gap between white and minority pension coverage. *The Public Policy and Aging Report, 8,* 10–11.

Older American Reports. (1997). *21,* 45. (Maximum federal SSI benefit is $484 a month for individuals.)

U.S. House of Representatives, Committee on Ways and Means. (1991). *Background material and data on programs within the jurisdiction of the Committee on Ways and Means.* Washington, DC: U.S. Government Printing Office.

4

Illness, Medical Care, and Income Maintenance

Becoming ill or disabled creates two major problems for those affected. If the inability to work cuts off income, the unemployed need income transfers to support themselves and their dependents. The primary problem of the sick or disabled is providing income. The other major problem is paying for medical care.

RISKS OF ILLNESS, DISABILITY, AND INADEQUATE INCOME

Several programs, all of which depend on the particular status of the individual, address the need for income. The Social Security program includes benefits available to persons disabled on a long-term basis. Some states provide short-term disability benefits as an element in their unemployment compensation program. Worker's compensation is available for those who have become ill or disabled on the job; this includes wage replacement and medical expenses. Many employers provide sick leave, which is a form of short-term disability benefit. The SSI program is available for the disabled who, for one reason or another, are not eligible for Social Security or any other income-producing programs.

Social Security Disability Benefits

Eligibility for Social Security benefits generally follows along the lines of eligibility for Social Security in general, as described in chapter 3. The major difference in eligibility between the two programs is a requirement for a longer attachment to the labor force. Although disability benefits are available to younger workers who meet the test of severity of disability, the law requires disabled persons to have worked under covered employment for a proportionately longer period of time than is required of deceased wage earners who die prematurely and leave survivors. The intention is to emphasize that the worker to be covered has made a significant financial contribution to the system before becoming eligible.

For purposes of determining the amount of benefits after disabled workers establish eligibility on the basis of severity of disability and length of time in the work force, they are considered retired. Their lifetime wages in covered employment are totaled and divided by the number of months of work. For younger workers, the number of months of covered employment may be small, certainly when compared to those of the retired person. However, the average monthly earnings of the younger worker could be as high as those of a retired worker. Indeed, the monthly average might well be higher, since the younger worker's wage history is more recent and covers a time when wages have been higher than those of a retired person whose wage history may go back 40 years. This peculiarity of the system has resulted in disability benefits generally running higher than those granted for retired persons.

Legislation enacted in 1980 set some ceilings on benefits for the disabled to ensure that benefits do not exceed previous earnings but reduce the gap between retirement and disability benefits. Benefits for disabled workers are increased if they have spouses and even more if they have dependent children. The procedure for determining the amount of these awards is similar to that used for retired workers, their spouses, and their young children, if any.

For claiming benefits, the definition of disability is a severe one. It attempts to limit the program to those persons with severe and long-lasting disabilities, either mental or physical. The words in the definition, "inability to engage in any substantial gainful activity," suggest that a test is to be made of the individual's ability to engage in "any gainful activity," not just a test of whether or not there is employment in the community in which the individual lives. This definition could conceivably result in the denial of benefits to people who might be able to do certain kinds of work even if there was no possibility of any work of that nature showing up.

The individual applicant is responsible for presenting proof of disability and, if medical examination or testing is involved, must pay for that cost. If the Social Security Administration is not satisfied with the proof offered, it will pay for additionally required examinations and reports.

When the program began in the 1950s, it was small and grew very slowly. In recent years it has expanded broadly. There is some disagreement over the reasons for the growth. Some observers feel that the administrators of the program have relaxed some of its standards. Others feel that applicants have become more knowledgeable about the various benefit programs and that they have been helped by experienced lawyers and encouraged by recipient advocate groups. Many instances of denial by the Social Security Administration have gone to appeal within the organization and, if that failed, have gone to the courts. A surprisingly large number of adverse administrators' decisions have been reversed by the courts.

Although the definition speaks in terms of long and severe disability, from the very beginning the assumption has been that some beneficiaries might be rehabilitated. For this reason, provision is made for each state's vocational rehabilitation agency to review all applications with a view toward identification of potential cases for vocational rehabilitation. The applicant who is recommended by the vocational rehabilitation agency for rehabilitation must accept the plan of that agency or forfeit rights to disability benefits. In some instances, the rehabilitation plan is financed by the Social Security Administration as a charge against Social Security funds. Those who are rehabilitated and who go off the program save the program a great deal of money over the years.

The cost of rehabilitation is usually regarded as a prudent investment. The actual record of rehabilitation cases shows that comparatively few applicants are able to be fully rehabilitated and return to work. Legislation under consideration would encourage beneficiaries to undertake work by assuring them of quick reentry to the program if the work does not prove feasible.

Under heightened review processes, an increased number of individuals receiving disability payments were terminated during the early 1980s. This included many older individuals who had received disability payments for many years. In fiscal 1983, the benefits of 182,074 workers were terminated, as compared to 80,956 in 1981 (U.S. House of Representatives, 1986). In response to mounting complaints about unjust terminations, the law now provides the individual with the right to a face-to-face hearing before benefits are terminated. Appeals procedures have also been clarified. The Disabilities Reform Act of 1984 specified the grounds on which disability benefits could be terminated, including standards of medical improvement.

Sick Leave

Important, but often overlooked, resources for providing income to people who are temporarily sick or disabled are the provisions many employers make for sick leave. Employers that provide sick leave tend to be those that employ white-collar workers. However, manufacturing companies have begun to provide this benefit as well. Government work of all kinds includes this form of illness protection. A specific and very important form of leave is now provided through the Family and Medical Leave Act enacted by Congress in 1993. Under this law, an employee is eligible for *unpaid* leave for up to 12 weeks within a 12-month period to care for newborn children or to care for a spouse, child, or parent with a serious health problem. A parent is defined as a biological parent, or an individual who was "in loco parentis" when the employee was a child, but not an in-law.

Worker's Compensation

Programs of worker's compensation are operated by the states or private insurance companies under state supervision. Typically, benefits include both financial assistance in lieu of lost wages and payment for medical bills. The illnesses and disabilities covered by this program are those incurred on the job, under the concept of no-fault; that is, no test is made to determine whether employees were careless or otherwise contributed to their own accidents. Benefits are often time-limited and are usually related to the severity of the disability. For the severely disabled, benefits include some form of rehabilitation, often in conjunction with the state vocational rehabilitation agency.

Not all employees are covered by worker's compensation. Since these are state programs, eligibility provisions differ around the country. In some states there are exemptions of small employers, usually defined as those with five employees. Typically, other employees not covered are domestic, casual, and farm workers. Because of these variations among the states and omissions from the program, there is some interest in enacting a federal law which would establish uniform standards for the nation.

Temporary Disability Insurance

Short-term disability benefits are available in about six states as an offshoot of the unemployment insurance program. These states include some of the large industrial states, such as New York and California.

Benefits are available for workers who are covered by the state unemployment insurance law and who are absent from work because of illness or disability. These would be people whose illness or disability is unrelated to their work (otherwise, they would be eligible for worker's compensation) and whose absence from work will be temporary, as contrasted with the long-term absences defined in the Social Security program. Workers covered by an employer's sick leave may not be excluded in some states; in others, disability benefits may be reduced or denied. Temporary disability benefits are not permitted to overlap unemployment insurance benefit payments.

All of the laws have minimum requirements for days absent or loss of wages before benefits will begin and, of course, set limits on the duration of benefits being paid. Benefits are related to the size of previous earnings, as in the case of unemployment compensation. The plans are financed by a state-imposed tax on employees and, in some states, on the employers. There is no federal financial support for these programs.

RISKS OF AGING, MEDICAL BILLS, AND INADEQUATE INCOME

Medical costs for the aged are increasing each year. This reflects not only the growing proportion of the gross national product devoted to medical care, but also the proportionately higher medical costs of the aged as compared with the population as a whole. Health care expenditures increased 11% annually in the 1980s. The aging of the American population accounts for part of this increase. Overall, individuals over the age of 65 account for one third of all personal health care expenditures in the United States (U.S. Senate, Special Committee on Aging, 1991). In addition, long-term care is costly and, by definition, long-lasting.

For these reasons, provisions to help the aged meet medical costs have been in the law for many years. From the earliest history of government and through the years, welfare programs have provided some medical care and some payment for medical care for poor people, especially the aged. That practice is now being carried out through the Medicaid program (Title XIX of the Social Security Administration).

Private insurance for health care costs has been available for decades, but has been especially prominent since World War II. The Blue Cross plan for hospital insurance was begun during the Depression and has had many individual subscribers as well as group subscribers. Private health insurance has become a fringe benefit of employment. While Blue Cross as a nonprofit community plan had a large number of old persons as subscribers, other private plans (especially the profit-making ones) shunned the elderly because of their poor risk record, and conducted all of their business through employers. Thus, if older persons remained in employment, they would have some financial help for medical expenses in this manner.

It became obvious over time that private health insurance could not be depended upon to provide protection for the aged. Indeed, there was doubt that private profit-making health insurance companies wanted a major role in insuring the aged. The high incidence of illness among the aged made them a poor risk for private health insurance. Although private Blue Cross plans have been an exception to this rule, even this group of nonprofit private insurers began to be concerned about the stability of their financial position, especially as the cost of hospital care began to escalate dramatically in the 1960s. Even though the private health insurance industry and private medical practitioners were opposed to further government involvement, the public interest and demand for hospital insurance for the aged prevailed, and Medicare was enacted in 1965.

Private programs vary widely in the protection offered, provisions for coverage, and circumstances of enrollment, but provide considerable protection for many elderly persons, especially those under the age of 65. For those over age 65, private health insurance is widely available to supplement the Medicare program. Although this program is universally available and is low in cost, older persons are currently spending 21% of their income on health care (Freudenheim, 1997a)

Medicare covers nearly all persons age 65 and over, those receiving disability benefits under Social Security, and a few other small groups. Eligibility and benefits will be discussed below. As the older population has continued to increase and the number of workers decrease, the problem of financing Medicare looms larger. One projection is that the hospital trust fund for Part A of Medicare will be in a "crisis" situation when individual "baby boomers" become eligible for Medicare in 2010 (Pear, 1997c). There are also projections that unless birth rates change, by the year 2050 only two workers will pay into Medicare for every one beneficiary. To combat this likelihood, changes have been discussed in taxes paid for Medicare, deductibles, and premiums paid by beneficiaries. The federal balanced budget bill passed in 1997 reduced reimbursements to hospitals and physicians.

To control hospital costs, a new system of prospective payment for hospital care has been introduced. This Diagnostic Related Group (DRG) system uses standardized payments for particular conditions. The results of this system have been controversial. Some critics have argued that older patients are being discharged prematurely. The Medicare Quality Protection Act of 1986 required hospitals to prepare discharge plans for patients who might be adversely affected by discharge. Patients must also be informed of their rights to in-patient hospitalization and have the right to appeal a decision for discharging them. By 1989, hospital stays for persons over age 65 had declined to 8.9 days (National Center for Health Statistics, 1991). A Rand corporation study undertaken in 1985–86 found no reduction in the quality of care after the introduction of the DRG system, nor a major increase in mortality, as a result of the new discharge policies (Kahn et al., 1990).

In contrast to the federally controlled Medicare program, Medicaid is a grant-in-aid program which is operated by the states and provides protection for some of the poor population. Coverage varies from state to state, and benefits also vary, but are broader than those of Medicare. The differences can be seen through a discussion of both Medicare and Medicaid.

Medicare

The Medicare program (Title XVIII of the Social Security Act) is an integral part of the Social Security program. Generally speaking, eligibility for Medicare is determined by eligibility for Social Security; Medicare benefits are provided to persons who have established eligibility for old-age benefits or disability benefits. No separate eligibility determination is made except for disabled beneficiaries, who must have been in receipt of cash benefits for 2 years prior to Medicare eligibility. Medicare is not available to persons who are below the age of 65, except for individuals suffering from end-stage renal disease or who are disabled.

The Medicare program is divided into two parts: Part A—hospital insurance—and Part B—medical insurance. All persons eligible for Medicare receive Part A benefits without any additional cost to them. Part B benefits are available only to persons who "join," that is, agree to pay a certain amount each month. This monthly fee is deducted from the check of persons who receive Social Security cash benefits. In the case of persons who are eligible for Social Security benefits but who do not receive a check because they are earning above the retirement level, a bill from the Health Care Financing Administration is sent for subsequent payment. In both parts, deductibles and coinsurance payments are required.

Part A

Under Part A, persons with a medically established need for hospitalization are entitled to 60 days of hospitalization. As a condition of eligibility, they must pay for the first day of the care. That amount is raised annually as the cost of hospitalization increases. It was $760 in 1997. If additional days of hospital care are needed, 30 more days are available upon the payment of a daily coinsurance fee, which in 1997 was $190. This fee is also raised annually. There must be a short period of time between hospitalizations before the 60-day and 30-day periods become applicable again. If additional hospitalization is needed beyond the 60- and 30-day limits, an individual can draw upon a lifetime reserve allowable for each eligible person. That life-time reserve is 60 days, with a daily coinsurance fee of $380 (in 1997). The services provided by the hospital are those usually included within a hospital's per diem charges, but not including the services of the anesthesiologist, pathologist, and radiologist. These services are charged separately by the doctors and are considered a Part B expense.

When patients have been hospitalized for at least 3 days and are found to be in need of medical care which cannot be provided in the home, but which is not as medically sophisticated as that offered in the hospital setting, they may receive care in an extended care facility (ECF). These facilities are high-quality nursing homes which must be closely related to or have working agreements with a hospital and must be able to provide the kind of care the patient needs. Without additional charge, patients may receive up to 20 days of care in an ECF. An additional 80 days of care will be provided upon payment of a daily fee of $95(in 1997). The service of an extended care facility shortens the length of stay of patients in hospitals; it is not intended to be long-term nursing home care. Indeed, the Medicare program as a whole does not respond to the need for long-term care.

Home health care is available, with no ceiling on days, if needed, and at no additional charge. Home health care must be medically ordered and must be of a medical nature, not homemaker service. The daily skilled care must be for a relatively short period of time or be seen as having an end within a predicted period. Medicare will reimburse hospices for the care they provide individuals with a terminal diagnosis of 6 months or less of life expectancy. The beneficiary may reside in a hospice for two 90-day periods and one subsequent 30-day period.

Part B

Part B of Medicare is called Supplemental Medical Insurance. As mentioned earlier, Medicare-eligible persons do not automatically participate in Part B. They agree to this insurance and pay $43.80 per month (in 1997) or accept that deduction being made from their Social Security checks. The monthly premium will rise to $105.40 by 2007.

Nearly everyone receiving Social Security belongs to Part B, which provides partial payment for physicians for medical services. There is an annual deductible amount which, in 1997, was $100. Expenditures for drugs, dental services, and the like are not included in Part B. Individuals who have joined Part B, have paid their deductible amount of medical expenses, and have maintained monthly payments into the Part B fund are required to pay 20% of the charges Medicare determines are reasonable for a particular service. This 20% limit, however, does not apply to outpatient hospital services. For these outpatient services, the Medicare patient must pay 20% of whatever the hospital charges, rather than 20% of the amount approved by Medicare. Because outpatient hospital services have increased dramatically in recent years, Medicare recipients are now paying 47% of the amount charged by hospitals for services such as radiology and outpatient surgery (Pear, 1997c). Outpatient psychiatric care had been reimbursed at a 50% rate with a $1,100 limit. This limit has now been removed. Medicare also now covers flu shots and routine mammograms every 2 years for women over age 65, Pap smears, screening for colon cancer, prostate cancer, and osteoporosis, and education for diabetics on self-testing and preventive treatment.

Physicians can be paid by making a direct charge to the Health Care Financing Administration through a system of intermediaries which has been set up to deal directly with doctors. If they follow this route, they will receive 80% of the fee set by the intermediary, following the rules and directives of the Health Care Financing Administration. These rules, reflecting the concern in the Congress over the rise in medical costs in general and physicians' charges specifically, are directed toward keeping the Medicare payment in the general range of average payments and not at the level of higher charges made by some doctors. The doctor must look to the patient for the remaining 20% of his charges. Physicians must now submit their bill to Medicare, regardless of whether they do or do not accept assignment.

In the past, the fee was based on "reasonable and customary charges" in the community. As of 1992, the rates are based on a fee schedule developed through the Department of Health and Human Services. The fee schedule covers 7,000 services, and reimbursement is based on "value units" assigned to each procedure or medical service. These value units take into account the doctor's time, overhead, and risk of malpractice suit, and are then multiplied by a conversion factor in dollars. The resulting amount will be the Medicare approved rate. Health and Human Services secretary Louis Sullivan termed the fee schedule "the most wide-ranging and fundamental change in Medicare's physician payment since the creation of the Medicare program in 1965" (Rosenthal, 1990).

The importance of Medicare to the American health system can be illustrated with a few statistics: In 1994, 37.6 million individuals were receiving Medicare benefits and the average annual benefit per person was $2,807 for Part A hospital insurance and $1,621 under Part B, supplementary medical insurance. In 1993, Medicare also accounted for 28.4% of hospital revenues and 20.3% of doctors' income. Between 1997 and 2003, Medicare expenditures are expected to increase by 50% (Pear, 1997b).

Medicare is now encouraging older persons to join Health Maintenance Organizations (HMOs) that provide a wide range of care to their members on a prepayment basis. Under the Tax Equity and Fiscal Responsibility Act of 1982, older individuals who join HMOs continue to pay their Medicare Part B payments, and the HMO receives payment from the federal government for each member equivalent to 95% of the average Medicare costs in that state. A range of services equivalent to that provided by Medicare must be provided by the HMO. By September 1986, 3% of Medicare beneficiaries had enrolled in HMOs. In 1997, it was estimated that 100,000 older people were enrolling in HMOs each month (Freudenheim, 1997a).

One of the attractions of HMOs has been that they cover many costs not covered by Medicare, particularly those of prescription drugs and eye-glasses. It is estimated that 25% of all older persons spend more than $500 a year on prescription drugs. This figure is increased by the cost of over-the-counter drugs. There were indications in 1997 that limitations by Congress in payments to Medicare HMOs were resulting in higher fees and the ending of coverage for prescription drugs by many of these health providers (Freudenheim, 1997b).

The federal government is also experimenting with Social HMOs (S/HMO) which provide additional social services to older recipients. The benefits provided by the S/HMO include home health care, homemaker services, respite care, day care, and chronic care benefits for skilled nursing. In addition to a premium paid by the enrollee, Medicare and Medicaid reimburse the S/HMO at a per capita rate (Newcomer, Harrington, Yordi, & Friedlob, 1988). Those individuals who do join the S/HMO appear to opt for more extensive benefits and less out-of-pocket expenses, particularly expenses for drugs, dental care, and eyeglasses (Newcomer, Harrington, & Friedlob, 1990).

The Program of All-Inclusive Care for Elders (PACE) is similar in its efforts. Begun by San Francisco's On Lok Senior Center in 1979, PACE now has 10 sites that target the frail elderly who are eligible for nursing homes. The services at the sites range from social and medical service through adult health day care and utilize multidisciplinary teams. Needed preventive and rehabilitation services are also provided. The S/HMO and PACE have been shown to reduce the burdens faced by informal caregivers, as well as improving the social and physical well-being of older persons.

A major element in excluded Medicare costs is long-term care. Long-term care is not included under Medicare not only because of its high cost, but also because it is a combination of both medical and domiciliary costs.

Medicaid

This program, known officially as Medical Assistance, is much more complicated than Medicare. This is because Medicaid is a grant-in-aid to the states and is not a national program like Medicare. The federal law offers states the choice of whether they wish to have a Medicaid program and a variety of options on the breadth of eligibility and services covered as well as the fees to be paid. The result is considerable variation in the kinds of programs which have evolved in the states.

Once a state decides to have a Medicaid program, it must first decide whether the program is to be available only to people who receive payments from welfare programs, or whether the program will also include some of the medically needy. The welfare groups are those recipients of Aid to Families with Dependent Children (AFDC) and SSI. With the inauguration of SSI in 1975, states were given a further option of excluding persons eligible under the expanded SSI program or including them. The "medically needy" are those people who would qualify for the payment programs because of their high medical bills but whose incomes exceed the stated limits for eligibility. This distinction explains the large number of medically needy people who are not included in the Medicaid program. Among the excluded groups are those below the age of 65 who are not disabled. Those over age 65 would qualify for SSI, as would those under age 65 who are disabled. Another example is the intact family in which the father is employed but earns very little. Since this family is not eligible for AFDC, the family is also not eligible for Medicaid.

About half of the states include some medically needy. In each of these states, a decision had to be made concerning the income level to be regarded as qualifying. Although federal law prevents states from being too liberal in making this decision, most states that include the medically needy have eligibility points below the federal maximum.

States must use Medicaid funds to pay for all Medicare premiums, co-payments, and deductibles for Medicare beneficiaries who are below the poverty line and have less than $4,000 in liquid assets. Beginning in 1991 the states were required to pay the premiums (but not other costs) of older persons whose income is below 110% of poverty and who have less than $4,000 in liquid assets. The income limit rose to 120% of poverty in 1995. The immediate cost to the Medicaid program is expected to result in significant savings in the long run.

The federal law sets up the classifications of services which states must or can offer to pay for. States must offer some institutional and some non-institutional services. In addition, states must offer:

- Inpatient hospital services
- Outpatient hospital services and other X-ray and laboratory services
- Skilled nursing home services for adults
- Early periodic screening services for children
- Physicians' services in the home, office, or hospital

For the medically needy, the states may offer a smaller range of services. In addition to those required services, there is a long list of other optional services, which includes drugs, home health care, dental services, and the like. A major optional service which the states may offer is intermediate care facility (ICF) care. An ICF provides services that range somewhere between those of a domiciliary facility and a nursing home. This obviously includes many nursing homes which offer only minimal services and often charge fees which the state Medicaid agency will pay. The federal share of

Medicaid costs ranges from 50%, in states with per capita income equal to or greater than the national average, to 83%, for the state with the lowest per capita income in the United States.

By far the largest sums expended by the states for Medicaid are for hospitals, skilled nursing homes, and ICFs. Medicaid is the major source of public funds for long-term care. In 1995, 52% of all nursing home costs and 13% of all home health care costs were paid by Medicaid (Moon & Mulvey, 1995). Inasmuch as all Medicare institutional services have time limits and the institutional services under Medicaid generally do not, many older persons find themselves receiving care in various kinds of nursing homes which are Medicaid-eligible. The federal law prohibits states from requiring that children be responsible for supporting parents. Even if older persons have resources in their own names, months of care in a nursing home will exhaust them. Thus, when the resources of the older persons diminish to the eligibility level for such resources as set by the state, they then become eligible for Medicaid.

Once a Medicaid recipient is institutionalized, states can place a lien on property to recover their Medicaid expenses, but not on the home of a spouse, children under the age of 21, or a blind or disabled child of any age. In addition, a lien cannot be placed on property where a brother or sister of the Medicaid recipient has equity if this sibling lived for at least 1 year in the home before the individual was institutionalized.

The Medicaid program has been engulfed in the rapidly rising cost of medical care. States have taken some steps to protect themselves, but even these measures have not been sufficiently effective to prevent the costs from becoming burdensome. In response to this, states have tended to trim services as best they can and have attempted to keep fees which they pay from rising too rapidly. The consequence is that many medical practitioners have refused to treat Medicaid patients. To some observers, the only answer to this problem of providing medical care for low-income people is national health insurance. To some degree, all national decisions made around Medicaid have been regarded as temporary, made in the belief that national health insurance will surely come to be and will help solve the problems. Even as proposals continue, the prospects of such a national health plan still seem to be far in the future.

Private Health Insurance

A major force for paying medical costs in the United States is private health insurance. Public policy has supported the notion of a strong private sector for paying for medical care. Medical practitioners have encouraged it; industry has looked to the private sector to provide help to employees with their medical bills, and tax laws have encouraged the development of private health insurance plans.

Significant as private health insurance is, its impact is much less on the aged than on younger workers. Since so few of the aged are employed, they tend to have less private health insurance than do younger people. With the advent of Medicare in 1965, the private health insurance industry was pleased to assume a smaller role for the aged, for obvious reasons. There is great risk that the aged will become ill and will need costly medical services. Private insurance provides policies that supplement Medicare ("medigap"). These policies pay for some of the deductibles and coinsurance charges and may provide payment for some additional hospital days, but they rarely cover long-term care. Thus, even the combination of Medicare and supplemental private health insurance does not provide the aged with full coverage. Long-term care insurance (discussed in Chapter 15) is becoming increasingly common among more affluent older persons.

Many older people purchase more than one "Medigap" policy. The result is extra expense without additional coverage. One estimate is that 25% of older persons with Medigap coverage have at least two policies. A reduction in these duplicate policies would save the older individual from $350 to $1250 per year, depending on the number of policies (Sinclair, 1990). Federal legislation now forbids the sale of duplicate policies and requires the salesperson to inquire whether the older person already has any medical policies. The salesperson must also list on the insurance application any other health insurance policies they have already sold to the older person, and the policies must return to the consumer at least 65% of what they bring in to the company.

Regulations adopted by the National Association of Insurance Commissioners now help to standardize Medigap policies. Under these regulations, 10 plans are offered. The basic plan offers "core" services. These services include the coinsurance for Medicare Part A; 365 days of hospital coverage after Medicare benefits end; the 20% of doctor's fees not covered by Medicare; and the first three pints of blood a patient needs each year. The more extensive plans cover a variety of options including coverage during foreign travel, home care, preventive care, and prescription drugs. Consumers are thus able to make comparisons of the costs of each of these plans as offered by different insurers (Crenshaw, 1991). Unfortunately, increases in health care costs and utilization by older people have resulted in dramatic increases in Medigap premiums. Between 1996 and 1997, the costs of a Medigap policy increased 31.4% in Arizona and 32.4% in Virginia (Freudenheim, 1997a).

Health insurance for older persons has become a complex, widely debated aspect of the American social welfare system. Clearly the existence of Medicare and other programs has provided a level of health care for older people that would formerly not have been possible. Despite the existence of all of these programs, however, the out-of-pocket medical expenses for older persons continue to be high.

REFERENCES

Crenshaw, A. (1991, October 16). Relief for Medigap confusion. *Washington Post,* Family and Retirement Section, p. 6.

Freudenheim, M. (1997a, August 2), Golden years for H.M.O.'s. *New York Times,* pp. A19, A20.

Freudenheim, M. (1997b, December 22).Medicare H.M.O.'s to trim benefits for the elderly. *New York Times,* pp. A1, A13.

Kahn, K., Rubinstein, L., Kosekoff, J., Rogers, W., Keeler, E., & Brook, R. (1990). The effects of the DRG based prospective payment system on quality of care for hospitalized patients. *Journal of the American Medical Association, 264,* 1953–1955.

Moon, M., & Mulvey, J. (1995). *Entitlements and the elderly: Protecting promises, recognizing realities.* Washington, DC: Urban Institute Press.

National Center for Health Statistics. (1991). *1989 summary: National Hospital Discharge Survey.* Hyattsville, MD: Author.

Newcomer, R., Harrington, C., & Friedlob, A. (1990). Awareness and enrollment in the Social/HMO. *The Gerontologist, 30,* 86–93.

Newcomer, R., Harrington, C., Yordi, C., & Friedlob, A. (1988). *Social/health maintenance organization demonstration evaluation: Summary.* San Francisco: University of California, San Francisco, Institute for Health and Aging.

Pear, R. (1997c, July 30). New options include shift into preventive benefits, and slightly higher costs, *New York Times,* p. A13.

Pear, R. (1997a, July 21). Elderly patients may get a break on medical costs. *New York Times,* pp. A1, 12.

Pear, R. (1997b, September 16). Modernization for Medicare grinds to halt. *New York Times,* pp. A1, 14.

Rosenthal, E. (1990, September 1). Medicare fee plan sent to Congress. *New York Times,* pp. 1, 9.

Sinclair, M. (1990, November 10). Fear of costly illness fuels "Medigap" waste. *Washington Post,* p. Bl.

U.S. House of Representatives, Committee on Ways and Means. (1986). *Background material and data on programs within the jurisdiction of the Committee on Ways and Means.* Washington, DC: U.S. Government Printing Office.

U.S. Senate, Special Committee on Aging, American Association of Retired Persons, Federal Council on the Aging, U.S. Administration on Aging. (1991). *Aging America: Trends and projections.* Washington, DC: Author.

Part III

Programs for the Aged

INTRODUCTION

Existing programs and services can be classified according to the dependence of the individuals assisted. Programs and services can also be classified in a format utilized by the Government Accounting Office* (Comptroller General of the United States, 1977): home help, medical, financial, assessment, referral, social-recreational, and transportation.

Many of the programs and services included in this list have common elements. Adult day care centers and multipurpose senior centers both utilize transportation and have major social components. Although this volume often discusses providing "services" or "serving" the elderly, the attempt is to differentiate between programs and services, terms often used synonymously. As defined, "programs" contain individual elements; "services" include many of these same elements combined under a larger umbrella. These programs and services are discussed as they are most commonly organized, but the existence of state-by-state variations means that descriptions of a program or service may be more applicable to one area than another.

In this part the focus is on individual programs vital to the well-being of the elderly: information and assistance, health and mental health programs, transportation, crime prevention and legal assistance programs, employment, volunteer, and educational programs, and nutrition programs.

---

* Comptroller General of the United States (1977). *Report to the Congress: The well-being of older people in Cleveland, Ohio.* Washington, DC: U.S. Government Printing Office.

59

5

Information and Assistance

GOALS

Creating an extensive network of services has no benefits for older persons unless they are informed about the availability of these services and how to make use of them. Information and assistance programs are thus a natural outgrowth of the tremendous increase in public and private programs for the elderly. The size of the agencies giving services, the size of the population being served in a given geographic area, and the number of different services available determine the need for an information exchange system that can identify appropriate services.

For the population at large, including the elderly, information and assistance is a social service in its own right: an activity by which a person in need is made aware of, and connected to, a service or resource which can meet the need. However, the simple concept of establishing a link between need and resource becomes complex as one takes a closer look.

The functions of information and assistance for the elderly are essentially the same as those for the general population, except for the focus on the specific needs of the elderly:

1. The assemblage and provision of information to link older persons with the services designed to help them meet their particular problems; and
2. The collection and reporting of information about the needs of older people and the adequacy of resources available to them.

Information and assistance systems link individuals to services and services to each other. The 1992 OAA amendments also emphasized follow-up to ensure that individuals receive the services they need.

HISTORY

Information and assistance programs began in the 1960s when monies were increasing for social programs. Some large federal and state agencies offered information and referral to the public in response to an expressed need. Information was provided in booklets and over the telephone as the need arose.

Official federal interest in information and assistance began in 1971, with the passage of legislation authorizing the Social Security Administration to provide information to wage earners who would soon be retiring. In 1973, under the Comprehensive Service Amendments to the Older Americans Act (OAA), priority was given to the development of information and assistance programs for the elderly. Similarly, the information and assistance needs of the general welfare population, including the elderly, were addressed under the 1974/1975 Title XX social services regulations, which designated these as optional services that states could elect to provide. However, information and assistance services were mandatory for SSI recipients. Title II of the Community Services Act of 1974 provided for urban and rural community action programs. Under a special section for Senior Opportunities and Services, provisions were made for information and assistance programs. Information and assistance programs could also be operated under the National Health Planning and Resources Development Act of 1974 and the Community Mental Health Centers Amendments of 1975. In addition, a series of interagency agreements have been developed at the federal level to promote coordination of information and assistance services through joint efforts at the federal, state, and local levels.

Information and assistance have grown in importance with each reauthorization of the Older Americans Act. The 1992 amendments required the AoA Commissioner to establish information and assistance as a priority service. In Title III, plans submitted by an Area Agency on Aging must not only discuss the establishment of information and assistance programs, but must also emphasize the linkage of isolated elderly suffering from Alzheimer's Disease or related disorders to programs and services. Demonstration grants related to information and assistance were also included in Title IV and many of the components of Title VII, involved information and assistance. A major example is the Outreach, Counseling, and Assistance Program.

OPERATION AND FUNCTIONS

A truly productive information and assistance system not only will be able to generate and respond to questions of need, but will be constantly testing the degree to which the belief that adequate services exist is based on fact. Information and assistance systems thus have the potential for generating beneficial changes in the service system. An effective information and assistance system cannot work outside the service system. The success of an information and assistance program is dependent, at least in part, on the extent and quality of the service system to which it refers.

An information and assistance system provides information about the service system and generates information through frequent contact with the services available. Information and assistance programs can be helpful to clients only if the service agencies have a clear understanding of what they are actually providing. Because the information given by agencies is not always an accurate portrayal of what is available, some information and assistance programs use client-supplied data to revise their descriptions. In addition, once the information about the agencies has been stored, it can be used as important data for planning and development purposes. Follow-up on clients receiving information from the information and assistance program can indicate the effectiveness of the service response.

ORGANIZATION

Scope

The diversity of information and assistance programs almost matches the number of information and assistance services available throughout the country, a number difficult to quantify because information sharing takes many forms. In order to identify a minimum requirement for an adequate information and assistance program, the federal Administration on Aging prepared policy guidelines to state agencies administering plans under the provisions of the OAA. Issued in August 1974, these guidelines also discuss long-range goals for the development of comprehensive information and assistance programs.

The nine service components were designed to build uniformity and comprehensiveness into the information and assistance programs and to provide some measure of adequacy. The service components emphasized:

1. Having an adequate facility to serve those seeking information;
2. making continuously updated resource files available to agencies needing service information;
3. making the service easily available to older persons;
4. providing outreach to those not familiar with using such a service;
5. following up on referrals; and
6. providing transportation when necessary to help the older person reach a service identified through information and assistance.

The individual who calls or walks into an information and assistance service is assured of anonymity, and usually no names are recorded on data forms. A casework approach is often utilized, in which the information and assistance worker explores the individual's problem and the alternative services available. As needed, the older person is referred to a specific service.

Schmandt, Bach, and Radin (1979) attempted to bring some clarity to the wide range of efforts that fall under the information and assistance label. Their attempt again indicated the complexity of the seemingly simple function of information and assistance. An information and assistance program may define its clientele on the basis of age, income, or specific problems. The program may confine itself to telephone assistance, or move into extensive outreach, including contact with individuals in their own homes. Limited research on the needs of the population within the community may also be undertaken. Within a defined city or metropolitan area, the agency offering the information and assistance program may adopt a posture which emphasizes a personal type of relationship with clients, or alternatively a relatively impersonal and highly professional one.

One of the difficulties in identifying and maintaining a minimum standard for information and assistance programs is the pressure to have these programs reflect the style, service system, and needs of the locale in which they are located. Schmandt et al. (1979) argue for both the standardized and localized programs. This would include a centralized telephone center as well as decentralized walk-in centers in local neighborhoods. A two-part system of this type can effectively respond to the multifaceted needs of a variety of clients in the local community.

There are a wide range of institutions involved in the planning and delivery of information and assistance programs. As indicated earlier, at the federal level, information and assistance responsibilities for the elderly are shared by a number of agencies. State and county social service departments represent a second layer of organizations responsible for information and assistance functions. At the community level, a variety of public and private organizations dispense information and assistance, generally to populations that include the elderly as well as other groups.

Types of Programs Available

The types of information generation, storage, and retrieval systems used are essential to determining the success of information and assistance. If local structures and community needs are taken into consideration when choosing a type of system, the system has a greater chance of success. A local walk-in information and assistance program has different information needs than a program that serves a large region and supplies data for planning. The service that can clarify its informational goals can be more effectively evaluated.

It has been suggested that the availability of late-hour and toll-free telephone lines would increase the success of information and assistance efforts. In 1990 the Administration on Aging awarded a grant to the National Association of Area Agencies on Aging to develop a toll-free 800 number which would refer callers to services in their area. The ElderCare Locator now sponsored by the National Association of Area Agencies on Aging and the National Association of State Units on Aging provides information on current services in an area, the location of the services, and the type of services being offered. It is also available online to individuals with access to the Internet.

The basic purpose of information and assistance programs is to provide information to individuals. The ability of these services to fulfill this function is difficult to evaluate from the perspective of users because "many users do not conceptually separate the information and referral service from the actual service provider" (Burkhardt, 1979, p. 30). Individuals tend to call an information and assistance service when faced with an immediate problem. In the vast majority of cases, they are referred to an agency or specialized service for assistance. Thus clients' perceptions of the effectiveness of information and assistance may be intertwined with how well they felt the agency to which they were referred dealt with their needs.

Information and assistance programs can, however, increase their perceived effectiveness by taking the necessary measures to insure that those clients who call actually make contact with appropriate services; that is, those who call an information and assistance program would have a better chance of getting the services they need if the program played a linkage and advocacy role. To facilitate referral, information and assistance can refer a client directly to one or more agencies; arrange for transportation or escort to insure that the client can reach the referred service; go to the client's home to provide direct assistance; call the service provider directly, giving information about the client, and then tell the client that the necessary contact has been made; or persuade a provider to handle a unique or difficult problem.

One of the big problems of information and assistance programs, as with any program available to the elderly, is accessibility to anyone who needs the service. The information and assistance program has the potential of being the most widely available of any service for the elderly because, by its very nature, it is relatively inexpensive and equally accessible to everyone. However, despite this relative accessibility, information and assistance programs are used by a disproportionate number of people who are already connected into the system in some way. The lack of awareness about many programs is probably most acute among lower-income minority elderly. A recent study of reservation-based, urban and rural Native American elderly in Michigan indicated that only 25% of these older persons knew about all of the services available to them (Chapleski, Gelfand, & Pugh, 1997). Unfortunately, direct outreach is expensive, and many such programs do not have adequate funds. When funds are limited, extensive use of the media appears the best way to reach isolated elderly populations. It is thus likely that most information and assistance services will not undertake the wide range of follow-up and client advocacy functions that are possible for information and assistance programs.

Several programs have been established in recent years to decrease the number of steps required before an individual obtains appropriate assistance from a variety of organizations. These programs utilize information and assistance programs as their base, but go further in their assistance. In Maryland, the Gateway I program is designed to provide a "single point of entry," usually through intake at senior centers. During fiscal 1985, the program served 14,260 older persons and provided information on Social Security, housing, income/financial assistance, health care, transportation, legal assistance, employment, nutrition/food support, home repair, and leisure activities (Bechill, 1987).

As the Maryland Office on Aging (1984) notes:

> Generally, each local site offers: toll-free (or collect) telephone service, in-person, walk-in service, full service five days a week, a coordinated system to provide information and assistance in obtaining available benefits and services, follow-up action to ensure that available assistance has been rendered, arrangements for comprehensive assessments of impaired elderly persons and current resource inventory files on aging services on local, state and federal levels in each local jurisdiction. (p. 30)

The National Long-Term Care demonstration begun in 1980 was designed to test the ability of a single point-of-entry system and case management approaches to identify and provide services to frail elderly. Based on 10 sites and over 6,300 clients, the evaluation team reported in 1986 that the "channeling" approach identified a very vulnerable older population. Among this group, over 22% were unable to perform the major activities of daily living such as eating, getting out of bed, or dressing (Mathematica Policy Research, 1986). An effective single point-of-entry system could also be combined with a case management unit within the information and assistance agency. As Applebaum and Austin (1990) suggest, the case management unit could receive referrals directly from information and assistance workers who would assess the clients to ascertain whether they would benefit from case management.

Funding

Funding for information and assistance programs comes from a variety of federal, state, local, and private sources, although state and area agencies contribute a larger percentage of funds to more information and assistance than other types of contributors. Major federal resources available include the Administration on Aging, or the Community Services block grant. Additional sources of funds include state and county taxes; civic and religious groups; private, nonprofit sources such as United Way and Community Chest Agencies; private groups such as local foundations, corporations, and unions; and income from the project itself, through the sale of items such as brochures, directories, and planning information.

IMPORTANCE

Information and assistance programs can be the link between the individual needing some type of service that can best meet that person's needs and relevant programs. According to the National Council on the Aging (1982), the effective information and assistance system must be:

- confidential
- accessible to all older persons
- sensitive to feelings and problems of older persons
- friendly to older clients
- reliable and accurate in the information it provides
- accountable and responsive to older persons and families
- neutral and nonpartisan in its referrals
- broad in the range of information it provides.

Many older people are unaware of the kinds of services available and how they can be found and, in many cases, are approaching the thought of professional assistance for the first time in their adult lives. A well-implemented information and assistance program can make older people aware of services, help them formulate their problem in the context of available services, and assist them in actually making the contact with the appropriate service. Organizing the maze of possible service systems, regulations, and eligibility requirements into a package of information, the information and assistance program is essential for responsive service delivery to the elderly, regardless of the size of the community. Just as information and assistance cannot be effective without a good service delivery system, service delivery systems cannot be effective without an efficient information and assistance program: one that reaches to everyone in need of problem solving.

REFERENCES

Applebaum, R., & Austin, C. (1990). *Long-term case management: Design and evaluation.* New York: Springer Publishing Company.

Bechill, W. (1987, March 9). *The reauthorization of the Older Americans Act.* Paper presented before the Subcommittee on Human Resources, Committee on Education and Labor, U.S. House of Representatives, Washington, DC.

Burkhardt, J. (1979). Evaluating information and referral services. *Gerontologist, 19,* 28–33.

Chapleski, E., Gelfand, D., & Pugh, K.(1997). Great Lakes American Indian elders and service utilization: Does residence matter? *Journal of Applied Gerontology, 16,* 333–354.

Maryland Office on Aging. (1984). *1984 annual report.* Baltimore: Author.

Mathematica Policy Research. (1986). *National Long-Term Care Channeling Demonstration: Final report.* Plainsboro, NJ: Author.

National Council on the Aging. (1982). *Comprehensive service delivery through senior centers and other community focal points: A resource manual.* Washington, DC: Author.

Schmandt, J., Bach, V., & Radin, B. (1979). Information and referral services for the elderly welfare recipients. *Gerontologist, 19,* 21–27.

6

Health and Mental Health

As noted in Chapter 1, the elderly suffer from a variety of chronic illnesses. The older adult does not suffer from the common cold as much as arthritis, the effects of strokes, and vision and hearing problems. Medical care for a population with these types of problems must stress not only efforts to cure, but treatment that allows the individual to adjust to living with a condition that may vary in intensity but will always be present.

Attempts to provide medical care for the elderly have met a variety of roadblocks including: (1) the lack of interest by physicians in treating individuals whose conditions are not "curable"; (2) the high costs of medical care; and (3) the inaccessibility of medical treatment. These problems are also endemic in mental health treatment of the elderly.

Medicare and Medicaid have helped to reduce the cost of medical care for many older adults, although the out-of-pocket share of medical expenses incurred by the elderly has been increasing consistently. Specialized transportation programs for older adults have also targeted medical appointments as a top priority. A major problem that remains to be addressed is the recruitment and training of professionals and paraprofessionals dedicated to providing medical care for seniors. Until the mid-1970s, there was little emphasis on geriatrics in American schools of medicine. The curriculum in most medical schools has only recently begun to include any appreciable content on the aging process.

Even if physicians show increased interest in treating the elderly, hospitals are oriented toward acute illnesses, and individuals who remain hospitalized for an extended length of time run up enormous bills. The alternative to acute care hospitals—a long stay in a nursing home—has not been attractive to the elderly or their families.

Only the introduction of in-home services and adult day care centers (to be discussed in Part IV) has made care possible outside of long-term facilities such as hospitals and nursing homes. The majority of health care programs serving the elderly are part of the extensive range of home care services that are becoming available. In this chapter we will examine health care programs available through clinics, hospitals, and non-home care agencies.

With the elderly spending substantial amounts of money for health care, the question has arisen as to whether separate services should be developed that are oriented to older adults. Separate services may require duplication of facilities and equipment. These facilities may be avoided by older individuals who feel stigmatized by attending special clinics. Alternatively, while encouraging the elderly to utilize existing services may avoid major capital outlays, older patients at large clinics often receive less attention from health professionals attracted to younger, more "curable" clients. With younger clients being generally more assertive about the health care to which they feel entitled, the net result is that the elderly are relegated to long waits and poor care.

HEALTH CARE PROGRAMS

Geriatric Clinics

A geriatric health clinic in a medical center is a compromise service delivery system that avoids setting up new facilities, but guarantees the elderly that their medical needs will receive attention. At Syracuse University, a geriatric clinic was integrated with other community health facilities. The clinic planners hoped that this integration would help to avoid ostracization of the elderly. Patients were assisted in establishing a relationship with a physician, but the clinic also maintained a referral service for specialized medical problems not treatable at the clinic (Syracuse University School of Social Work, 1971).

A similar model was utilized at the geriatric clinic opened in 1970 at Worcester State Hospital in Massachusetts. Patients were referred to the clinic by neighborhood workers. At the clinic, medical histories, physicals, and laboratory tests were undertaken. Based on the results of these tests, a decision was made by clinic medical personnel either to treat or to refer the client to other medical services. Clients with no regular physician were referred to an outpatient clinic or a local hospital, or they remained as patients of the geriatric clinic (Worcester State Hospital, 1972).

These screening programs are now common at senior centers, and many are held in May during Older Americans Month. In a medically underserved rural area of southwestern Pennsylvania, the Area Agency on Aging uses a 35-foot van for mobile health screening (Goughler, Lange, & Broggi, 1986).

The Worcester clinic provided treatment, but other programs have been primarily oriented to either screening, publicizing medical needs of the elderly, or encouraging the elderly to obtain adequate medical care. In Hawaii, difficulties in reaching facilities, together with psychological fears resulting from limited fluency in English or low education, resulted in underutilization of health services by the elderly. To meet this problem, a senior center health screening program was instituted. Conducted on a bimonthly basis in Honolulu, the program was able to screen 100 individuals in 3-4 hours. Counseling was provided to the individual about existing medical conditions and abnormal results. Abnormal results were also reported to the individual's primary care physician. In some cases where serious conditions were noted, the screening program instituted follow-up to insure that the individual obtained the necessary medical treatment (Hawaii Senior Services, 1975).

In Baltimore, the Veterans Administration Medical Center operates a Geriatric Assessment and Continuity of Care Outpatient Clinic. The GAP program provides evaluation, management, and continuity of care to frail older veterans who have a number of chronic illnesses or mental health problems. The Waxter Senior Center in Baltimore has an affiliation with the University of Maryland Department of Internal Medicine. The department operates a health clinic at the senior center.

Health Promotion

Local primary prevention programs have been built around educational programs informing the elderly about nutrition, care of chronic illnesses, correct drug usage, and a variety of other medical issues. These educational programs have been run at senior centers, nutrition sites, and adult day care centers. Short television and radio announcements have also been utilized in efforts to alert the elderly to potential health problems and appropriate treatment. Health fairs have been inaugurated in many localities. These one-day fairs provide information on a variety of health conditions and programs and offer basic screening of blood pressure, vision, and hearing. The Health-O-Rama held each year in the Detroit metropolitan area offers a variety of free screenings each year for individuals of all ages.

Exercise Programs

In recent years, it has become evident that regular exercise is an important element of illness prevention for individuals of all ages. Increasing numbers of senior centers, as well as day care programs, are offering exercise classes and activities for their clients. In West Virginia, the Prevent-care program offers three-day-a-week exercise sessions at senior centers, nutrition sites, churches, mental health centers, hospitals, and nursing homes in 51 of the 55 West Virginia counties (National Institute on Senior Centers, 1978). The Adult Health Development clinic at the University of Maryland offers older adults regular Saturday morning exercises and physical activities in which they are assisted by individual students. The relationships developed through this one-to-one contact often extend into close friendships between students and older persons. Similarly, the Senior Actualizations and Growth Exploration (SAGE) program begun in California works with small groups of older persons, who join together for an extended involvement. A variety of techniques are used including exercise, meditation, yoga, massage, and gestalt therapy. SAGE's efforts show that many of the newer growth and therapy techniques can be effective with any age group, given the individual's willingness to undertake the intensive commitment required.

Dental Care

Dental problems increase with age, and a lack of visits to the dentist only exacerbates dental problems. In 1979, 33% of older Americans had not visited a dentist in the last year and 44% had not been to a dentist in the past 5 years. In 1985–86, 37% of Americans aged 65–74 were edentulous—without any natural teeth. While this figure may seem high, it is a significant improvement from the 55% found in 1957. Among groups such as native Americans, however, over half of the group age 65–74 were edentulous (Phipps, 1989). Dental care is not reimbursed through Medicare, and only eight states cover dental care through Medicaid. Other efforts are being fostered to make regular dental care affordable for older adults. In some states, dental societies are beginning to work with senior centers and Area Agencies on Aging to offer dental care to elderly clients at reduced rates. This reduced-rate dental care may be provided at the dentists' offices, but some senior centers are also incorporating dental suites into their facilities. These dental facilities also serve as training sites for dental students.

Drugs

As major consumers of both prescription and over-the-counter drugs, the elderly are faced with the problems of absorbing the enormous costs of these medications, even when assisted by Medicare and Medicaid. The shift in many states to utilization of generic rather than brand-name drugs is helping to lower costs. Since 1958, the American Association of Retired Persons (AARP) has operated direct-mail pharmacies for its elderly members. In 1978, AARP pharmacies were located in eight cities and offered a full line of over-the-counter and prescription drugs.

Beyond providing drugs at lower costs, a number of programs are now directed to providing more consumer education about the potentials as well as the dangers of drugs. The Elder-Ed program at the University of Maryland pairs retired pharmacists and students in drug education efforts at senior centers and apartment complexes for the elderly. A corollary effort, Elder Health, uses students and retired pharmacists to train other caregivers who can provide drug education to older consumers. Through its pharmacies, AARP is providing more detailed leaflets with the drugs it sells (Lipton & Lee, 1983). In addition, increasing numbers of pharmacists are maintaining personal profiles that keep an inventory of the drugs the older consumer may be utilizing. This effort enables pharmacists to alert consumers when drugs, often prescribed by different doctors, may cause dangerous drug interactions.

All of these diverse efforts will need to be greatly expanded in the future if the requisite health care for the elderly is to be provided. As the numbers of elderly living in the community increases, a larger complement of health care programs will be needed to prevent and treat acute and chronic illnesses prevalent among older adults.

MENTAL HEALTH PROGRAMS

In the United States, mental hospitals have often functioned as quasi-homes for the aged. Although the number of patients in state mental hospitals has lessened dramatically in the past 30 years, many of the elderly released from the hospitals had been patients for 20 years or more. Community-based treatment programs, psychotropic drugs (Bloom, 1975), the tightening of legal grounds for commitment, and the growth of nursing homes has dramatically curtailed the number of older patients in state mental hospitals. At Oregon State Hospital, (1998) for example, 114 of the licensed 727 beds are set aside for patients served by the geropsychiatric program.

Community Mental Health

Community mental health programs took root in 1963 with the passage of the Community Mental Health Centers Act. The intention of the Act's supporters was to enlarge mental health expenditures at all levels and develop a network of community-based treatment facilities. These treatment facilities would be located in geographic areas that had a maximum population of 175,000. Each state, however, had to determine appropriate catchment-area boundaries. In each catchment area an organization was to be designated as responsible for providing community mental health services.

As originally specified in 1963, the services included five major components. In 1975, this list was enlarged to a total of 12 different services:

1. Inpatient care
2. Outpatient care
3. Partial hospitalization (day care)
4. Emergency services
5. Consultation and education
6. Specialized services for children
7. Specialized services for the elderly
8. Screening of individuals considered for referral to a state mental hospital
9. Follow-up services for discharged inpatients
10. Transitional halfway houses for former mental patients
11. Programs for prevention and treatment of alcoholism if not already in existence in the catchment area
12. Programs for the prevention and treatment of drug addiction, if not already available in the catchment area.

Under the block grant program initiated in 1981, the number of required services was placed at five: outpatient services, 24-hour-a-day emergency services, day treatment, screening of patients for state mental health facilities, and consultation and education.

The actual proportion of effort and funds allocated by a mental health center to any one of these components was to be determined by the needs of the community. While 675 centers were in operation by 1979, the goals of having a center in all 1,500 catchment areas in the country remains a long way from being realized.

Primary prevention, as embodied in the consultation and education programs, was one of the major assumptions of this "bold new approach" (Kennedy, 1963) to mental health services. Treatments for individual mental health problems were supposed to be supplemented by primary prevention programs that located the sources of stress in the environment and worked with community groups to alleviate these negative influences. Primary prevention efforts focused on at-risk populations would include the elderly in many communities.

The 1987 OAA amendments explicitly added the term "mental health" at many points where formerly only the term "health" had been used. Any mental health services provided with AAA funds were to be coordinated with community mental health center programs and those of other public and nonprofit agencies.

Mental Health Prevention Programs

Unfortunately, adequate appropriations to replace federal funding have not been forthcoming, and cutbacks in programming have been made at many centers. These cutbacks have often been at the expense of primary prevention programs. Primary prevention programs are often seen by traditional trained mental health professionals as irrelevant to therapeutic intervention with individuals.

One innovative approach that is becoming increasingly common is the development of peer counseling among older people. In Santa Monica, California, a peer counseling program was begun in 1977. By 1990, 208 counselors had been trained. Each counselor must volunteer for 8 hours per week for one year after training (Bratter, 1986). Part of the growth of peer counseling programs can be explained by the belief that older people will more readily talk to their age peers than to younger age cohorts. Peer counselors can also serve as positive role models for the individuals they counsel (Bratter & Freeman, 1990). Although peer counseling for older adults has often begun as a way to provide services at limited costs, its benefits have quickly established them as worthwhile efforts. A survey of peer counseling programs indicated that counselors saw most of their clients once a week. Counseling was conducted at an agency or senior center (44%) or at the client's home (33%)(Bratter & Freeman, 1990).

Tertiary prevention programs aimed at reintegrating discharged patients into family and community life have also encountered difficulty in becoming well-established and accepted. Part of this difficulty can be traced to the methods used by advocates of these programs in obtaining support for deinstitutionalization. During the 1960s, mental hospitals were derided, not only for their effects on individuals and the lack of adequate treatment, but for their supposedly high costs.

Deinstitutionalization

Proponents of community-based programs argued that individuals could be treated outside the state mental hospital without creating an "institutional personality" and at a lower cost. Actual experiences have not always shown these cost claims to be true. While state mental hospital costs are evident upon careful auditing, accounting for the costs of a community-based program are more difficult.

Mrs. S. provides a good example. A woman in her early 70s, she had been in the state hospital for 20 years. Discharged under the new community approach of the 1960s, Mrs. S. has been living in an old hotel in a beach-front community in New York. Because of her lack of any other means of support, she receives financial aid from the state as well as casework services from the Department of Social Services. The mental health services she obtains are provided through the Department of Mental Hygiene. If any vocational training is included in the supports she receives, this will be provided by the Department of Vocational Rehabilitation.

Mrs. S. is thus receiving a variety of services, most of which are not provided under mental health auspices. Unless this is taken into account when cost-effectiveness studies of institutionally based versus community-based programs are compared, the figures will show that the costs of the community services are considerably cheaper, which may not be true, given the number of paid professionals involved in assisting Mrs. S. to remain in the community. As the reality of the costs involved in providing quality aftercare services in mental health has become evident, claims about cost-effectiveness have become muted. The opening of new programs to serve released patients has also been retarded.

Discharged mental patients living in old hotels and domiciliary facilities operated by state mental health departments continue to make headlines, as many communities protest these problems being "dumped" in their neighborhoods. As some communities pass zoning regulations, making it difficult to open new facilities, discharged mental patients become concentrated in areas such as Long Beach, New York; South Miami; or parts of Chicago. If the ex-patients themselves do not create problems, their assumed vulnerability attracts individuals who prey on them.

Thus the promise of deinstitutionalization has not been fulfilled. As Curtis (1981) has commented, it was not unreasonable to think that community programs could replace state hospitals when the enrollment of these hospitals was shrinking. The resistance of communities to deinstitutionalized patients, the instability of many small community programs, and the preference of the private sector for working with less impaired individuals were not anticipated.

Aided by the impetus of the Community Support Program of the National Institute of Mental Health, community-based foster care and group homes have become available in many states. Many of the basic costs of housing and feeding individuals in these programs are met through the availability of federal SSI funds for disabled individuals. With this base of federal funds, states have been willing to provide the additional case-management services needed to enable a chronically mentally ill older person to live in a community setting.

ELDERLY IN THE MENTAL HEALTH SYSTEM

There are now three major groups of elderly involved in the mental health system: (1) elderly who have been long-term residents of state hospitals and are attempting to live outside the controlled hospital environment; (2) elderly who have been utilizing mental health services for a period of time; and (3) elderly who begin to exhibit major mental health problems only as they become older. These problems may include depression, insomnia, hypochondria, paranoia, and organic brain disorders. We will examine the present condition of mental health services for former residents of state hospitals and for older persons exhibiting mental health problems often associated with aging.

Discharged Patients

Individuals who have been in a mental hospital for a long period of time may have major difficulties readjusting to any form of independent life in the community. As Kirk and Therrien (1975) have argued, family members are often opposed to long-term mental patients living in their homes. An added complication is that mental patients often have few employable skills and minimal financial resources. Watson (1976) has shown, however, that the morale among elderly psychiatric patients being treated on an outpatient basis was significantly higher than among elderly inpatients. For elderly outpatients to function adequately in the community, extensive supportive services are needed, including a means for obtaining regular medications.

Mental Health and Nursing Homes

The hue and cry about the lack of aftercare programs would be even greater if the 1960s had not seen a major growth in the number of nursing homes. Nursing homes have now taken a major share of the burden of caring for the institutionalized elderly. The drops in individuals in state hospitals since 1960 was matched by an equivalent increase in nursing home patients.

The National Center for Health Statistics 1973 survey of nursing home patients found that the largest percentage were labeled "senile," a label that now appears to be as vague as it is overused (Glasscote et al., 1976). Whatever the mental condition of nursing home patients, few are actively receiving psychiatric care. Glasscote et al. (1976) summarized a 1976 investigation of the mental health needs and treatment of nursing home patients:

Our sample of nursing facilities estimated that about three quarters of their patients are either formally diagnosed with a psychiatric disorder or are "de facto psychiatrically impaired"; if this figure can be projected to the 1,100,000 population of all nursing homes, then there are more than three quarters of a million nursing home patients with psychiatric disability, most of whom have had no contact at all with psychiatrists. (p. 71)

In 1987, Congress required that applicants for nursing homes be screened for mental health problems. Screening may be partly responsible for the 108% increase between 1977 and 1987 in the number of nursing home residents diagnosed with a mental health disorder (Smyer, Shea & Streit, 1994). Individuals who need treatment must be provided this treatment by a nursing home. Prior to passage of this legislation it is estimated that only 4.5% of nursing home residents were receiving mental health treatment, a figure much lower than any available estimates of need. Among those receiving treatment, the most common diagnosis was schizophrenia (Burns et al., 1993).

Elderly in Mental Health Centers

For the majority of the over-60 population, mental health services must be obtained from community mental health centers. As already shown, services to the elderly were a requirement for federally funded mental health centers. Despite this mandate of 1975, mental health centers have still not shown a major interest in providing extensive mental health services for older adults. For the majority of mental health professionals, the most desirable clients remain youthful, attractive, verbal, intelligent, and successful individuals (Schofield, 1964). In contrast, the elderly are often perceived as depressed individuals whose problems are merely the product of "getting old." Whereas the younger persons have an extensive future ahead of them, mental health professionals may view older persons as having their "best years" behind them, and thus as less deserving of attention.

The present generation of elderly may also fail to utilize mental health services because of their limited education and fluency in English. Other more complex reasons are that they may (1) not recognize some behaviors as mental health problems; (2) believe that many mental health problems are the responsibility of the family unless extremely serious (Fandetti & Gelfand, 1978); (3) stigmatize mental illness and be fearful of being labeled "crazy" if it becomes known that they are utilizing mental health services; (4) be unaware of the services available at mental health centers; or (5) have difficulty reaching mental health centers and clinics because of lack of transportation. At present, the mental health needs of the elderly are much greater than the services provided. The prevalence of mental illness and emotional distress is higher among those over age 65 than in the general population. The incidence of depression (the most common mental health problem among the elderly) among older persons living in the community is 1–4%. This figure rises to 10% among elderly hospitalized for medical reasons and to 20–25% among older persons who are cognitively intact but living in nursing homes (Katz, 1997).

Widowed Persons and Peer Counseling Programs

The widowed persons programs are important efforts run independently of mental health centers. These programs provide counseling on an individualized basis to men and women who are recently widowed. These widows and widowers are paired with volunteers who provide support on emotional issues relating to the loss of a spouse and practical information about preparing to lead a life as a single person. This practical information may cover finances or even learning to drive for the first time. The AARP runs the largest widowed persons program in the United States. In 1987, the program was available at 190 locations.

SPECIALIZED AGING SERVICES

Flemming, Buchanan, Santos, and Rickard (1984) have examined the effects of the switch in mental health funding from a "categorical" system to the block grant system that removed specific requirements for mental health services for the elderly. Under the block grant system, decisions about specific priority groups for mental health services are now made at the state level.

The data collected indicated a decline since 1981 in the specialized services available to older persons in 55% of the centers participating in the Flemming et al. Study (1984). It thus remains questionable whether the mental health services available to older persons from mental health providers have improved.

An encouraging sign is the integration of mental health services in services provided by Area Agencies on Aging. In Washington, a service agreement between the Spokane Community Mental Health Center and the Eastern Washington Area Agency on Aging has been based on the assumption that "mental health needs of the elderly, especially frail, vulnerable, or moderately to severely dysfunctional cannot be separated from physical, social and economic needs" (Raschko, 1985, p. 461). Among the older individuals participating in the program, 95% have received no prior mental health care.

The Michigan Office of Services to the Aging and the state Department of Mental Health have implemented a program ("Building Ties") through which participating counties designate a liaison person to help coordinate mental health services for older persons. In Indiana, a mental health center staff person is placed for a half day per week at a senior center, nutrition center, or public housing project. This staff person conducts educational programs, in-service training on mental health, group discussions, case and program consultation, as well as reduced-fee individual counseling ("Michigan program." 1990).

The Psychogeriatric Assessment, Treatment, and Teaching program in Baltimore utilizes two nurses and two psychiatrists to conduct mental health outreach efforts in public housing with a large population of older residents. The residents are referred to the PATCH team by building management (Roca, Storer, Robbins, Tlasek, & Rabins, 1990). A similar program in Ventura County, California, relies on an interdisciplinary mobile geriatric team. These mobile teams have had success in reaching minority elderly who feel unable to seek services at a mental health center or who have transportation problems (Hernandez & Sweon, 1989).

As the President's Commission on Mental Health (1978) emphasized, the lack of outreach to older persons is a major factor in their representation in mental health services. Medicare coverage for mental health services remains limited. Medicare provisions emphasize hospital treatment and nursing home care, with only limited coverage for outpatient mental health services. Changes in these provisions to emphasize community-based treatment might provide the transfusion necessary for financially strapped community mental health centers and clinics to turn their attention to the mental health needs of the elderly.

REFERENCES

Bloom, B. (1975). *Community mental health*. Monterey, CA: Brooks/Cole.
Bratter, B. (1986). Peer counseling for older adults. *Generations, 10*, 49–50.
Bratter, B., & Freeman, E. (1990). The maturing of peer counseling. *Generations, 14*, 49–52.
Burns, B., Wagner, R., Taube, J., Magaziner, J., Permutt, T., & Landerman, R. (1993). Mental health service use by the elderly in nursing homes. *American Journal of Public Health, 83*, 331–337.
Curtis, W. R. (1981). Commentary. *New England Journal of Human Services, 1*, 4–6.
Fandetti, D., & Gelfand, D. (1978). Attitudes towards symptoms and services in the ethnic family and neighborhood. *American Journal of Orthopsychiatry 48*, 477–486.
Flemming, A., Buchanan, J., Santos, J., & Rickard, L. (1984). *Mental health services*

for the elderly. Washington, DC: Action Committee to Implement the Mental Health Recommendations of the 1981 White House Conference on Aging.

Glasscote, R., Biegel, A., Butterfield, A., Jr., Clark, E., Cox, B., Wiper, J. R., Gudeman, J. E., Gurel, L., Lewis, R. V., Mila, D. G., Raybin, J. B., Reifler, C., & Vito, E., Jr. (1976). *Old folks at homes*. Washington, DC: American Psychiatric Association and the Mental Health Association.

Goughler, D., Lange, B., & Broggi, A. (1986). Health screening van solves access problems for rural Pennsylvania elderly. *Aging, 353*, 33.

Hawaii Senior Services. (1975). *Health screening for the elderly*. Honolulu: Author.

Hernandez, A., & Sweon, C. (1989). Mobile mental health team reaches minorities. *Aging, No. 359*, 12–13.

Katz, I. (1997, Spring). Late life depression. *Inside ASA.*.

Kennedy, J. F. (1963). *A message from the President of the United States relative to mental illness and mental retardation*. Washington, DC: Government Printing Office.

Kirk, S., & Therrien, M. (1975). Community mental health myths and the fate of former hospitalized patients. *Psychiatry, 38*, 209–217.

Lipton, H., & Lee, P. (1983). Innovative drug information sources for professionals and elders. *Generations, 8*, 54–56.

Michigan program links aging services with community mental health providers. (1990, December 7.) *Older American Reports*. 474.

National Institute on Senior Centers. *Senior Center Report, 1978, 1*, 3.

Oregon State Hospital (1998). *Child adolescent and geropsychiatric treatment services*. Available: omhs.mhd.hr.state.or.us/ogh/index.html.

Phipps, K. (1989). *Oral health status of native-American elders*. Washington, DC: Gerontological Society of America Fellowship Program in Applied Gerontology.

President's Commission on Mental Health. (1978). *Report to the President (Vol. 1)*. Washington, DC: U.S. Government Printing Office.

Raschko, R. (1985). Systems integration at the program level: Aging and mental health. *Generations, 25*, 460–463.

Roca, R., Storer, D., Robbins, B., Tlasek, M., & Rabins, P. (1990). Psychogeriatric assessment and treatment in urban public housing. *Hospital and Community Psychiatry, 41*, 916–920.

Schofield, W. (1964). *Psychotherapy: The purchase of friendship*. Englewood Cliffs, NJ: Prentice-Hall.

Smyer, M., Shea, D., & Streit, A. (1994). The provision and use of mental health services in nursing homes: Results from the national medical expenditure survey. *American Journal of Public Health, 84*, 284–287.

Syracuse University School of Social Work. (1971). *Concerns in planning health services for the elderly*. Syracuse, NY: Author.

Watson, C. (1976). Inpatient care or outplacement: Which is better for the psychiatrically medically infirm patient? *Journal of Gerontology, 31*, 611–616.

Worcester State Hospital. (1972). *Two year activities of a geriatric clinic in the Worcester area*. Worcester, MA: Author.

7

Transportation

Transportation programs are a necessary support for community-based aging services, including day care centers, senior centers, mental health centers, and nutritional and educational programs. Transportation is also a crucial factor in elder's ability to obtain medical care, maintain relationships with family and friends, and attend social and cultural events.

Many communities lack any transportation system designed to serve the general public. This lack of public transportation programs will be a more significant problem in the future as the elderly population living in suburban communities increases. Dependence on the automobile is difficult for many older persons, who feel a lessening sense of security behind the driver's wheel as their reflexes slow. Visual problems also preclude many elderly from driving at night, limiting the social events they can attend. For the elderly on fixed incomes, the cost of purchasing and maintaining an automobile may also prove to be too burdensome. At present, reports indicate that the majority of elderly living in urban areas depend on walking to reach their destinations. The mobility problems of the isolated rural elderly are intensified because of inadequate and often poorly maintained road systems.

Data collected by the United States Department of Transportation (1997) indicates that transportation-related fatalities rise significantly among individuals over the age of 75. Although only 9% of pedestrians are over the age of 70, 19% of pedestrian fatalities occur among this age group, a percentage higher than among any other age group.

A variety of approaches to the transportation needs of urban, suburban, and rural elderly are thus required. To place the present thrust of transportation programs in an appropriate framework, we need to examine the goals of these services and the factors that impinge on realization of these goals.

OPTIONS

Transportation systems can vary in their extensiveness, their frequency of operation, and their ability to meet the individualized interests of potential consumers. In the language of transportation planning, these systems can be "demand-responsive," "need-responsive," or "desire-responsive." While demand-responsive systems respond to calls for service on the part of individuals, need-responsive systems attempt to service transportation requirements felt to be important to the individual's maintenance of a satisfying life. The demands placed on transportation services by elderly individuals may be less than what they "need" for an independent, healthy lifestyle. Need-responsive systems are close to desire-responsive systems, and planners usually confine their analyses to these two groups.

The optimal transportation system for the elderly and the handicapped would be need-responsive, increasing the options of these populations for interactions with a range of individuals and programs. In densely populated areas, an inexpensive, properly designed mass transit system may enable the older person to reach a variety of important destinations. In suburban and rural areas with low density and dispersed services, a system responsive to the older person's needs is more difficult to implement.

MODELS

The major variables in transportation systems are routing, schedules, and loading points. Four major combinations of routing and scheduling are possible: (1) fixed-route services with fixed scheduling, a model corresponding to mass transit; (2) fixed routing with varied scheduling; (3) variable routing with fixed scheduling; and (4) variable routing with variable scheduling. As we examine both existing and newly developing transportation systems, we will note examples of all four of these alternatives.

Aggregate trips taken by individuals to different sites, and the costs or subsidization that must be borne for each trip taken, are major factors in choosing transportation models appropriate to a community. As transit authorities around the country have discovered, public transit systems cannot be expected to run at a profit if fares are to be kept at a reasonable level. The growing understanding that public transit of any form needs to be subsidized has retarded its development in many areas. Unfortunately, many transit authorities attempting to stop the rise of deficits have become involved in a cycle of raising fares, resulting in a lower number of riders and subsequent fare increases. With each fare increase, the differential between the costs of mass transit and driving decreases, and increasing numbers of individuals therefore turn to their automobiles for commuting and pleasure trips. Transportation systems of all kinds must face the issue of the maximum subsidies that the community will tolerate and optimal methods for financing these subsidies.

FORMS OF TRANSPORTATION FOR THE ELDERLY

Mass Transit

During the 1960s and 1970s, an effort was made to encourage the use of existing mass transit facilities by the elderly. Under the 1974 National Mass Transit Assistance Act, the Urban Mass Transit Administration was authorized to allot funds for capital and operating costs of mass transit systems. Communities attempting to qualify for these funds were required to institute programs for the elderly that reduced fares in nonpeak hours to no more than one-half of peak-hour fares. A number of major cities had already instituted this approach before the federal legislation was enacted. By 1974, 145 cities had already instituted half-fare programs (U.S. Administration on Aging, 1975).

Cantor's interviews (1970) with a sample of New York City elderly indicated that they felt they used the subway and bus system more extensively because of the low-fare privileges. This increase in ridership creates some methodological problems in evaluating the costs of this type of program. Half-fare rides are obviously not matching the operating costs for each ride. If, however, the ridership increases at nonpeak hours, even at half-fare, is this increase reducing the subsidization? Alternatively, have some of the individuals now riding at off-peak hours switched their riding patterns from peak hours, reducing the number of full fares collected by the system and thus increasing the number of heavily subsidized rides?

Answers to these questions have been difficult to obtain, but the positive effects of the program for elderly riders have been demonstrated. These include increased use of the mass transit systems by the elderly to attend social activities and programs and to obtain medical care. Unfortunately, available studies do not reveal the reasons many elderly still refrain from using the transit system. The stress of the elderly on convenience and accessibility, rather than costs of transportation, may account for reduced ridership among older people, who have to walk long distances to reach transit stops or take buses even to reach the subway. Having accomplished this task, they then must surmount obstacles posed by steps on buses or stairways in subway stations.

The Urban Mass Transportation Act (UMTA) specifies that elderly and handicapped persons have the same rights to utilize mass transportation facilities and services as other individuals. In 1975, regulations were issued requiring recipients of UMTA funds to build their facilities in a manner that would not create physical barriers for the elderly and handicapped. Installation of elevators at all new subway stations has been one major outgrowth of this requirement.

The physical barriers on buses are more difficult to overcome. In East Orange, New Jersey (Rinaldi, 1973), an escort service was provided during the early 1970s to help elderly individuals negotiate the steps of buses and other public transit barriers. In 1973, a negative report on this effort was issued. Despite the assistance made available by the escorts, the costs of this service were prohibitive. Costs were doubled, since fares were required for both the elderly person and the escort. The service was also not found to promote new trips by elderly individuals.

Regulations issued by the Department of Transportation required all new buses purchased with UMTA funds after September 1979 to have boarding ramps or hydraulic lifts, floor heights no more than 22 inches off the ground, and an ability to "kneel" to 18 inches. The regulations were rescinded in 1981, and local communities were allowed to demonstrate that they had made reasonable efforts to meet the needs of the elderly and the handicapped. Under the Americans with Disabilities Act passed in 1990, all new buses ordered after August 26, 1990, must be accessible to people with disabilities.

New Transportation Systems

Building public transportation systems is an extremely costly process, and these systems do not always provide the most direct route to a destination. In some cases, a bus trip to a medical center may require 50 minutes and a transfer of buses and cost $1.00. A taxicab ride to the same destination might occupy 10 minutes, cost $1.50, and be door-to-door.

The problems involved in creating new transportation systems for the elderly are more complex than reductions in fares on existing mass transit facilities. Critical examination of the potential of new systems is necessary because of the increasingly decentralized living patterns of Americans. The Federal Aid to Highways Act of 1973 emphasized the need to take the mobility needs of rural elderly and handicapped into account in highway planning and improvements (U.S. Department of Transportation, 1976).

Financial assistance for transportation programs has been available under Section 16(b)(2) of UMTA grants to assist nonprofit organizations in providing services to the elderly and handicapped when mass transit systems are unavailable, insufficient, or not appropriate (U.S. House of Representatives, 1976). In 1990, 1400 vehicles were purchased with these UMTA funds. Under the UMTA program, 20% of these vehicle costs must be contributed by the local agency or transit authority. Supplementing the UMTA funds in many communities are funds from Title III of the OAA (which, as noted in Chapter 2, now places a strong emphasis on issues of access); revenue-sharing funds; and purchase of care arrangements among individual social service agencies.

Substantial amounts of Title III funds have been channeled into transportation programs, although the AoA discourages the use of these monies for the purchase of vehicles. AoA officials fear that many agencies will not be able to afford the expenses of maintaining and operating these vehicles after using Title III funds to purchase them. The difficulties of meeting operating expenses is a common theme among organizations running extensive transportation efforts and facing mounting repair costs for heavily used vehicles. The costs of repairs plus high gasoline prices continue to make transportation an expensive service.

Obtaining adequate insurance at reasonable rates was previously a major headache for agencies attempting to implement transportation services for the elderly. In 1980, this major block to the expansion of transportation programs began to be resolved by new insurance ratings agreed upon by the federal government and the insurance industry. Under this new grouping, insurance ratings for vehicles owned by a program, or owned by employees or volunteers who transport the elderly, were placed midway between those for school buses and city buses. The new rates also provided excess liability insurance for the agency and the owner of the vehicle when transportation was provided for clients of a program. The excess liability was set at a low premium ("Vehicle insurance rates," 1980). These new rates were the result of work on the part of the federal government and community groups to convince the insurance industry that the elderly were not more prone to injury when transported than other groups. In Janesville, Wisconsin, a transportation program staffed primarily by volunteers over the age of 55 uses a combination of the driver's own insurance (usually $300,000) and a blanket policy purchased by the program (Green Associates, 1984).

Fixed-route, fixed schedule services are available in a number of cities. In Denver, Colorado Metro Mobility operates a fixed-route system that provides transportation to medical or dental appointments, congregate meal sites and adult day care programs.

A more flexible system is needed by many older people. In Austin, Texas, the Reserve-A-Ride system charges $1 a ride for transportation to doctors or dentists, lawyers, banks, pharmacies, hair appointments, a friend in the hospital, volunteer work sites, or social engagements. The older person must call at least 24 hours in advance of their request date and riders are scheduled on a first-come, first-served basis.

An extensive transportation system is operated in Santa Barbara,

California. Begun in 1987 with four vans, the Santa Barbara effort provided over 7,000 rides in August,1996. During Fiscal year 1995 the program provided 70,000 rides to 1,500 people who were unable to use available mass transit. As in Austin, $1 is charged for each ride, and rides are provided on a first-come, first-served basis. The program operates on a 7-day-a-week schedule and provides curb-to-curb service. Drivers are not allowed to enter private homes or go past the lobby in nursing homes.

In Tennessee, the Mid-Cumberland Human Resources agency has implemented a "demand-responsive" system that offers rides to older people after 24 hours notice. These rides are free to individuals over the age of 60 and 10,000 trips per month are now being undertaken through this program (Takas, 1996).

RIDERSHIP PROBLEMS

Encouraging frequent utilization of these transportation services is important in reducing the average cost per ride. A shuttle system developed in Washington, D.C. in 1978 to transport the elderly to shopping on Thursdays found it difficult to attract new riders to the 13-passenger wheelchair-accessible vans. As the director of the program commented: "So far, I think we haven't been reaching the people. Many of them remain isolated in their apartments, so how can we reach them?" (Bernhard, 1979, p. A15).

Faced with the problems of financing $15,000 vans and then obtaining sufficient numbers of riders to keep subsidization at a reasonable level, it would appear that taxicab usage would be more economical and more convenient. Taxicab-based systems might also reduce any negative feelings that elderly residents have about riding special buses and would make use of existing dispatching systems.

In the early 1970s, a shared taxicab service was implemented in Arlington, Virginia. By 1975, this system had been abandoned on the basis of excessive costs. Each passenger paid $.15 for the taxicab, but the actual cost per taxi trip was $2.74. Although 45% of the eligible elderly were using this service, it was hard to persuade passengers to share the taxis, or that a reservation 2 hours in advance was not an arbitrarily imposed requirement. As the program reached its final stages, only 1.4 passengers were being transported in each taxicab ride (Kast, 1975). Aside from cost problems, many cab drivers may not want to pick up elderly passengers who live in poor inner-city or rural areas. The flexibility and convenience of the taxicab has thus been difficult to match with a program that is economical and efficient. "User side" subsidies do, however, appear to have strong support among older persons. Montgomery County, Maryland, has instituted taxi vouchers that older persons can purchase at a rate based on their income.

Depending on the length of the ride, these vouchers can substantially reduce the cost of the ride. The city of Baltimore also provides taxi vouchers for older persons.

Teal, Rooneys, Mortazari, and Goodhue (1983) found shared-ride taxi systems the most effective. Fostering cost-effective shared-ride systems would require the abolition of existing strictures on ridership. Abolishing these strictures, however, would double the costs of the program. In the middle 1980s, the authors estimated the increased costs at from $50,000 to $150,000.

COORDINATION OF PROGRAMS

Many of the transportation programs for special groups are mandated under federal legislation. Medicaid legislation specifies that each state plan must include provisions for assuring the transportation of Medicaid recipients to and from medical services. This provision can be satisfied by reimbursement of recipients for their transportation costs. Title III of the OAA requires the provision of transportation for clients to and from nutrition sites if transportation is otherwise unavailable.

An indication of the proliferation of transportation programs was provided by a study in Chattanooga, Tennessee, where 40 agencies were found to be operating transportation programs in 1975 (U.S. Department of Transportation, 1975). Coordination of these individual agencies' efforts in order to pool resources for capital outlays and operating costs is one step that promises to reduce the constantly increasing financial burdens of these programs. In Roanoke, Virginia, a nonprofit transportation agency was formed in 1975 to pool all the transportation resources and needs of individual agencies. Funds received by the transportation agency (Roanoke Dial-A-Ride) are then distributed to the participating organizations. In California, the local Transportation District provides 64% of the expenses for transportation programs in Marin County. The Transportation District also coordinates transportation programs for senior citizens, a medical transportation program, and a system of transportation for service and charitable organizations. Cleveland, Ohio, has acted to create a more efficient transportation system for older people by consolidating four providers into one system that offers both fixed route and demand services ("Three Ohio AAA's," 1990).

FUTURE TRENDS

The transportation needs of the older person will continue to increase as the proportion of older persons living in suburban communities also increases. The emphasis on outpatient treatment for many health problems means that older persons will need to be able to reach their health providers on a regular basis. Many communities will attempt to provide fixed route transportation systems, but a more common model will be the type of system now in place in Austin, Texas.

The federal government is attempting to assist transportation programs through both subsidization of vouchers and capital assistance funds that allow organizations to buy vehicles. The Federal Transit Administration is placing a special emphasis on support for the development of special transit programs in rural areas. In these communities, 36% of the riders are elderly.

Even with this support, the provision of adequate transportation will remain a major issue for providers of services for older persons. The expenses associated with this service will not decrease, although the spiral in insurance premiums noted in the late 1970s has largely abated. Transportation will continue to consume a major portion of the budget of service agencies, even with proper coordination, and program planners must be aware of the costs and difficulties of providing adequate transportation.

For the elderly, we can expect transportation programs to remain demand-responsive rather than need-responsive. Although flexible schedules and route services may be officially available, priorities of shopping and medical trips may consume most of the van and bus capacity available in many areas. It is thus doubtful that any new public transportation system will be able to open up major new opportunities for elderly individuals to expand their range of activities. The realistic goals of transportation services should be to enable: (1) formerly isolated elderly to reach the variety of agencies and programs now available; (2) elderly individuals to obtain the medical and mental health care they require; and (3) the elderly to undertake the necessary shopping trips to avoid doing without important goods. Visiting or attendance at cultural events requires a flexible and individualized service not within the resources of transportation systems presently in operation. Rural elderly and the increasing numbers of frail individuals over the age of 85 are two groups for whom specialized transportation services will need to be directed.

The goals mentioned are major, and their fulfillment will not be a simple task. Their attainment promises an improvement in the isolating conditions under which many elderly and handicapped now live, but it will remain an expensive effort. Subsidization of transportation services will always be necessary. Providing adequate transportation services may prove to be a major test of the general public's commitment to maintaining the network of services needed by older individuals.

REFERENCES

Bernhard, M. (1979, January 8). Giving a lift to the elderly. *Washington Post*, p. A15.

Cantor, M. (1970). *Elderly ridership and reduced transit fares: The New York City experience.* New York: New York City Office on Aging.

Green, D., Associates. (1984). *Use of volunteers in the transportation of elderly and handicapped persons.* Washington, DC: Urban Mass Transit Administration.

Jones, P., Rott, E., & Murphy, M. (1976). *A report on services to the elderly: Part 1. Transportation: A low-cost fair-fare transportation program for the elderly and disadvantaged.* Washington, DC: Aging Program, National Association of Counties Research Foundation.

Kast, S. (1975, January 2). Arlington elderly about to lose those free rides. *Washington Star-News*, p. B-2.

Vehicle insurance rates lowered for elderly programs. (1980). *Older American Reports, 4,* 4.

Three Ohio AAA's use state funds for local initiatives. (1990). *Older American Reports, 14,* 399.

Rinaldi, A. (1973). *Aid to senior citizens' mobility in East Orange, New Jersey: An escort service.* Millburn, NJ: National Council of Jewish Women.

Takas, T. (1996). My father must stop driving. *Elder Law Fax,* January 8.

Teal, R., Rooney, S., Mortazari, K., & Goodhue, R. (1983). *Taxi-based special transportation studies.* Washington, DC: Urban Mass Transit Administration.

U.S. Department of Transportation. (1975). *Transportation for the elderly: The state of the art.* Washington, DC: U.S. Government Printing Office.

U.S. Department of Transportation. (1976). *Rural passenger transportation: Technology sharing.* Cambridge, MA: Transportation Systems Center.

U.S. Department of Transportation. (1997) *Transportation for a maturing society.* Washington, D.C.: Author.

U.S. House of Representatives, Select Committee on Aging. (1976). Transportation: *Improving mobility for older Americans.* Washington, DC: U.S. Government Printing Office.

8

Crime and Legal Assistance Programs

While programs related to crime attempt to protect the older adult from victimization, many of the legal services being stressed in aging attempt to protect the elderly from themselves. Legal services have increased since they became the focus of attention at the 1971 White House Conference on Aging and in the 1975 amendments to the OAA.

Legal programs for older persons are diverse in nature. As we shall see, even the laws on guardianship and protective services differ from state to state. While it is impossible to cover all of these rapidly growing and changing programs, this chapter will provide an overview of the types of programs now in existence. It will also outline the legal issues involved in programs designed to protect the elderly from doing harm to themselves, either physically or financially.

THE ELDERLY AND CRIME

Concerns and Figures

Concern about crimes against the elderly has intensified in recent years. Reports of elderly people being mugged and murdered have made front-page headlines. In 1977, the report of a Brooklyn, New York, couple who committed suicide after leaving a note stating that death was better than living in continual fear received major coverage throughout the United States. It remains unclear, however, whether the reality of the crime rate matches the concern that it raises among older people or in the media.

Data collected on crimes committed against elderly victims are impre-
cise, as are criminal statistics in general. The FBI compiles its widely relied-
upon statistics from incidents of crime reported to local police
departments, which have varied reporting requirements. There is also wide-
spread belief that older individuals fear dealing with the police or retalia-
tion by attackers who live in the neighborhood, and therefore often avoid
reporting crimes against them. Finally, if a crime is reported to the police,
the age of the victim is not always recorded.

Patterns of Crime

The rates of criminal acts perpetrated against the elderly are different from
those perpetrated against younger individuals (U.S. Department of Justice,
1994). Although 20% of crimes against individuals under age 65 are robberies, 38% of crimes against older persons fall into this category. Older
crime victims are twice as likely to be raped, robbed, or assaulted in or
near their own homes (U.S. Department of Justice, 1994). Elderly individuals with limited access to transportation may develop life styles that do not
involve traveling great distances. The likelihood of any attacks occurring in
or near the home is therefore increased.

The consequences of crime are more severe for people over the age of 65
than they are for younger individuals. Nine percent of older crime victims
are likely to suffer broken bones in comparison to 5% of younger individuals. Half of older victims of crime, compared to 25% of younger victims,
undergo some treatment at a hospital after a crime. Older African Americans
are more likely to be crime victims than Whites of the same age.

There is an inverse relationship between the risk of personal and household victimization and age. A 1997 report on criminal victimization between
1994 and 1995 indicated that personal crime victimization rates have continued to fall (U.S. Department of Justice, 1997). As Table 8.1 indicates, personal crime victimization of older persons occurs much less frequently than
it does among younger individuals. It can be argued that the number of
crimes against older persons would be more extensive if many elderly did
not remain at home in the evening, thus also restricting their involvement
in the social life of the community.

Vulnerability

Do special legal programs need to be developed to protect the elderly from
victimization? This question can be answered only by examining the effects
of crime on people in different age groups. As an official of the Justice

TABLE 8.1 Personal Crime Victimization, by Sex, Age, Race, Hispanic Origin, Household Income, Region and Location or Residence of Victims, 1995

	Rates of personal crime in 1995 (per 1,000 persons) Violent Crimes					
Age	Total	Total	Rape/ Sexual Assault	Robbery	Total Assault	Personal Theft
12–15	110.9	107.1	2.2	9.5	95.4	3.8
16–19	110.3	107.7	5.7	9.0	93.0	2.7
20–24	79.8	78.8	3.0	10.8	65.0	1.1
25–34	55.9	54.7	2.0	6.9	45.8	1.2
35–49	5.6	33.8	1.4	4.7	27.7	1.8
50–64	15.6	14.0	.1	1.8	12.1	1.6
65 or older	6.9	5.9	0.0	1.3	4.6	1.0

Note: From *Change in Criminal Victimization, 1994–95.* (pp. 1–2) by Bureau of Justice Statistics, National Crime Victimization Survey, U.S. Department of Justice, 1997, April, Washington, D.C.: Author. Adapted.

Department testified to the U.S. House of Representatives Select Committee on Aging (1976):

> While there may be some uncertainty about crime victimization among senior citizens, there is, I believe, little question about their vulnerability— physical, psychological and financial. Take, for example, the instance of the theft of a television set. The effect on a younger person does not carry the same impact as it does upon a person who is 65 years and older and of limited means. Take the instance of physical violence. It has a particularly debilitating effect on the older person. The theft of a social security check has a tremendous impact upon a person of lower income. (p. 5)

This testimony points to a number of factors that make the elderly especially vulnerable to crime. A low income makes it difficult for many older persons to recoup from robbery, and it also makes them susceptible to confidence games that hold out the promise of quick wealth. Older individuals faced with the threat of violence may not have the physical strength to fight off a potential attacker, and thus may be viewed as easy victims. The elderly also tend to reside in changing areas of the city where unemployment and general social problems abound. Many of these elderly residents receive their checks for Social Security, SSI, or pensions on fixed dates of each month. These dates are often common knowledge in the neighborhood and become red-letter days for attackers. The development of a system of direct deposit of checks is helping to reduce this problem. The elderly are also easy prey for attackers because they often live alone and go out shopping by themselves rather than in groups.

Confidence Schemes

In addition to the physical weakness and living habits that increase the vulnerability of the elderly to violent crime, the American aged have a number of other characteristics that make them "marks" for consumer fraud. Especially important is their fear of growing older and of the loss in functioning that they assume to be a part of aging will include. Devices that promise to prevent or repair losses in hearing or vision may be especially attractive to older adults, and those who suffer from chronic illnesses frequently jump at the opportunity to purchase medications that promise to relieve their pain. All of these factors are most at play among the less-educated elderly. Older individuals with more education show less interest in overpriced merchandise and less susceptibility to fraudulent schemes.

The most common of confidence games is the "pigeon drop." In this scheme, an elderly person is approached by someone on the street who informs him or her that a bag of money has been found. The money will be shared if the older person shows good faith by going to the bank and withdrawing some funds, which will be held by an attorney until the bag of money is legally released to them. The con artist, once given the money, disappears. Other con games are variations on this theme, which promise the elderly some easy reward for providing some of their funds as a sign of good faith or as security.

A second form of fraud is engaged in by unscrupulous retailers and salesmen who encourage the elderly to buy items that are unnecessary, inadequate, or overpriced. The most common consumer frauds perpetuated against the aged involve hearing aids, eyeglasses, funeral arrangements, dentures, and health insurance. In many cases, the elderly are encouraged to buy prosthetics, such as hearing aids, that will not make up for their auditory losses; or they are encouraged to buy overpriced aids. Some major insurance companies have been sued for making false claims about life insurance policies they marketed to older persons.

Among the large concentration of older persons in Miami, Florida, fraud against the elderly has become a significant problem. Between 1992 and 1993, these crimes increased 12% (Seeman, 1993). The various forms of fraud include bogus telemarketing of a variety of products, as well as home repair and cleaning fraud, in which services are contracted for, but not delivered adequately by the provider.

CRIME PREVENTION AND ASSISTANCE

Robberies, attacks, consumer frauds, and confidence swindles can beset the elderly individual. Because victimization can take so many forms, the programs that have been devised to protect the victims are also extensive. They are run under a variety of auspices, including general or special units of the Police Department. Some programs are operated by the local Area Agency on Aging or a social service agency.

Educational Programs

Educational programs about crime for older persons focus on the avoidance of street crimes and confidence swindles. A second type of program related to crime prevention encourages increased cohesion in the community and the implementation of support services, such as an escort service. Finally, most areas now have some form of "victim assistance" program that provides both financial compensation and counseling to victims of crime.

At the national level, the AARP has worked to develop a training program that is available to senior citizen organizations. In four 2-hour sessions, this program informs the elderly about methods of avoiding street crime and burglary, about the most common types of confidence schemes, and how to work with the police to reduce crime. In Evansville, Indiana, the police department holds a two-day symposium every year for the elderly which is geared to common crime problems (International Association of Chiefs of Police, n.d.). In Philadelphia, North West Victims Services (NWVS) conducts programs at senior centers on how to prevent fraud. NWVS also visits local banks as part of its Bank Session Project. During these visits, seniors are counseled about safe banking habits and general safety. Between 1990 and 1991, 2,000 older people were counseled at 10 banks (Tomz & McGill, 1997). The Cottage Grove, Oregon, police department has developed a program that trains senior citizens to be crime-prevention specialists. Having completed training, they contact other elderly residents in the community, informing them about building security and how to mark their valuables for identification. In Baltimore, Maryland, the mayor's office has developed videotapes dealing with assault, robbery, and burglaries. These tapes concentrate on techniques that can be used when the individual is confronted with these crimes.

In Los Angeles, the Interagency Task Force on Crime against the Elderly has been formed from the law enforcement agencies, the Area Agencies on Aging, social service agencies, libraries, and educational institutions in the area to design educational programs dealing with victimization of the elderly. The task force's efforts have included the use of television and radio announcements. California has also attempted, through its Consumer Information and Protection Program for Seniors, to provide education for the elderly on prevalent types of consumer fraud.

Security Programs

In many areas with a high concentration of elderly, educational efforts have been combined with increased security measures. The Law Enforcement Assistance Administration (LEAA) funded a project in Syracuse, New York, to establish security units in eight low-income-elderly housing projects. In Plainfield, New Jersey, a $6,000 program was developed to control access into senior housing units through the use of closed-circuit TV systems. In South Bend, Indiana, $3,000 was spent for the installation of door locks for elderly residents who could not afford them. This project was operated by the South Bend police.

The federally funded "Blow the Whistle on Crime" program made efforts to provide whistles to individuals in over 300 cities. In the Crown Heights section of Brooklyn and in high-crime areas of Milwaukee, Wisconsin, and Wilmington, Delaware, "security aides" provided escort services for the elderly. The Wilmington program utilized both older individuals and teenagers as escorts. With funding cuts in fiscal 1982 and the disappearance of LEAA as an independent agency, the emphasis became focused on technical assistance through dissemination of materials rather than direct program funding.

Victim Assistance

A final group of programs is aimed at providing assistance to individuals who have been the victims of crime. Many of these programs began with funding through the 1984 Victims of Crime Act (see page 97). By 1994, 2,400 victim assistance programs were receiving federal funds. Between 1990 and 1991 these programs serviced over three million people. Many of these programs intervene to help elderly crime victims cope with their "reactions", which are often more severe than among younger victims (Lurgo & Resick, 1990).

A variety of services are provided through these programs ranging from emergency assistance, to counseling and help with the legal system or obtaining compensation due crime victims. A survey of 319 victim assistance programs indicated that the most common form of assistance was information about the legal rights of victims. Among individuals served, 8%

were over the age of 65 (McEwen, 1995). In Santa Ana, California, the victims assistance program has a Senior Victim of Crime Specialist who may go to an older person's home to offer help. In Minneapolis-St.Paul, the program staff visit older victims of crime homes and board up damaged windows and secure damaged doors (Tomz & McGill, 1997).

"Victim centers" in major cities serve all age groups and are often located within police departments. In Colorado Springs, Colorado 40 older volunteers serve on the Senior Victim Assistance Team and act as liaisons with older victims. They offer emotional support, visit victims who are hospitalized, assist them in obtaining new credit cards, and help them with the paperwork needed to obtain compensation from victim assistance programs. If someone has been arrested for the crime, the team helps the victim understand the legal process and notifies them of court dates.

Many of the elderly who become crime victims are reluctant to serve as witnesses. To cope with this problem, there are also "witness centers" in conjunction with the local courts. The witness is informed about court procedures as well as provided with necessary services, such as transportation. The centers will provide protection for witnesses if necessary.

As Jaycox (1981) notes, it was difficult to evaluate the victim witness programs beyond an expression of satisfaction by clients and observers, some time savings for witnesses, and "modest improvements in the witness appearance rates" (Jaycox, 1981, p. 4). The Victims of Crime Act, passed in 1984, has helped to fund state compensation and victim assistance programs throughout the country. In 1986 the funds collected from fines and distributed to states supported 1500 programs. Besides this federal legislation, since 1980, 35 states have passed legislation related to victims (Davis & Henley, 1990). Unfortunately, many elderly people find that they are not reimbursed by insurance for what they lose as a result of victimization. Many states have not instituted victim compensation laws which provide reimbursement for the costs sustained by all individuals.

The state-by-state variation in these victim compensation laws is great. The maximum amount of compensation for medical expenses or loss of earnings varies, as does the maximum time within which a victim may file a claim vary.

In Baltimore, the Commission on Aging has established a victim's assistance unit composed of a director, attorney, and counselor. The unit works with elderly individuals who have been victimized. The majority of these elderly victims are referred to the unit by the police.

Despite all of this activity, the effectiveness of these programs is not yet clear. The loss of a feeling of community and the general fear that pervades many American cities is still strong. This fear can also be found among suburban elderly even if they have not personally experienced criminal victimization (Cantor, Brook, & Mellor, 1986). Crime rates have been lower during the 1990s in many major cities. In 1994, the National Crime Victimization Survey found that crime rates for personal theft and household crime against older persons was lower in 1992 than it had been in any of the 20 years of the survey's existence (U.S. Department of Justice, 1994). Between 1994 and 1995 personal crime rates fell 13%, the rate of violent crime fell 12.4%, and the rate of property crime declined by 9.1% (U.S. Department of Justice, 1997). It remains unclear whether this reduction is the result of new punitive policies that stress longer prison sentences or fewer numbers of younger individuals, the group most likely to commit crimes. Some analysts predict a rise in crime rates as the adolescent population begins to increase during the next decade.

LEGAL REPRESENTATION

As services for this population have increased, the elderly have become more involved with a variety of public and private bureaucracies which determine their eligibility for these programs. Disputes about eligibility may necessitate legal representation. For older people, legal issues which most often arise are questions about Social Security and SSI benefits, landlord-tenant disputes, Medicare claims, food stamp certification, and wills and probates.

There is little doubt that the elderly have not received adequate legal assistance, partially because lawyers are not likely to earn high fees working with the elderly. Many older persons also remain unaware of their legal rights, or are afraid of dealing with lawyers, just as they do not report crimes out of fear of dealing with the police. Even elderly individuals who do possess higher educational backgrounds and who are more confident about legal transactions may lack the transportation necessary to reach a lawyer's office.

Legal representation for the elderly has begun to improve in recent years, mainly through the efforts of the Legal Services Corporation (LSC), authorized under federal legislation in 1975. This corporation is an independent successor to the poverty law program that existed within the now-defunct Office of Economic Opportunity. The LSC has lawyers in offices throughout the country and services all individuals including the elderly who fall below the federal poverty level. Specialized programs for the elderly have been supported by funds from a variety of federal programs and local funds from organizations such as the United Way. In Memphis, Tennessee, $220,000 from revenue-sharing funds was allocated by the city for a legal program for the elderly, and $150,000 was set aside in Sacramento, California, for a similar program. In San Diego, California, the Bank of America has supported a program to increase legal representation for the elderly. The LSC and the AoA have provided support to the National Senior Citizens Law Center (NSCLC) and Legal Counsel for the Elderly at the American Association of Retired Persons.

Approximately 11% of Legal Services Corporation clients are over the age of 60. The cases these older clients bring to court usually involve questions of eligibility for government benefits. The threat of legal action is also helpful in situations where private pension plans contain major loopholes and possibilities of abuse by employers. In one case, a truck driver for a major supermarket chain retired after 34 years of work, expecting a pension of $300 a month. When his first check arrived, he found that it was for only $250. The employer informed him that his pension had been reduced because he retired a month too early, even though his date was advised by an official of the firm. A student at the Protection for Elderly People program of the George Washington University Law School wrote to the supermarket chain informing them of the problem. After two months, the retired driver received a check for $1,200, an apology from the company for the mistaken advice, and credit for the additional month.

In the 1990s funding for LSC was cut substantially, reducing the availability of LSC personnel and the type of cases the agency could handle. LSC is now ineligible to bring class action suits and must involve itself only with individual cases. The budget reductions resulted in 300,000 less cases being handled by LSC in 1996 and the closing of 300 offices.

While the efforts of the LSC, the NSCLC, and Legal Counsel for the Elderly are admirable, these three organizations alone are unable to provide sufficient legal representation to serve the multiple needs of the elderly. Some law schools have set up special clinics to serve the elderly, but it is unlikely that in the upcoming years we will see any rush on the part of lawyers toward major private practice with older populations. A number of other approaches to utilizing lawyers are now being tried. In Tennessee, a legal aid program sends lawyers on a regular circuit of 3 to 15 counties in the state. On these trips, the lawyers visit senior centers and conduct seminars for the elderly on important legal issues. In addition, the NSCLC provides "support and information" for lawyers representing elderly clients. The NSCLC will provide information on previous cases of draft pleadings for legal aid lawyers who request this assistance. NSCLC also provides technical assistance to states on a variety of issues, including housing for the elderly and formulations of pension plans.

One innovative approach to meeting the legal representation needs of older persons is the Legal Hotline. The first such hotlines were developed in 1985 by the Legal Counsel for the Elderly. Attorneys are paid a per diem rate to offer legal information or advice to a caller. They can also refer the caller to a publicly funded legal program or a program that offers services for a reduced fee. If the attorney decides that the caller's problem is not a legal problem, he or she may refer the older person to a local social service agency (Kolasa & Soto, 1990). Legal hotlines may be funded through organizations such as AARP or through community organizations using AoA funding.

As Kolasa and Soto note, the hotlines overcome transportation problems facing the elderly, and help the older person define the problem more carefully without facing major legal fees (Kolasa & Soto, 1990). There have been some problems with the hotlines. Most prominent has been high turnover rates among the staffing attorneys. Hotlines have also had difficulty working with hearing-impaired older callers (Porter & Affeldt, 1990).

Pro bono representation is now a policy of the American Bar Association, but attempts to specify the amount of time lawyers should donate to clients have been resisted. While efforts are being made to increase lawyers' gratis representation of the elderly, it is likely that much of the increased legal counseling will be undertaken by paralegal counselors.

Paralegal Assistance

As of 1977, over 100 paralegal programs existed in the United States, with many focusing attention on the legal problems of the elderly. The common definition of a paralegal as "any person who deals with the products of the legal system, that is, statutes, regulations administrative agencies and court" has been objected to by Buford (1977, p. 109). This definition, he contends, is vague and omits the crucial fact that the "paralegal is an employee of an attorney who has been trained to work on tasks formerly done by attorneys" (1977, p. 109). Although paralegals are not licensed by bar associations, they are allowed by federal regulations to handle cases of individuals seeking such public benefits as Social Security, SSI, welfare, public housing, and food stamps. In cases where a lawyer is required, paralegals may prepare the briefs for lawyers.

A second group of individuals who can provide assistance to the elderly are what the Paralegal Institute has termed community services advocates (CSA). CSAs may be individuals with backgrounds in many other fields; the common denominator is that they come into frequent contact with the elderly. Caseworkers or home health workers may thus play an important role as CSAs, and the National Paralegal Institute has made efforts to train social service workers as CSAs. Since CSAs are not employed by an attorney, they are limited in the legal representation they can provide the elderly in actual hearings. However, they can be strong advocates for the elderly who are having legal problems, particularly in relation to public benefits.

Legal services were classified as one of the three priorities in the 1978 OAA amendments. As part of its plan for the aging, each state was required to show that the Area Agencies on Aging (AAAs) were contracting for legal services while making efforts to involve private bar organizations in legal services at reduced rates or for free. The emphasis on legal services was deleted from the 1981 amendments in line with the concept that localities should exercise control of programs.

Data from 1980 reveal that the average AAA spent 6% of its Title IIIB funds on legal services (American Bar Assocition, n.d.). Under the 1987 OAA amendments, state units on aging must require AAAs to expend a specified percentage of their funds on legal services, and must document that the actual providers of legal services are attempting to meet the needs of low-income minority elderly (Section 306). Although no data have been collected since 1980, the percentage of AAA funds spent on legal services is presumed to have declined (American Bar Association, n.d.).

Some of the funds for legal services have been allotted to the ombudsman programs. In fiscal 1995, 565 ombudsman programs funded by a combination of federal and nonfederal funds were operational. The 1987 OAA amendments included a specific authorization of $20 million for the ombudsman program and specific guidelines for establishing a long-term care ombudsman program with the State Offices on Aging. The State Office on Aging, or contractor, is charged with using the ombudsman program to investigate complaints by residents of long-term care facilities and to establish procedures for access by the ombudsman to the long-term care facility. The amendments also prohibit retaliation by a long-term care facility against an individual or employee who files a complaint or provides information to an ombudsman. In FY 1995, funds from Title VII accounted for 15% of the funding for the ombudsman programs, but 48% of all of the funding came from Title III programs funds of Area Agencies on Aging or state agencies on aging. States also contributed a substantial amount of funds to the long-term care ombudsman efforts (21.8%). Despite the commitment of funds from a variety of sources, a report on the long-term care ombudsman program by the Institute of Medicine found the funding levels to be inadequate (Institute of Medicine, 1995).

In 1995, 162,000 individuals lodged complaints with an ombudsman. Ombudsmen investigated 218,000 complaints. Of these, the vast majority were in nursing facilities, followed by board and care and other residential facilities.

PROTECTIVE SERVICES

While in many cases legal representation of an elderly person can increase the person's self-sufficiency, protective service measures remove many of the rights an individual has to make his or her own decisions. Elderly persons who are thought to be unable to manage their personal or financial affairs in their own best interests are subject to the imposition of protective services designed to protect them from themselves and from unscrupulous third parties (Horstman, 1977, p. 227).

Elements of Protective Services

Protective services have two major components: (1) intensive services provided, with the individuals' consent, to those who appear to need major supportive assistance; and (2) services provided for individuals, without their consent, after a hearing, which involve "legally enforced supervision of guardianship which, temporarily depriving the client of certain rights, enables an agency to assist the person" (Regan & Springer, 1977, p. 4). These services and guardianship may be imposed on individuals of any age, but the concept of protective services has been most widely applied to individuals over 60.

Recipients

We can define the type of person for whom protective services might be appropriate by examining an individual case.

Mr. E., 73, a tall powerfully built man with no surviving family, formerly a skilled iron worker, had become settled, but not rooted in one area of town after an early adulthood of country-wide transiency. He had never married but was proud of earlier feminine conquests. Inarticulate, having had a large investment in his body image, he now lacked the kind of strengths which formerly had helped him achieve his goals. With a foreign upbringing and little formal education, Mr. E. was now frustrated by the ravages of illness and old age. He reacted behaviorally with extreme intolerance of others, suspicion, and severe verbal abusiveness. At the point of referral, Mr. E. was in grave danger of dying and was thwarting efforts of interested agencies to induce him to accept proper medical attention through hospitalization. Despite his cleanliness of person, his disabilities had affected the maintenance of his small apartment which was cluttered and dirty. A friendship of 20 years with a male friend indicated some underlying capacity for human attachment. The grave medical problems were compounded by the limitations of an income of $105 monthly from Social Security (Wasser, 1974, pp. 103–114). Mr. E. can obviously benefit from many forms of assistance, including a variety of personal services. He may also be one of the 25% of the elderly often estimated to have major mental health problems.

During the famous social experiment in protective services at the Benjamin Rose Institute of Cleveland, individuals such as Mr. E. were provided with intensive casework assistance from experienced social workers with master's degrees in social work. These social workers functioned under one overriding directive: "Do, or get others to do, whatever is necessary to meet the needs of the situation" (Blenkner, Bloom, Nielsen & Weber, 1974, p. 68). In order to be effective, the social workers had to utilize a variety of concomitant services needed by clients of the protective services program. These included financial assistance, medical evaluations, home aides, and psychiatric consultation. In 20% of the cases, legal consultation was utilized; in 12%, guardianship proceedings were instituted and completed. The Benjamin Rose program provides a model for the types of assistance that protective services might supply, its basic assumption being that clients of the program require more intensive assistance than is normally provided by most agencies.

GUARDIANSHIP

Contemporary legal guidelines for guardianship and commitment are inadequate. The complex questions raised by protective services have been outlined by Blenkner et al. (1974):

1. If the services provided to an individual such as Mr. E. are inadequate and are resisted by Mr. E., who should have the right to define Mr. E. as a problem and deprive him of his ability to make decisions?
2. If older persons resist services, does provision of services against their will provide them with assistance, or merely satisfy the "psychological discomfort" of the social worker?
3. Is providing protective services the answer to the problems of Mr. E., or is the real issue for the elderly the conditions that are imposed on them, and under which they are forced to live?
4. If the proposed solution to Mr. E.'s problems is placement in a long-term care setting, will this solve the problems for the family and neighbors upset by his behavior, but be destructive to his own personal functioning?
5. Can any services, whether voluntary or imposed, help many of the individuals who come under the wing of protective services improve to a "normal" functioning level?

Even if answers to these questions affirm the need for protective services, there remains the necessity of careful criteria for legal intervention models. There are increased signs of an understanding of the complexity and importance of guardianship. Among the eligible supportive services included in Title III of the 1992 OAA amendments are "representation in guardianship proceedings by older individuals who seek to become guardians . . . " and "information and training for individuals who are or may become guardians . . ." [Sec. 312].

Consequences of Guardianship

An individual placed under "guardianship" can suffer a variety of losses. These include the right to sue, charge purchases, engage in contracts, deed property, marry, divorce, open a bank account, or vote. In some states, the individual's eligibility for program benefits, including Medicare and pensions, will come under scrutiny when a guardian is appointed.

An incompetent is defined traditionally as one who by reason of mental illness, drunkenness, drug addiction, or old age is incapable of self-care, of managing business, or of exercising family responsibilities, or as one who is liable to dissipate an estate or become the victim of designing persons (Regan & Springer, 1977).

In most states, the individual must be declared incompetent in order for a guardian to be appointed. Vague bases for declarations of incompetence such as "old age" have contributed to the abuses now associated with the protective services approach. Despite these changes, there are still variations across states in the procedures required in guardianship hearings. In 15 states, the presence of the older person being considered for guardianship is mandatory. Many other states dispense with the older person's attendance in the "best interest of the clients." On a national basis, only 8% of older people actually attend the guardianship proceedings in which they are involved. A 1978 examination of state statutes reveals that 34 states had public guardianship legislation (Schmidt, Miller, Bell, & New, 1981) and that considerable progress has been made toward defining the grounds for guardianship and the public entities' responsibility in the guardianship process. In contrast to "plenary" guardianships, which award all decision-making rights to the guardian, limited guardianships are possible in many states, but are not frequently used. Under limited guardianship, the guardian's "ward" retains some authority over decisions. Temporary guardianships can also be used in emergency situations.

Incapacity is defined as the inability of the person to care for his or her person or property or the imminent danger to the person of physical harm or material waste. This is the standard for making decisions about the need for guardianship. The criteria for determining incapacity range from "clear and convincing" evidence to vaguer standards that stress the "best interests of the ward." In over half of the 34 states, a medical examination is required, and 14 states include a psychological examination. Minnesota employs a more comprehensive approach, requiring a separate evaluation by a physician, a psychologist, and a social worker with recommendations about the type of guardianship best suited for the individual.

In some states, this interdisciplinary approach has been formalized through the development of Geriatric Evaluation Services (GES). The GES evaluates clients being considered for commitment to a mental hospital, appointment of a conservator, emergency protective services, or protective placements. In many of the states, the terms "guardian" and "conservator" are used interchangeably, and only careful reading of the statutes indicates the responsibility of the individual appointed by the court. One-third of the states initially prefer to utilize an adult child, parent, or relative of the person as a guardian. If none of these choices is available, then a public guardian is called upon. In 20 states, a specific state or county agency is designated in the legislation as the public guardian of the older person. In seven states, the ward has an opportunity to participate in the selection of the guardian.

In the view of Schmidt et al. (1981), those states that appoint a public agency providing services to the ward as a guardian are developing a conflict of interest. The agency's priority may be efficient and low-cost service delivery rather than protection of an individual. Seventeen states have the same agency providing services and acting as a guardian. Few of the states explicitly mention the funding of the guardian, and 20 of the 34 states make some provision for review of the guardianship. These alterations, while not sufficient, are clear evidence of changes in philosophy concerning protective services and guardianship.

The guardianship-conservator model is long-term in nature. There is, however, a rationale for an emergency intervention model for individuals whose needs are immediate or expected to be temporary. In most states, individuals believed to be dangerous to themselves and others may be confined for a period which averages 72 hours. After that time, a formal hearing must be held to determine whether an individual should be committed for a longer period. In Maryland, three criteria must be evident before individuals can be committed to a state mental facility: the individuals must (1) be dangerous to themselves or the community, (2) require inpatient treatment, and (3) be mentally ill.

Alternatives to long-term commitment have not existed until recently and have not always been explored by protective service workers. Alternative settings were a major point in the landmark *Lake v. Cameron* (1966) decision, in which the D.C. Court of Appeals ruled that Mrs. Lake could not be held in St. Elizabeth's Hospital unless all other possible less restrictive alternatives were explored. Unfortunately for Mrs. Lake, no alternatives available at that time (1966) were deemed appropriate, and she was remanded to St. Elizabeth's.

Changes in Protective Services

The potential for abuses in protective services is obvious, and a number of major changes are being promoted throughout the country to prevent undue restriction of the elderly's civil rights. These include:

1. Changes in the law to redefine competency according to the level at which an individual is capable of functioning, rather than by a vague medical diagnosis;
2. requirements that the individual be informed of the importance of guardianship hearings, the right to counsel, and the right to cross-examine witnesses; It is interesting to note that one study in Los Angeles found that in only 2% of the guardianship hearings was counsel present for the subject. In Ohio, a negative correlation of .94 was found between representation by counsel and decisions to commit an individual to a long-term care institution);
3. legislation to authorize a full range of protective social services throughout the country; and
4. establishment of a system of public guardianship for people without private guardian resources.

Horstman (1977) argued for a "bill of rights" for all aged people which would define their constitutional rights in relation to confinement. Under his plan, confinement would be utilized only when the following five conditions were present:

1. The individual had been declared mentally incompetent to determine the viability of seeking or refusing treatment, and
2. Less restrictive alternatives to total institutionalization have been fully explored and found to be inadequate to protect and maintain the individual, and
3. The individual is unable to live safely in freedom either by himself or with the assistance of willing and responsible family members or friends, and
4. The individual is untreatable, and
5. Institutionalization is in the individual's best interest. (p. 288)

It could be argued that a nationwide development of protective services might cut down the need for guardianship or commitment hearings. The Benjamin Rose Institute study stressed caution in aggressively expanding protective services. The research did not show significant differences on a number of measures between individuals in the experimental and control groups. As summed up by Blenkner, Bloom, Wasser, and Nielsen (1971):

For the participant, himself, however, there was no significant impact with respect to increased competence or slowed deterioration and greater contentment or lessened disturbance. Furthermore, although he was more "protected," the participant was no less likely to die when given protective services than when left to the usual and limited services of the community. In fact, the findings on functional competence together with those on death and institutionalization force consideration of the hypothesis that intensive service with a heavy reliance on institutional care may actually accelerate decline. (p. 494)

This negative evaluation placed a brake on the development of protective services and raised important questions in many social workers' minds about the degree to which the development of extensive services promoted dependency of the aged on the worker. A reanalysis by a new group of researchers at the Benjamin Rose Institute (Bigot, Demling, Shuman, & Schur, 1978) indicates, however, that the original staff may have underestimated the positive effects of the intensive social work services. The federally funded "channeling" demonstration provided a single point of access to coordinated services. Reports on the effects of this project were released in 1986. These data raise again the issue of whether extensive services to older persons may not produce dependency and reduce functioning levels (Mathematica Policy Research, 1986). The positive and negative effects of protective social casework services offered by agencies remains unclear. The effects of legal procedures for the elderly that remove their rights are much clearer in their negative implications. Legislative enactments as outlined by Regan and Springer (1977) will afford due process for the elderly and restrict the power to unduly remove the civil liberties of the elderly. These legislative revisions should be a prime concern for advocates of aging programs and practitioners in aging.

Elder Abuse

In recent years abuse and neglect of older persons has become a major topic of concern for protective service workers. Elder abuse is defined by the Administration on Aging (1998) as including physical, psychological, and financial abuse and neglect.

The 1984 amendments to the OAA required AAAs to assess the need for elder abuse services in their jurisdictions, and the 1987 amendments authorized a $5 million program of grants for elder abuse services and education. Title VII of the 1992 OAA amendments authorized at least $15 million for elder abuse programs. These funds were earmarked for education about elder abuse, receipt of reports about elder abuse, outreach to older persons who may be the victims of elder abuse, and referrals of complaints about elder abuse to law enforcement agencies [Sec. 705(a)(6)].

Reported elder abuse cases numbered 117,000 in 1986 but had increased to 241,000 in 1994. Partly because of the stigmatized behavior it represents, the actual prevalence of elder abuse and neglect remains in question (National Center on Elder Abuse, n.d.). A 1994 study found 820,000 cases of elder abuse. When cases of self-neglect were added to this number, the total was 1.86 million individuals. Self-neglect was the most common form of abuse (58.5%) followed by physical abuse (15.7%) and financial exploitation (12.3%). Among the reported cases of abuse, 65% of the abused older persons were White, 21.4% African American, and 9.6% Latino. Surprisingly, the proportion of male and female abusers was almost equal and 37% of these abusers were adult children of the older person. Other family members account for 15% and spouses an additional 14% of the abusers.

By 1997, 42 states had passed legislation requiring professionals to report elder abuse. In 1990 Mississippi enacted legislation making elder abuse and neglect in nursing homes and hospitals a felony offense (NARCEA Exchange, 1990). Pennsylvania has enacted a law providing legal protection for individuals who report suspected elder abuse. This diversity in response across states remains one of the major problems in combating elder abuse. Wolf's (1988) list of problems at the state level include: "no consistency with regard to groups covered, definitions, mandatory reporting, investigation procedures, penalties, immunity, confidentiality and services" (p. 12).

Although this legislation has an important protective function, it may also lead to more guardianship cases. Guardianship results if a public agency required to investigate report of abuse or neglect finds that the older person is uncooperative with the investigation, refuses to accept the services the agency recommends, rejects a recommended move to a nursing home, or opts to stay in an environment where he or she is being abused. If there are inadequate services available in the state to help the abused older person, then guardianship may be seen as the only alternative.

A number of programs around the United States can serve as models for elder abuse initiatives. In New York, Mt. Sinai Medical Center has developed a comprehensive assessment and treatment program for abused elderly. Besides providing the treatment available in the hospital, the program helps abused older persons learn about their legal rights. The New Ventures program teaches volunteers to assist in managing finances and negotiating the health and human services system. In San Francisco, Community Agencies Serving the Elderly has developed a consortium of 55 community agencies that provide extensive services in cases of elder abuse ("Models from Manhattan to Oahu," 1991). In Massachusetts, the Elderly Protection Program is a collaboration between local police departments and local adult protective service offices (U.S. Department of Justice,

1994). Under this program local police are provided background about issues in aging, financial exploitation of older persons, domestic violence, and other issues related to elder abuse. By 1993, 445 police and 58 protective service workers had completed this training. In Suffolk County, New York, the Victims Information Bureau assists victims of elder abuse. The Bureau provides in-home counseling, information and referral, court advocacy and accompanies elder abuse victims to court. Begun in 1990, the program has served 100 clients per year.

REFERENCES

Administration on Aging. (1998). *Elder abuse prevention: What is elder abuse.* Available: aoa.dhhs.gov/factsheets/abuse.html

American Bar Association. (n.d.). Committee on Legal Problems of the Elderly. *White Paper: Legal assistance under the Older Americans Act: Current status and recommendations.* Washington, DC: Author.

Bigot, A., Demling, G., Shuman, S., & Schur, D. (1978). *Protective services for older people: A reanalysis of a controversial demonstration project.* Paper presented at the annual meeting of the Gerontological Society, Dallas, TX.

Blenkner, M., Bloom, M., Nielsen, M., & Weber, R. (1974). Final report: *Protective services for older people.* Cleveland, OH: Benjamin Rose Institute.

Blenkner, M., Bloom, M., Wasser, E., & Nielsen, M. (1971). Protective services for older people: Findings from the B.R.I. study. *Social Casework, 82,* 483–522.

Buford, A. D., III. (1977). Non-lawyer delivery of legal services. In M. Rafa (Ed.), *Justice and older Americans.* Lexington, MA: Lexington Books.

Cantor, M., Brook, K., & Mellor, M. J. (1986). Growing old in suburbia: *The experience of the Jewish elderly in Mount Vernon.* New York: Fordham University Third Age Center.

Davis, R., & Henley, M. (1990). Victim service programs. In A. Lurgio, W. Skogan, & R. Davis, (Eds.), *Victims of crime: Problems, policies & programs* (pp. 157–171). Newbury Park, CA: Sage.

Horstman, P. (1977). Protective services for the elderly: The limits of pare IS patriae. In J. Weiss (Ed)., *Law of the elderly.* New York: Practicing Law Institute.

Institute of Medicine. (1995). *Real people, real problems: An evaluation of the Long-Term Care Ombudsman Program of the Older Americans Act.* Washington, DC: Author.

International Association of Chiefs of Police, Technical Research Services Division. (n.d.). *Crime prevention programs for senior citizens.* Gaithersburg, MD: Author.

Jaycox, V. (1981). *Creating a senior victim/witness volunteer corps: An introductory brochure.* Washington, DC: National Council on Senior Citizens.

Kolasa, M., & Soto, M. (1990, October). *Legal hotlines to serve older people.* Paper presented at Third Annual Joint Conference on Law and Aging, Washington, DC. Unpublished.

Lake v. Cameron, 364 F. 2d 657 (N.C. Cir. 1966).

Laub, J. (1990). Patterns of criminal victimization in the United States. In A. Lurigo, W. Skogan, & R. Davis (Eds.), *Victims of crime: Problems, policies & programs* (pp. 23–49). Newbury Park, CA: Sage.

Lurgo, A., & Resick, P. (1990). Healing the psychological wounds of criminal victimization: Predicting postcrime distress. In A. Lurigo, W. Skogan, & R. Davis (Eds.), *Victims of crime: Problems, policies & programs* (pp. 50–68). Newbury Park, CA: Sage Publications.

Mathematica Policy Research. (1986). *National long-term care channeling demonstration: Final report.* Plainsboro, NJ: Author.

Models from Manhattan to Oahu. (1991). *Aging Today, 12,* 15.

McEwen, T.(1995). *Victim assistance programs: Whom they serve, what they offer.* Washington, DC: U.S. Department of Justice, National Institute of Justice.

NARCEA Exchange. (1990). Legislation and Policy Notes. [Brochure] Wilmington, DE: Author.

National Center on Elder Abuse (n.d). *Elder abuse information series: 1. Elder abuse in domestic settings.* Washington, DC: Author

Porter, D., & Affeldt, D. (1990). Legal services delivery systems: An overview of the present and a look at the future. In P. Powers & K. Klingensmith (Eds.), *Aging and the law: Looking into the next century* (pp. 89–112). Washington, DC: Public Policy Institute, American Association of Retired Persons.

Regan, J., & Springer, G. (1977). *Protective service for the elderly: A working paper prepared for the U.S. Senate Select Committee on Aging.* Washington, DC: U.S. Government Printing Office.

Schmidt, W., Miller, K., Bell, W., & New, B. (1981). *Public guardianship and the elderly.* Cambridge, MA: Ballinger.

Seeman, B. (1993, July 8). Swindlers target lonely unwary seniors. *Miami Herald,* p. 1.

Tomz, J. & McGill, S. (1997) *Serving crime victims and witnesses* (2nd ed.) Washington, DC: U.S. Department of Justice, Office of Justice Programs, National Institute of Justice.

U.S. Department of Justice (1994). *National Crime Victimization Survey: Some findings from the Bureau of Justice Statistics Elderly Crime Victims.* Washington, DC: Author.

U.S. Department of Justice (1997). *Bureau of Justice Statistics,National Crime Victimization Survey: Changes in Victimization, 1994–95.* Washington, DC: Author.

U.S. House of Representatives, Select Committee on Aging. (1976). *Elderly crime victimization (Federal Law Enforcement Agencies—LEAA and FBI).* Washington, DC: U.S. Government Printing Office.

Wasser, E. (1974). Protective service: Casework with older people. *Social Casework, 97,* 103–114.

Wolf, R. (1988). The evolution of policy: A 10-year retrospective. *Public Welfare, 46,* 7–14.

9

Employment, Volunteer, and Educational Programs

For many elderly, retirement is a long-awaited event that promises to allow them to engage in long-postponed activities. Retirement may also mean relief from the drudgery of a job that has been endured but never enjoyed. For other older workers, retirement is a dreaded moment, a termination of a career with its attendant status, a loss of important collegial relationships, and a future that promises to consist of hours of unfilled time. Activities for the elderly must therefore include both paid jobs and volunteer opportunities. Jack Ossofsky, former Executive Director of the National Council on the Aging, attempted to place the issue of employment and volunteer activities in a framework that transcends purely economic issues:

> Maintaining options for the older American is the heart of the issue. . . The greatest loss among the elderly is not economic status, income or health, serious as these may be. It's the loss of options, the opportunity to stay employed, volunteer for social work, start a second career (Cattani, 1977, p. 13).

In this chapter we will examine both paid employment programs and volunteer opportunities available to the elderly.

EMPLOYMENT LEGISLATION

Age and Retirement

In 1900, two-thirds of men over 65 were still in the labor force. In fact, until 1950, over one-half of men over 65 were still working (National Council on the Aging, 1978). While many workers elect early retirement, others feel forced out of jobs without any considerations being given to their experience and competency.

Social Security regulations have restricted the work options of the elderly since benefits have been reduced in proportion to earned income for persons aged 65–69. The removal of any Social Security limitations on earned income might encourage more older individuals to seek employment. The problem of employment for the elderly has thus been twofold: (1) finding employers who did not discriminate against them and (2) finding sufficient numbers of part-time jobs which provide additional money without exceeding the limit allowed by Social Security regulations.

Age Discrimination Legislation

The major ally of the elderly in their effort to obtain employment has been the Age Discrimination Employment Act of 1967 (ADEA), which outlawed discrimination based on age unless age was a bona fide requirement of the job, and the Age Discrimination Act. Originally the provisions of the ADEA covered employees in private firms, public agencies, and labor organizations who were between 40 and 65. In 1977, 86 suits were filed under this act; but in 1978 and 1977, over 5,000 complaints were registered with the Department of Labor, the agency formerly responsible for enforcing the act's provisions (U.S. Department of Labor, 1977).

For the elderly, the most important changes in the ADEA took place in 1978. The 1978 amendments increased coverage of the act to individuals up to 70 years of age in private and nonfederal employment. Mandatory retirement for most federal employees was abolished. The 1986 amendments to the ADEA outlawed mandatory retirement at the age of 70. It is estimated that there will be 195,000 more older workers by the year 2000. In 1986, 1.1 million workers were over the age of 70 (Durso, 1986). Since 20.9 million workers have been employed under compulsory retirement provisions, the effects of these changes will need to be carefully observed. Regulations accompanying the passage of the 1978 amendments to the ADEA transferred the enforcement of the act from the Department of Labor to the Equal Employment Opportunities Commission. This shift brought the ADEA enforcement under the wing of the agency charged with overseeing all other antidiscrimination activities.

EMPLOYMENT PROGRAMS

Attaining part-time and full-time jobs requires well-coordinated placement services that match skills of the worker to possible positions. Efforts in this direction are underway. Much less common are efforts to retrain older workers for new positions which require the attainment of extensive new skills.

Counseling

The first stage of employment efforts in many areas entails helping older workers gain a better understanding of their skills. This type of counseling has been part of the programs of voluntary agencies in Cleveland and Baltimore since the middle 1960s (Health and Welfare Council, 1965; Occupational Planning Commission of the Welfare Federation of Cleveland, 1958). The counseling clinics attempt to provide the worker with supportive help, foster the development of self-assurance, and help with occupational adjustment. Meeting these goals involves attempting to overcome some of the common problems found among older individuals interested in working. These may include poor motivation or poor work histories, a long lag period since their last job, and a lack of appropriate skills for a changing labor market. Added to these deficits may be physical or emotional problems. Once counseling has helped to overcome these problems and enabled workers to achieve a realistic understanding of their own work potential, adequate placement becomes critical.

Using a variety of federal and local funds, placement programs are operating in a number of states and localities. This number could easily be expanded. Many of these programs are funded through provisions of the OAA, but a number of the most well-developed programs predate AoA's funding for employment programs. In 1959, the Atlanta branch of the National Council of Jewish Women (Cattani, 1978) started a placement program for older workers. In Evanston, Illinois, Senior Action Services has placed older workers in a variety of centers. This placement record represents one out of every three applicants. These workers hold jobs as typists, house sitters, companions, and chauffeurs. Locally funded, Senior Action Services' efforts are coordinated through Operation Able, a coordinating group for all Chicago-area senior programs. Operation Able also operates similar programs in other states.

Older Americans Act Employment

On a national scale, the largest provision of funds for the older worker stems from Title V (formerly Title IX) of the OAA. Prior to the emphasis on employment in the OAA, Title X of the Public Works and Economic Development Act of 1965 provided some job opportunities for the elderly. This program, targeted for high-unemployment areas, made some funds available for older workers. By 1975, approximately 4,800 seniors had obtained employment under this funding mechanism (Braver & Bowers, 1977).

The original Title IX of the OAA authorization of 1975 was aimed at helping needy older persons obtain a higher income level. It was also hoped that employment would provide these workers with a renewed sense of involvement with the community while they acquired new skills or upgraded existing ones. The 1992 OAA amendments emphasize older persons with "the greatest economic need" "who have poor employment prospects" [Sec. 502].

The OAA also saw older persons as resources able to provide communities with needed additional human service workers, especially to fill major gaps in providing services to the elderly. The Senior Community Service Employment Program (SCSEP) of Title V has been contracted by the Department of Labor to a number of major organizations including the American Association of Retired Persons, Green Thumb, National Asian Pacific Center on Aging, National Association of Hispanic Elderly, National Caucus and Center on Black Aged, National Council on the Aging, National Council of Senior Citizens, National Indian Council on Aging, National Urban League, the U.S. Forest Service, and individual states. In 1975, 22,440 slots were authorized under the program (U.S. Department of Labor, 1977), but this figure had risen to 64,933 by 1990 and the total budget to approximately $367 million.

In 1994 the "slots" available for the 10 national contractors ranged from a high of 16,000 positions for Green Thumb to a low of 836 positions at the National Indian Council on Aging. Individual states receive funds in accordance with the percentage of state residents over age 55 and the per capita income of the state. A major concern of the program is to avoid political problems that would result if SCSEP workers filled job classifications normally held by full-time employees and were seen as competitive with these workers (National Council of Senior Citizens, 1987).

The SCSEP program grew dramatically in the last part of the 1970s. There were nearly 12 times as many participants enrolled in 1980 as compared to 1976. Approximately half of all of the workers were in jobs providing services to the general community. This breakdown parallels the types of jobs being emphasized in other elderly employment programs. A concrete example of these efforts is the assistance seniors in Los Angeles have provided elderly Filipinos in obtaining citizenship. The SCSEP administered through the AARP provides similar opportunities for individuals in public or private nonprofit organizations. The National Council on Senior Citizens Senior Aide program provides limited employment in 53 areas for older persons working in community service organizations for the elderly. This includes activities such as delivering meals to the homebound or providing shopping services. In all SCSEP efforts, the older adult has been limited to a maximum of 1,300 hours of work per year, averaging 20–25 hours per week, and payment of either the federal or state minimum wages, whichever is higher.

The Green Thumb program, operated by the National Farmers Union, administers activities in mostly rural areas in 43 states and Puerto Rico. Inaugurated in 1965 to do highway beautification, it now arranges for older men and women to serve in host agencies. About 70% serve the community at large and 30% target services to the elderly. Focusing on intergenerational involvement, enrollees serve young people through assignment in the field of education, mostly in small rural schools. In 1995, 38% of Green Thumb participants were 70 years of age or older, 17% had disabilities, 43% had never finished high school, 73% were women, and 18% were from minority backgrounds. After participating in Green Thumb, the agency was able to place 30% of its participants in unsubsidized jobs (Kilborn, 1995). The U.S. Forest Service utilized low-income individuals over 55 in a variety of projects in National Forest lands in 1990.

The Job Partnership Training Act (JPTA), which replaced CETA, earmarks 3% of its funds for poorer workers over the age of 55. The Act provides training and remedial education as well as counseling and job search assistance. The training and assistance are oriented to private businesses. Title III of JPTA offers job search assistance to workers about to be laid off or at the end of their unemployment compensation eligibility. In the 1989–90 program year, over 38,000 older participants were served through the "setaside" and 9,500 workers over age 55 were involved in Title III services.

Meeting Employment Needs

SCSCEP participants are primarily women. There is substantial participation of minority elderly, particularly Black elderly. Although 30% of the participants are over age 70, the majority are in their 60s. Unsubsidized job placements now account for 20–25% of all placements.

Despite an inability to overcome the problem of obtaining unsubsidized jobs, the self-esteem and well-being attested to by SCSEP participants has been seen as a testimony to its importance. The demographic profile of the United States is shifting, and fewer younger workers are available. Increasing numbers of employers may soon move on their own volition to hire older workers to meet their labor force needs. An interest in hiring older workers is in evidence among fast-food and retail outlets, and is expected to increase during the remainder of the century. Hirshorn and Hoyer's (1992) research confirms the interest of private sector firms (with more than 20 employees) in hiring retirees. Regardless of the new interest among employers in older workers, there is no indication that the majority of older Americans are interested in working. In its national study of retired Americans, the National Health Interview Survey found only 12% who wanted to work, and the figure was lower among those individuals who had retired for health reasons (Kovar & LaCroix, 1987).

Many older people may welcome the opportunity to develop new skills and talents if the working conditions are not onerous or the employment opportunities are interesting. One example of this type of effort can be found in Chicago, where Roosevelt University has trained older Hispanics to work in bilingual day care for children. This program meets the need of community programs for bilingual workers. The program also provides older adults with opportunities for advanced education, since the prospective workers are enrolled in the university for courses (Winkelstein & Olson, 1985).

VOLUNTEER AND INTERGENERATIONAL PROGRAMS

There are numerous opportunities available to older people who wish to serve as volunteers. The emphasis on older persons as volunteers has increased as the pool of women outside the paid labor force has shrunk. Older persons are thus recruited to assist museums and community organizations as well as traditional volunteer organizations such as the Red Cross. In addition to these general voluntary efforts, there are a number of programs oriented specifically to recruiting older persons as volunteers. At the federal level, the most important efforts are those administered through the National Senior Volunteer Corps, a component of the Corporation for National and Community Service. The programs more directly oriented toward the older person include the Retired Senior Volunteers Program (RSVP), the Foster Grandparents Program, the Senior Companions program, and the Service Corps of Retired Executives (SCORE).

RSVP

RSVP roots can be traced to a pilot program developed by the Community Service Society of New York in 1965. This project attempted to enlist older adults in volunteer work in the community and make use of their neglected talents and experience. The planners of project SERVE (Serve and Enrich Retirement by Volunteer Experience) hoped that the involvement of the elderly in the program would provide them with a renewed sense of self-esteem and satisfaction as well as filling important gaps in community resources.

The present RSVP program continues this tradition. Programs are locally planned and sponsored. Local communities must also provide 10% of the costs of the projects for the first year, 20% the second, and 30% for the third year. Individuals enrolled in RSVP work in "volunteer stations" which include courts, schools, libraries, nursing homes, children's daycare centers, and hospitals. Volunteers in the program include a retired minister who operates a commissary cart at a local nursing home and a retired lawyer who works one day per week at an Indian community center providing legal advice. Many volunteers are reimbursed for transportation to and from their assignments and for out-of-pocket expenses. The programs also provide the volunteers with accident and liability insurance. In FY 1995 RSVP projects were utilizing 453,000 volunteers ("Elderly volunteer programs," 1997).

Foster Grandparents

The Foster Grandparents Program is designed to provide low-income elderly with important social experiences while they assist children who have special physical or psychosocial needs: "Foster Grandparents do not displace salaried staff, but complement staff care to special children with the love and personal concern essential to their well-being" (ACTION, 1979). Foster Grandparents work 4 hours a day in a variety of settings including correctional facilities, pediatric wards of general hospitals, homes for the mentally retarded or emotionally disturbed, schools, and day care centers. Foster Grandparents receive a nontaxable stipend in compensation for their efforts, reimbursement for transportation and meals, and accident insurance. To participate in Foster Grandparents, the older person's income must be no greater than 125% of the federal poverty level. The recruitment and training of Foster Grandparents is the responsibility of the individual program. The local programs also provide the older individual with counseling and referrals on personal matters. In FY 1995, the Foster Grandparents Program budget enabled 24,000 volunteers to be recruited to work with approximately 83,000 children around the country. Because of its emphasis on assisting poverty-level elderly, Foster Grandparents programs have been emphasized in low-income areas.

Senior Companions

The Senior Companion Program, which was authorized in 1973, is modeled after the Foster Grandparents Program, except that its stress is on low-income elderly working with other elderly: "Senior Companions may provide services designed to help older persons receiving long-term care, deinstitutionalized persons from hospitals and nursing homes, and others with special needs for companionship" (ACTION, 1979). The main emphasis of the program is on chronically ill homebound elderly. The volunteers must agree to serve at least 20 hours per week and at least 10% of project funds must be obtained from non-federal sources. By FY 1995, over 34,000 elderly were being assisted by 13,800 Senior Companion volunteers in 142 projects. Legislation enacted in 1986 now makes it possible for older individuals who exceed the income limits of the Foster Grandparents or Senior Companion program to join the program under certain conditions (U.S. Senate, 1991).

SCORE

The fourth program for older Americans is the Service Corps of Retired Executives (SCORE). Sponsored by the Small Business Administration, SCORE places retired executives in small businesses such as groceries, restaurants, bakeries, pharmacies, and other organizations which can benefit from their managerial experience. In Wharton, Texas, a SCORE volunteer is helping a bottling company revise its accounting system. In Chicago, a SCORE volunteer helped a small supermarket qualify for a Small Business Administration loan. SCORE volunteers are reimbursed for out-of-pocket expenses (ACTION, n.d.). In 1997, almost 13,000 older persons belonged to 389 SCORE chapters. These members provided services in a variety of formats including one-time counseling sessions, follow-up counseling sessions, and workshops. The members assisted 250,000 businesses. In 1996 SCORE volunteers counseled 257,000 entrepreneurs, donating about 1 million hours of service overall.

Besides these efforts, intergenerational programming is now being implemented under the auspices of numerous agencies. Some of this programming is based on the premise that younger as well as older people benefit from intergenerational contact. Some of the increase in intergenerational programming is also due to the difficulties community programs have in obtaining adequate funds to pay staff.

Intergenerational programs can utilize youth to assist older people, as in the service-learning efforts on college campuses undertaken by the National Council on the Aging in the early 1980s (Firman, Gelfand, & Merkel, 1983). A more common approach is the utilization of older adults in programs for children, as in the Foster Grandparents model. In San Francisco, the Seniors Enriching Educational Roles brings older retirees into local schools as tutors and instructors in a variety of courses (Siegel, 1985). One of the most well-known intergenerational efforts is the Teaching-Learning Communities program in Ann Arbor, Michigan (Tice, 1985). Since the 1970s, older volunteers have been brought together with children in the Ann Arbor schools who have learning and emotional problems. The range of intergenerational programs is already impressive, and has been shown to have major benefits for children as well as older adults (Lowenthal & Egan, 1991).

In order to assist in the recruitment and recognition of volunteers, the 1992 OAA amendments permit Area Agencies to hire a volunteer services coordinator. If more than 50% of the AAAs in a state develop a volunteer services coordinator position, the State Office on Aging must also develop a volunteer coordinator position. Expanded intergenerational programs in schools are also supported by a new section in Title III. The intent of this authorization is to provide intergenerational school-based programs, oriented to students with limited capacity in English and at risk of either leaving school, drug abuse, remaining illiterate, or living in poverty. At the same time, by locating intergenerational programs in schools, older persons can obtain access to school facilities such as libraries, gymnasiums, theaters, and cafeterias (Congressional Record, 1992).

Older people who volunteer as tax counselors can serve individuals of all ages. The American Association of Retired Persons Tax Aide program works in 9,000 sites and provides tax advice for individuals at libraries, senior centers, and community centers. Nationwide, 28,000 volunteers are involved in this program each year.

EDUCATIONAL PROGRAMS

Educational opportunities for seniors have increased as institutions of higher education have recognized the potential for having adults of all ages on campus and the need to move some of their educational programming into the community. As the cohort aged 18–24 decreases, the opportunities for adults to fill their places in the classroom become more apparent.

Community Colleges

Community colleges have become community educational centers, not only for people seeking Associate of Arts degrees, but for individuals wanting to upgrade skills and explore new areas of learning. Responding to this interest, many colleges have developed extensive noncredit programs that are offered both at the college and at sites in the community. For example, reading, literature, history, and art classes are often taken into nursing homes, senior daycare centers, and nutrition centers. Many of these noncredit programs, freed from semester structure, can be offered on a flexible time schedule. They are geared to the older person and often designed in conjunction with groups of seniors.

Community colleges have also encouraged older persons to take courses on campus through tuition waivers, precampus counseling, and remedial supports. For example, Dundalk Community College in Maryland offers a full semester of orientation for older persons. During orientation, each department is visited, time is spent in the labs and with the faculty, and remedial materials are made available. The campus-based courses include some geared particularly towards the elderly, as well as regular offerings which can be taken for credit or audit. The tuition waiver can come either through the decisions of the college itself or as part of a city, country, or statewide program of tuition waivers. Because of the unique nature of the community college, it has done more to encourage older persons to become involved in education than any other educational group.

College and University Programs

Universities and four-year colleges have also expanded their participation in educational programming for older persons. The most common way to expand opportunities is through tuition and fee reductions or waivers. Universities have provided everything from a minimum reduction in fees for audit only to full waiver of tuition and fees for any course or program of study. This latter approach usually offers all courses, degrees, and recreational facilities without cost to any state resident aged 60 and over. The first 2 years of the program often offer a full range of courses with the strongest emphasis in languages. Evaluation of these programs is showing that seniors who participated in these programs integrated themselves into the overall student body and did not ask for any special orientation, group meetings, or activities at the time they enrolled or at any later time. The university programs also appear to be attracting primarily older adults with previous college experience.

The extent to which a college or university can offer free programs is dependent upon the size and status of the institution. For large state universities, the effect of 300 tuition-free students on the overall class structure will be minimal. For a small college or university, 300 students could make a significant difference in the course offerings and the size of classes. It is partly for this reason that educational opportunities for older persons vary greatly.

ElderHostel

ElderHostel is a national educational program that is gaining in popularity among older persons and educational institutions. This educational program sponsors 1-week courses on college campuses during the summer months. ElderHostelers interested in participating in the program stay in dormitories with other summer students on the particular college campus during the week of courses. The purpose of the program is to create opportunities for ElderHostelers to live with other students, participate in campus activities, and take courses from regular campus faculty. The courses, designed for the 1-week program, are similar to those that would be offered to full-time undergraduates during the school year, and may include an introduction to music or astronomy, special history courses, or the flora of New England. Three courses are offered in each of the one-week segments. A campus can offer as many weeks as it wishes for Elderhostelers, depending on the resources available.

The Elderhostelers come from throughout the nation and can go from campus to campus across the country. Each ElderHosteler must pay his or her own transportation and toward the costs of the course, room, and board; there are no additional charges for the program. By 1997 there were 250,000 ElderHostelers participating in programs at over 2,300 campuses throughout this and 70 other countries. The enthusiasm among seniors for ElderHostel should not be surprising. As the numbers of older adults with extensive educational backgrounds continues to grow, there will be more demands on their part for advanced educational opportunities.

REFERENCES

ACTION. (1979). *Senior Companions Program history*. Washington, DC: Author.
ACTION. (n.d.). *Service Corps of Retired Executives*. Washington, DC: Author.
Braver, R., & Bowers, L. (1977). *The impact of employment programs on the older worker and the service delivery system: Benefits derived and provided*. Washington, DC: Foundation for Applied Research.
Cattani, R. (1977, January 9). The elderly: Fight for job rights. *Christian Science Monitor*, pp. 12–13.
Cattani, R. (1978, January 11). Government job programs provide limited help to elderly. *Christian Science Monitor*, p. 15.
Congressional Record. (1992, September 22). *Older Americans Act*, Part II, H8969–H9006.
Durso, L. (1986). Reagan expected to support mandatory retirement ban. *Older American Reports*, *10*, 3.
Elderly volunteer programs would see more money in FY '95. (1997). *Older American Reports*, *18*, 47.
Firman, J., Gelfand, D., & Merkel, K. (1983). Students as resources to the aging network. *The Gerontologist*, *23*, 185–191.
Health and Welfare Council. (1965). *Older workers project: A demonstration on the job training program for workers over 50*. Baltimore: Author.
Hirshorn, B., & Hoyer, D. (1992). *The private sector employment of retirees: The organization experience*. Detroit, MI: Wayne State University Institute of Gerontology.

Kilborn, P. (1995, September 15).Threat to job program for the elderly poor. *New York Times*, p. A7.

Kovar, M., & LaCroix, A. (1987). Aging in the eighties: Ability to perform work-related activities. *Advance Data* (No. 136). Hyattsville, MD: National Center for Health Statistics.

Lowenthal, B. & Egan, R. (1991). Senior citizen volunteers in a university day-care center. *Educational Gerontology, 17*, 363–378.

National Council of Senior Citizens. (1987). *Senior aides: A unique federal program*. Washington, DC: Author.

National Council on the Aging. (1978). *Fact book on aging*. Washington, DC: Author.

Occupational Planning Commission of the Welfare Federation of Cleveland. (1958). *Measuring up: A career clinic for older women workers*. Cleveland: Author.

Siegel, E. (1985). Intergenerating in San Francisco's Public Schools. In K. Struntz, & S. Reville, (Eds.), *Growing together: An intergenerational source book*. Palm Springs, CA: American Association of Retired Persons, The Elvirita Lewis Foundation.

Tice, C. (1985). Teaching-Learning Communities: An investment in learning and wellness. In K. Struntz, & S. Reville, (Eds.), *Growing together: An intergenerational sourcebook*. Palm Springs, CA: American Association of Retired Persons, The Elvirita Lewis Foundation.

U.S. Department of Labor. (1977). *Age discrimination in Employment Act of 1967*. Washington, DC: U.S. Government Printing Office.

U.S. Senate. (1991). *Developments in aging, 1990*. Washington, DC: U.S. Government Printing Office.

Winkelstein, E., & Olson, G. (1985). A community/university day care training model: A bilingual intergenerational approach to adult learning. In K. Struntz, and S. Reville, (Eds.), *Growing together: An intergenerational sourcebook*. Palm Springs, CA: American Association of Retired Persons, The Elvirita Lewis Foundation.

10

Nutrition Programs

The Elderly Nutrition Program was formally authorized under the 1973 amendments to the OAA and provides at least one hot meal a day, primarily in a congregate setting, for those age 60 and over. Originally criticized by some as a new version of the Depression soup kitchen this program has become the most popular and universally well-received program of the Older Americans Act. Its success can be attributed, at least in part, to the fact that it provides a measurable service (namely, the preparation and serving of a meal) in a setting that brings people together informally while integrating its efforts with other available services in the community.

The goals of the program identified in 1973 by the AoA illustrate the dual emphasis of the program:

1. Improve the health of the elderly with the provision of regularly available, low-cost, nutritious meals, served largely in congregate settings and, when feasible, to the homebound.
2. Increase the incentive of elderly persons to maintain social well-being by providing opportunities for social interaction and the satisfying use of leisure time.
3. Improve the capability of the elderly to prepare meals at home by providing auxiliary nutrition services, including nutrition and homemaker education, shopping assistance, and transportation to markets.
4. Increase the incentive of the elderly to maintain good health and independent living by providing counseling and information and referral to other social and rehabilitative services.
5. Assure that those elderly most in need, primarily the low-income, minorities, and the isolated, can and do participate in nutrition services by providing an extensive and personalized outreach program and transportation service.
6. Stimulate minority elderly interest in nutrition services by assuring that

operation of the projects reflects cultural pluralism in both the meal and supportive service components.

7. Assure that Title VII (changed to Part C under Title III in 1978) program participants have access to a comprehensive and coordinated system of services by encouraging administration coordination between nutrition projects and Area Agencies on Aging (AAAs). (Cain, 1977)

The first two goals also provide a summary of the success of the program. Nutrition is essential to good health but is greatly affected by the social situation. Eating is a social activity, and regardless of other resources, the older person is less likely to prepare adequate meals when eating alone. The last goal was strengthened in the 1978 OAA, which brought the administration of the nutrition program under the direction of the AAAs for the first time. Before 1978, the formal links with the AAAs were optional.

THE CONGREGATE NUTRITION PROGRAM

History

There has been conflicting data on the nutritional deficiencies of older Americans, conflicts based largely on the differences in urban, rural, ethnic, and economic variables. However, some general patterns of deficiency have emerged (Rawson, Weinberg, Herold, & Holtz, 1978):

Calcium appears as the most common denominator, noted as deficient in most of the studies cited. Iron and Vitamins A and C are the next most commonly identified deficiencies . . . within the elderly, the problems of nutrition intake increase as the individuals grow older and are based as much in quantitative dietary shortcomings as in qualitative deficiencies. (p. 27)

The malnourished elderly have been a part of our society for a long time, but formal, sustained programs to provide for those who do not have personal or financial resources are relatively new. The most significant research prior to the planning and development of a national nutritional program was the 1965 National Study on Food Consumption and Dietary Level sponsored by the Department of Agriculture. This study showed that 95 million Americans did not consume an adequate diet; 35 million of these had incomes at or below the poverty level. Subsequent analysis indicated that 6–8 million of those age 60 and over had deficient diets. These data laid the foundation for a federal nutrition program for the aged (Cain, 1977).

A task force set up to develop recommendations based on the results of the national study recommended demonstration projects for a 3-year period to determine the best mechanisms for delivering nutritional services. Demonstration projects were needed because of the lack of information on how such programs should be designed and, more important, the extent of their effectiveness (Bechill & Wolgamot, 1972). The purpose of the demonstration projects was to "design appropriate ways for the delivery of food services which enable older persons to enjoy adequate palatable meals that supply essential nutrients needed to maintain good health . . . in settings conducive to eating and social interaction with peers" (Cain, 1977, p. 142).

While this overall goal seems straightforward, the demonstrations were expected to examine multiple issues. Besides the major effort to improve the diet of older adults, the meals were to be served in social settings which would allow for the testing of the effects of different types of sites. These sites would be evaluated in terms of their ability to promote increased interaction among the older clients. The effects of a nutrition education program on the eating habits of the elderly would be evaluated as well as the general ability of the congregate meals approach to reduce the isolation of older persons. Of course, the AoA was also concerned about the comparative costs of different methods of preparing and delivering meals, and the problems that were entailed, in any effort to increase the nutritional quality of the older person's diet (Cain, 1977).

The AoA funded 32 demonstration and research projects under Title IV. An intensive evaluation of the demonstrations produced the support for the national nutrition program first authorized in the 1973 OAA Amendments. The 32 demonstration projects were designed to control for variations in income, living conditions, ethnic background, environmental setting, staffing, and record keeping. This intricate design allowed national guidelines to be developed that would incorporate the successful components of each project. More important, the Title IV projects indicated to the AoA and the U.S. Congress that the proper provision of congregate meals for groups of elderly people fostered social interaction, facilitated the delivery of supportive services, and met emotional needs while improving nutrition.

Program Operation

Under the provisions of the OAA, the AoA is mandated to develop a nutrition program for older adults

> 1. which, five or more days a week, provides at least one hot or other appropriate meal per day and any additional meals which the recipient of a grant or contract may elect to provide, each of which assures a minimum of one-third of the daily recommended dietary allowances as established by the Food and Nutrition Board of the National Academy of Sciences. . .

2. which shall be provided in congregate settings; and
3. which may include nutrition education services and other appropriate nutrition services for older individuals. (Title III, Part C)

The nutrition program was developed at the federal level under the authorization of the AoA and administered through a single agency. The guidelines for operation have thus been clearer than in other programs, such as home-delivered meals, which have developed out of different local and national program units.

Each state is allotted funds in proportion to the number of older persons in the state as compared with the older population nationally. However, each state is guaranteed a minimum of .5% of the national appropriation. The federal government pays 90% of the cost of establishing and operating nutrition services. The nutrition program is administered by the state agency on aging, unless another agency is designated by the governor and approved by the Secretary of the Department of Health and Human Services. Based on a previously approved state nutrition plan, the moneys are allocated to AAAs or public and nonprofit agencies, institutions, and organizations for the actual provision and delivery of meals. Before the 1978 amendments, one-half of the local nutrition programs were under the sponsorship of the AAAs, the other half under the local sponsorship. Within 2 years of the 1978 amendments, all nutrition programs were to be administered through the local AAAs to ensure service delivery coordination. However, AAAs are authorized to contract the nutrition programs to other local groups as appropriate.

The state units on aging and local nutrition administrative units must provide for advisory assistance that includes consumers of the service at the state level, members of minority groups, and persons knowledgeable in the provision of nutrition services. Nutrition advisory groups can advise on all aspects of the program as well as play an advocacy role for the continuation and growth of the program. Programming, allocations, recruitment of participants, meal sites, and service linkage are common areas of concern for nutrition advisory committees.

All persons age 60 and over and their spouses are eligible for services under the nutrition program. Special emphasis is placed on serving the low-income and disadvantaged elderly. This is achieved by locating nutrition centers, when possible, in areas that have a high proportion of low-income elderly. Through this system, any variation of a means test is avoided, thus increasing the general acceptability of the program to the elderly, who often avoid programs that appear to be "charity." Actual centers or sites are located in any space appropriate for the serving of congregate meals. The centers can serve as few as 5 or as many of 250 participants on a given day; however, the average center serves between 20 and 60 participants each day.

Church basements, schools, high-rise apartments, senior centers, and multipurpose centers are the more common locations for nutrition sites. Because transportation is so important to the success of the program, centers are usually located in high-density areas, where walking is possible, or on bus or subway lines. In suburban and rural areas, the centers are located in areas where some form of transportation to and from the center can be provided by the site. Unless the nutrition program is incorporated into senior centers that offer all-day programming, nutrition sites or centers are open up to 4 hours a day. The location of the center, transportation available, and additional resources affect the length of time of the daily operation of the program. For example, programs held in school cafeterias are often sandwiched between student lunch programs.

Location also affects the type of programming developed by the site. Sites that are not used for other purposes allow greater freedom for alterations, decorating, and storage space than do locations that have other activities scheduled in the same space. Shared space has posed a hardship for many nutrition programs in meeting the national guidelines for program development.

The meals themselves are either prepared on site, delivered to the site in bulk, or delivered to the site in individual trays or containers. Because of cost and health code regulations, the on-site preparation is the least popular form of meal preparation. Catering services contracting with many nutrition sites in a given area can provide 6- to 8-week-cycle menus that both meet the nutritional requirements of the program and are interesting to the participants. Private firms, hospitals, and long-term care institutions are the most likely sources for meals because they can incorporate special diets into the program and already have an understanding of the nutritional needs of older persons. School cafeterias and restaurants are less successful meal sources. Catered meals arriving in individual trays provide the most flexibility for nutrition center locations, as health code requirements are minimal.

Eating and Socializing

Because the purpose of the nutrition program is to provide both meals and socializing, programming is an important part of the services offered. When the nutrition site is incorporated into a high-rise for the elderly, a senior center, or a recreation center, programming is usually part of the additional available resources. When the nutrition site is its own center, programming responsibility rests with the nutrition site managers under the direction of the nutrition project director for the region.

Programming is diverse and related to the interests and backgrounds of the participants. The programming available is similar to that found in senior centers, but with special emphasis on nutrition education, meal preparation, buying practices, health maintenance, and physical fitness. Not all participants become involved in the programming. Nutrition screening, assessment, education, and counseling are, however, basic components of the program.

Eating and Needs

People who attend the nutrition centers very often have other service needs. Because of this, the nutrition program has had to reach out and develop linkage with other community services in order to respond to the needs of its participants. The nutrition programs have not built a duplicate service system but have, instead, integrated other agency services into their programs. Visits by Social Security representatives, health department officials, and recreation leaders are part of nutrition programming.

The limit on service funds has also been a factor in the location of nutrition sites. Many times, priority is given to sites located in existing community programs. For example, the nutrition program has led to the expansion of the multipurpose senior center system and has made possible many geriatric day care programs. County departments of recreation have been able to expand their programming because of the available lunch program. Housing developments for the elderly have also been able to build around the lunches being served.

Funding limitations have necessitated links to other programs to fulfill the mandates of nutrition programs. Project directors have reached to other programs to supplement nutrition center staffing needs and have, in some cases, used senior aides and RSVP volunteers to provide support staff. Guidelines indicate that staffing preference should be given to older persons. In locations where the nutrition center or site is separate from other services, the staff usually consists of one part-time site manager assisted by volunteers. In this manner, the participants themselves become involved in the actual operation of the program, and see it as "their program" for which they feel responsible.

Funding

Funding for the basics of this program came from the federal government, with an initial outlay fund of $98 million. In 1975 and 1976, the amount was raised to $125 million and has continued to grow dramatically since then. The nutrition program is now the largest single component in AoA funding. In Fiscal 1994, the Elderly Nutrition Program provided 127 million meals to 2.3 million older persons at congregate meal sites (Administration on Aging, 1996). Over $364 million was appropriated by Congress for congregate meals in FY 1997. Even with this funding, 41% of AoA providers of meals have waiting lists of people who need this program. To help compensate for these funding limitations, sites are requiring reservations, advance notice of cancellations, and in some cases, a 3- or 4-day rotating system of attendance, all of which create hardships for older persons who have become dependent on these programs for an adequate diet.

Participants are encouraged to contribute something for the meal. The guidelines provide that individuals, from their own consciences, shall determine how much they should and can afford to pay (Cain, 1977). Nutrition centers furnish envelopes or have similar systems in which participants pay what they feel is appropriate. The 1984 OAA amendments forbid programs from charging for their meals. Voluntary contributions, however, account for about 20% of the costs of congregate and home-delivered meals. Some congregate nutrition programs have adopted the use of posters to encourage older people to contribute for their meals. Others, such as the Columbus County Office for the Aging in New York State, have a suggested contribution scale. State offices on aging also receive surplus commodities or cash to supplement the cost of the meals they provide. The funding provided by the Department of Agriculture is based on the number of meals served with Title III funds. With the limited funding in some local areas in relation to the participant demand, participants have decided among themselves to contribute higher amounts in order that more people can be served. Local donations and volunteers also help to defray about 14% of the costs of this program. The average cost for a meal is $5.17.

HOME-DELIVERED MEALS

Home-delivered meals ("Meals on Wheels") are provided to homebound persons, and enable those persons who cannot buy food or prepare their own meals to have good nutritional meals on a regular basis. Approximately 90% of all those receiving homebound meals are aged 60 and over. The purpose of the program is to provide either one or two meals per day, 5 days a week. These delivered meals may enable many of these aged to remain living in the community.

History

Programs of home-delivered meals began in England immediately following World War II. The first program in the United States began in

Philadelphia in 1955. The longest continuously operating program is "Meals on Wheels" of Central Maryland, Inc., which began in 1960 in Baltimore and was modeled after the English programs.

The early models of home-delivered meal programs were operated locally and largely by volunteer organizations. Originating in a church kitchen, these programs would serve from 15 to 100 clients, generating payment from clients either through a fixed fee or on a sliding scale. From 30 to 300 volunteers would be involved in any given local program. Referrals would come from friends, families, professionals in the field, or the elderly themselves. The number of daily meals and the costs of these meals both depended on the facilities available for meal preparation. Menus, number of meals served, amount, and cost were determined by the local organization sponsoring the program. Volunteers were primarily retirees and non-working women, each of whom volunteered approximately 2 hours a week. The hot meal was delivered at noontime, and if a second meal was provided, it was a cold evening meal delivered at the same time as the hot meal. The early programs were sponsored by local churches, community groups, or nonprofit organizations and were largely self-sufficient based on the fees charged the participating clients.

In the early 1970s, government funds resulted in either new programs under government sponsorship, or links between nonprofit local programs and government agencies. With the introduction of these new support mechanisms, uniform standards, quality control, and uniformity began. The 1978 amendments to the OAA for the first time designated a separate authorization for home-delivered meals. This program was to be administered through the nutrition program. In some situations, there were no pre-existing home-delivered meal programs. AoA-funded home-delivered meal services served primarily clients who were congregate-site participants, while locally funded programs served other eligible clients. Because congregate nutrition participants often pay only when they feel they can, while those being served by a locally self-supporting home-delivered meal program pay a fixed fee, the Meals-on-Wheels cost to a client is often as much as five times higher. This can cause confusion when a client moves from one program to the other.

The 1978 legislation with separate authorization for home-delivered meals brought this issue of privately operated, largely volunteer groups vis-a-vis federally sponsored programs to a head. The authorizing legislation stated that home-delivered meal programs under the separate authorization were to be administered through the federal nutrition program, with preference for funding given to local preexisting voluntary home-delivered meal programs. Since 1978, OAA funding for home-delivered meals has grown dramatically.

Program Operation

In a home-delivered meal program, two volunteers—one acting as a driver, one as a visitor—visit 8 to 10 different clients each day. The volunteers spend 5 minutes with each client while delivering the meal. The home-delivered meal program's primary function is to prepare and deliver the meals, but it also provides a few minutes of friendly visiting. If additional services are needed, the client is referred to other support systems.

The meals are prepared by volunteers in church kitchens or are catered by private services, hospitals, long-term care institutions, schools, or colleges. When catered, the meals are either packaged by volunteers (delivered in bulk) or packaged by the meal-producing agency. The extent to which special-diet meals are available is determined by the amount of funds available and the source of the meal preparation. Low-salt and diabetic diets are the more common special diets available. The development of better serving boxes for keeping food warm and of better individualized food-storage containers have improved the system of food delivery. Appropriate delivery equipment is essential to keeping the food at the right temperature without spoilage. Either a 6- or 8-week-menu cycle ensures the variety necessary in such a program, while guaranteeing that the one-third required daily nutritional allowance is met in each meal.

For many of the home-delivered meal programs, the volunteer aspects of the program are themselves a service to older persons. In a study of the volunteers in "Meals on Wheels" of Central Maryland (Olsen, 1979), one-half were over 60 years of age themselves and indicated that being able to serve in this program gave meaning to their lives; 29% of the volunteers were widows and living alone. Although primarily intended for the home-bound clients, the program obviously also provides a service to those preparing and delivering the meals.

When the home-delivered program is attached directly to the nutrition congregate site, the nutrition participants themselves often package and deliver the meals. In this way, those that are attending can keep in touch with participants who are unable to attend. As was pointed out in Congressional testimony (Cain, 1977), the longer the congregate nutrition program is available, the greater potential for home-delivered meals as part of the program. One project found that after 3 years, up to 30% of the participants were receiving the home-delivered meals because of changes in their physical condition. The interrelation of the two programs is important in order that those who are eligible for the nutrition program can have an opportunity to continue, even when physical limitations temporarily make visiting the center impossible. The home program can speed recovery and perhaps, in many situations, make a return to the congregate site possible.

The 1978 amendments allowed individuals under 60 years of age to utilize AoA services. Because home-delivered meal programs have served anyone homebound, this legislation allows the younger homebound to continue to be eligible for the programs.

Funding

Nationally, the actual cost per day for the one hot meal and one cold meal delivered through the Meals on Wheels programs averaged $5.31 in FY 1994. Funding to cover these costs has always been diverse. Either a fixed fee based on the cost of the meal, or a sliding scale that averages the cost of the meal has been the common method. Recently, eligible clients have been able to use food stamps in most locations to supplement the cost of the meals. Currently, funds from Title III of the OAA ($105 million in FY 1997) are the key sources for revenue. These funds can be used not only for the cost of the meals themselves, but to pay those who prepare, package, and deliver the meals. Because of the availability of federal funds, there is a shift from volunteer to paid help for meal preparation and delivery. Local United Way, church, community service, and neighborhood groups also contribute money, equipment, or transportation to the program. With the inclusion for the first time of home-delivered meals into the OAA and the separate authorization for funding, the home-delivered meal program continues to expand its important role in the community service delivery system. Overall, funds from Title III enabled 877,000 homebound elderly to receive delivered meals in FY 1994. Through Title VI an additional 47,500 older persons received home-delivered meals.

It is clear that elderly participating in nutrition programs have some major needs and that these programs are helping to meet some of these needs. Between 80 and 90% of nutrition program participants have incomes less than 200% of the federal poverty level, and are also twice as likely to live alone as other elderly. Possibly related to this social situation is the fact that two-thirds of these participants are either under- or overweight and have twice as many physical problems as other age peers (Administration on Aging, 1996).

Despite the growth of nutrition programs, it is clear that there will be increased demand for its services, particularly among individuals over the age of 85 and home-bound. Earlier hospital discharges will also result in many older persons being at home but unable to prepare the meals they need for proper convalescence.

REFERENCES

Administration on Aging (1996). *Serving elderly at risk: The Older Americans Act nutrition programs, National evaluation of the Elderly Nutrition Program, 1993–95.* Washington, DC: Author.

Bechill, W. B., & Wolgamot, I. (1972). *Nutrition for the elderly: The program highlights of research and development nutrition projects funded under Title IV of the Older Americans Act of 1965, June 1968, and June 1971.* Washington, DC: U.S. Government Printing Office.

Cain, L. (1977). Evaluative research and nutrition programs for the elderly. In *Evaluative research on social programs for the elderly.* Washington, DC: U.S. Government Printing Office.

Olsen, J. (1979). *The effect of change in activity in voluntary associations on life satisfaction among people 60 and over who have been active through time.* Unpublished doctoral dissertation, University of Maryland, College Park, MD.

Rawson, I., Weinberg J., Herold, J., & Holtz, J. (1978). Nutrition of rural elderly in southwestern Pennsylvania. *Gerontologist, 18,* 24–29.

Part IV

Services for the Aged

In contrast to programs, existing services in aging offer a large number of components, and always seem to be under pressure to expand. Since these services are community-based, these expansionist pressures often come from seniors in the community and their families. Pressures are also being generated by a federal government that is demanding more accessibility to services for seniors and more accountability on the part of service providers.

This part will examine some complicated and vital service delivery systems, including multipurpose senior centers, housing services, in-home services, adult day care centers, and nursing homes. These services are being presented in this chapter in sequence that relates to their orientation to elderly with differing levels of need. Multipurpose senior centers serve ambulatory elderly, while housing services may be oriented to ambulatory elderly with some housekeeping and personal needs for which they require assistance. In-home services and adult day care centers serve seniors with more extensive physical or emotional problems. Finally, nursing homes are oriented toward a population which cannot survive in the community, even with the provision of extensive services.

It should be noted that although these services are discussed here individually, they are not mutually exclusive. Seniors may be taking advantage of more than one service. Ambulatory elderly who attend a senior center may also be living in elderly housing and receiving some homemaker assistance. Clients of adult day care centers may also be recipients of extensive in-home services.

Because of the variety of funding sources and varying eligibility standards, programs around the country have attempted to combine various sources of money with other local resources in order to be able to provide as broad a base of service as possible. In many areas this has blossomed into full-scale case management programs. The National Advisory Committee on Long-Term Care defines case management as

a service that links and coordinates assistance from both paid providers and unpaid help of family and friends to enable elderly or disabled individuals with chronic functional and/or cognitive limitations to obtain the highest level of independence consistent with the capacity and their preferences for care. (Quinn, 1995, p. 8)

The committee has also defined six core functions of case management:

1. Comprehensive assessment of the older person;
2. Development of a care plan based on the assessment;
3. Implementation and coordination of the care plan;
4. Monitoring of consumer and provider services to ensure their appropriateness and quality;
5. Comprehensive reassessment as needed; and
6. Discharge from case management.

In some communities, some of the needed services may not be available locally, creating problems for the case managers. As appropriate "packages" of services become more evident around the country, there has been increased effort to expand programs to enable case management to be effective in keeping the older individual in the community.

In Maryland, the Gateway II program serves moderately and severely health-impaired persons over 65. Comprehensive assessment of the older individual and assignment of a case manager to help coordinate services are the basic components of the program. Limited "gap filling" funds are available when other programs are not sufficient to meet the older client's needs. The program is means-tested. Only individuals within 80% of the state's median income and with assets of $11,000 are eligible for the program (Bechill, 1987).

The Triage experience in Connecticut indicates that a well-conducted case-management approach can diminish the cost of providing service by reducing inappropriate institutionalization of the older person as well as the use of inappropriate community-based services. As a federally funded demonstration, Triage was allowed to waive some Medicare requirements for clients. Triage cost estimates were well below those of long-term residential care (Quinn, Segal, Raisz, & Johnson, 1982).

In many areas, case managers have no ability to affect the quality of a service except by refusing to refer individuals to a particular agency. Case-management programs in Monroe County, New York, and in San Francisco employ an approach that enables them to control the quality of programs they utilize. In Monroe County, the ACCESS program controls funds for the purchase of services. The On Lok program in San Francisco offers comprehensive services for its clients (Grisham, White, & Miller, 1983). Case-management services can also be an integral part of other programs, such as adult day care. In one national survey (Weissert et al., 1989), 79% of the day care centers under the auspices of general hospitals and social service agencies offered case-management services.

Case-management and supportive services may be even more crucial where family members live at a distance from their older relatives. The Jewish Family and Children's Agencies around the country have developed an Elder Support Network. Family members are able to arrange for case management and supportive services to be provided to their relatives living throughout the United States. The services are provided through local Jewish Family and Children's Agencies. Charges are on a sliding scale based on the family member's income. Similar services are available through networks of private social workers.

REFERENCES

Bechill, W. (1987, March 9). *The reauthorization of the Older Americans Act.* Paper represented before the Committee on Education and Labor, U.S. House of Representatives, Washington, DC.

Grisham, M., White, M., & Miller, L. (1983). Case management as a problem-solving strategy. *Pride Institute Journal of Long Term Home Health Care, 2,* 21–28.

Quinn, J. (1995). LTC case management: What it is and where it's going. *Aging Today, 26,* 7–8.

Quinn, J., Segal, J., Raisz, H., & Johnson, C. (1982). *Coordinating community services for the elderly: The Triage experience.* New York: Springer Publishing Company.

Weissert, W., Elston, J., Bolda, E., Cready, L., Zelman, W., Sloane, P., Kalsbeek, W., Mutran, E., Rice, T., & Koch, G. (1989). Models of adult day care: Findings from a national survey. *The Gerontologist, 29,* 640–649.

11

Multipurpose Senior Centers

The multipurpose senior center is probably the most diverse service now available to the elderly. This diversity is emphasized in NCOA's definition of a senior center:

> a community focal point on aging where older persons as individuals or in groups come together for services and activities which enhance their dignity, support their independence and encourage their involvement in and with the community. (National Council on the Aging, 1979, p. 15)

This definition emphasizes the senior center as a community focal point, the key ingredient of present senior-center philosophy. Senior-center programs operate from a separate facility, serve as a resource for information and training, and promote the development of new approaches to servicing the older adult.

The OAA emphasizes the multipurpose senior center's role as a community facility for the organization and provision of a broad spectrum of services for the older person. The success of senior centers, however, lies not only in the breadth of services they provide, but also in the voluntary participation of the center's users in center activities. Seniors can choose not only whether they want to participate in a center program, but in what way they want to become involved. Individuals thus maintain their independence while reaching out to others and to the community in a variety of activities.

HISTORY AND LEGISLATION

Associations of peers have always been sources of support for individuals. Clubs organized for older people can be traced as far back as 1870.

However, centers for older people began with a program in New York City in 1943. The idea came from workers in the New York City Welfare Department, who felt that the older people with whom they were working needed more than a club. The organizers of the project, besides securing a meeting place, had contributed games, had suggested the serving of refreshments to foster sociability, and having gathered the old people together, expected that they could manage by themselves. They had in this way provided them with a more sociable means of passing time, which then seemed adequate provision. No one had thought beyond this point (Maxwell, 1962, p. 5)

The idea of this form of association quickly spread, as private groups began setting up centers throughout the country. The San Francisco Senior Center, begun in 1947, was created through efforts of the United Community Fund, the American Woman's Volunteer Services, the Recreation Department, and individual local citizens (Kent, 1978). In 1949 the new "Little House" in suburban Menlo Park, California, was able to attract while-collar and professional clients (Maxwell, 1962).

Senior centers grew primarily as locally supported and directed institutions. Established either by local nonprofit groups or by local units of government (departments of social service or departments of recreation), centers were designed to be primarily responsive to local needs. However, most of the growth in senior centers has occurred since 1965. Before that time, small clubs were the most common form of social organization. Even in 1970, there were only 1,200 centers, as opposed to 10,000 in the 1990s (Krout, 1995).

In the 1970s, federal legislation made more funds available for the development of senior centers. The most important piece of authorizing legislation was Title V of the OAA. The 1973 amendments, Section 501, inserted into the act the new "Multipurpose Senior Centers" title. Although not funded until 1975, this title identified senior centers as a unique and separate program. Because Title V provided funds for "acquisition, alteration, or renovation" of centers, but not for construction or operation of centers, Title III made it possible to fund senior centers for the development and delivery of a variety of specific services. Title V provided resources for the facilities, while Title III provided operational monies.

The 1978 amendments to the OAA consolidated the Title V program into Title III, repealing the Title V. With this change, Title III can "provide for acquisition, alteration, renovation, or construction of facilities for multiple purpose senior centers as well as provide for the operations of these centers." This consolidation provides for a greater opportunity to organize senior centers under the direction of the AAAs. The new Title III also allows the AAAs to fund senior centers from their beginning to fully operational stages.

A number of other legislative enactments provide mandates for senior centers:

1. The local Public Works Development and Investment Act of 1965 provided funds which may be used for the development of multipurpose senior center facilities. Under Title I of this act, funds may cover 100% of the cost of construction, renovation, and repair of buildings to be used as centers.

2. Title XX of the Social Security Act, authorized in 1974, provided funds for group services for older persons in senior centers. Many of the programs offered through senior centers were eligible for funds under Title XX, because Title XX's purpose was the provision of social services for low-income persons. Only individuals who met the eligibility requirements could receive services. Because of this requirement, it was often difficult to coordinate Title XX programs with those funded through the OAA, which had no eligibility requirements other than the age of the recipient.

3. The Housing and Community Development Act of 1974 provides funds for the expansion of community services, principally for persons of low and moderate income. Construction funds are available through this act (U.S. Administration on Aging, 1977).

CHARACTERISTICS

Senior Center Users

By 1990 the senior center concept had grown to a point where between 5 and 8 million older persons were participating in 10–12,000 centers around the country (Krout, Cutler, & Coward, 1990). In 1984, senior center participants represented 15% of the population over age 65. The attendance at senior centers represents a usage rate 4 to 12 times greater than that of any other community-based programs for older persons.

There has been a strong interest in differentiating users from nonusers of senior centers. Krout's (1988) review of research on this issue does not provide any definitive answers. The variables that did not differentiate users from nonusers of senior centers include sex, age, marital status, degree of loneliness, and lack of transportation.

Studies of the effects of race and ethnicity on senior center usage have produced mixed findings; as have variables including occupation, income, educational differences, health status, and degree of social contact with others. While these reported studies were based on local samples, an analysis of national data (Krout et al. 1990) found senior center participation related to "higher levels of social interaction, lower income, increasing age up to 85, living alone, fewer ADL and IADL difficulties, higher education up to post-high school, being female, and living in central city or rural nonfarm areas" (p. 79). Miner, Logan & Spitze (1993) attempt to clarify the determinants of attendance by analyzing data from the 1984 Supplement on Aging to the National Health Interview Survey. They found that individuals who participate and use senior centers most frequently are poorer, more socially active, and older. The age variable is complex in its effects, since after a certain age, individuals are less likely to attend a senior center. Neither race, subjective health status, or frequency of usage were found to be determinants of center attendance. There was also no relationship between functional disability and frequency of usage, although the most disabled individuals are less likely to participate in senior center activities.

Although race was not a predictor of senior center usage, Ralston (1989) points out that there are major gaps in data on the use of senior centers by Asians and native American elderly. Nationally, participation of African American and Latino elderly are senior centers has been low. A survey of 424 senior centers (Krout, 1994) found that 24% had an increased number of non-White participants. Ralston and Griggs (1985) found a significantly higher commitment to senior center programs among African Americans than among Whites. Although African Americans may have more difficulty in getting to the centers, African American women were more encouraged by children to attend the senior center than were white women.

Models

The early centers in New York and Menlo Park became the prototypes for the two conceptual models of the senior center that are now dominant. One conceptual approach embodied in the social agency model views senior centers as "programs designed to meet the needs of the elderly and postulates that the poor and the disengaged are the more likely candidates for participation in senior centers." The alternative "voluntary organization model hypothesizes that the elderly who are more active in voluntary organizations and who manifest strong attachments to the community are also the ones who make use of senior centers" (Taietz, 1976, p. 219).

Early research identified the social agency model as the most commonly developed. As Taietz notes, the social clubs for the elderly have been most meaningful to individuals who are isolated from social relationships, the clubs helping to relieve the older person's loneliness. For the older person who is active in a number of informal and organizational roles, the existence of age-graded social clubs may not seem an exciting opportunity.

The voluntary organizations are usually groups that have many social activities but also possess regular memberships, have organizational bylaws, and conduct scheduled meetings of the members on a variety of topics (Taietz, 1976). In a study of senior centers in 34 communities, Taietz noted the similarities between senior centers and other voluntary organizations which include both service components and professional staff. One major difference, however, was that, while veterans and fraternal groups tend to be sex-exclusive, senior centers provide men and women with equal access to programs. However, because the centers under this model are similar to formal voluntary organizations, their major clientele will tend to be active elderly rather than the more isolated senior.

In an exploratory study, Sabin (1993) found support for both models, with different types of programs and clientele patronizing the respective programs. While centers that utilized the social agency model had more of an emphasis on services, centers oriented to the voluntary agency model had more focus on self-expression, recreation, and collective action. These centers were more attractive to higher-income and more active older persons.

Fowler (1974) proposed three different criteria for categorizing senior centers. The first defines centers in terms of activities generated. The center can be identified by whether it provides primarily services, activities, individual services and casework, or a combination of the three. The second mechanism for categorizing centers is by administration. The center administrative core may be either centralized (everything in a central facility); decentralized (located in several neighborhood facilities); combined (central location, with satellites); or a multiplicity of operations with some linkage. Finally, centers can be classified by the origin of their services. The services can be offered exclusively by center staff, by center staff and community agencies, or by community agencies with the center staff providing coordination. The descriptions of the models themselves show how complex and diversified the structure can be and still come under the rubric of "senior centers".

As part of the National Council on Aging (1979) study of centers, another model emerged, one based on size and complexity of operation and including four levels:

1. Multipurpose senior center
2. Senior center
3. Club for older persons
4. Program for all persons, with special activities available for elderly

The differences between centers and clubs do not rest solely in their activities or membership, but rather in the breadth of services available to clients, the permanent nature of the physical facility, and the numbers of unpaid staff. Many senior centers are also incorporated entities. In the NCOA survey, 51% of the responding organizations were centers, 46% clubs, and 3% could not be placed in any existing category (Leanse & Wagner, 1975).

Cohen (1972) attempted to further delineate the center from the club. The center was viewed as having the following five characteristics:

1. Community visibility based on a good facility and easy identification
2. A central location for services, through either central site or satellites
3. An ability to serve as a focal point for concerns and interests
4. An ability to serve as a bridge to the community
5. A program purpose that focuses on the individual, family, and community

The diversity of structure, size, and functioning capabilities are a result of the origins of senior centers. The centers have emerged from the community; are sponsored primarily by voluntary, nonprofit, or public community-based organizations; and still receive a substantial percentage of funding from locally determined sources.

PROGRAMMING

Although center programming is diverse, it falls into two basic types: recreation-education and service. The programming provided is most likely to be successful when it is built as part of the larger community structure and under the direction, or at least with the support, of the older people who will be served by the center.

Recreation and Education

Recreation-education is the type of programming most commonly conceived as the central component of a senior center. It is this that sets it apart from other service delivery agencies in the community, and builds the center as a neighborhood focal point for seniors.

The development of activity and the selection of the activities to be offered are related to the target group identified by the center. If the center plans to serve everyone within a given geographic area, the programming should reflect the diversity of the population served. Whether clients are men or women, people of high or low income, people of various ethnic backgrounds, or from urban or rural settings should be reflected in the activities designed for the center. If not, unrepresented components of the population potentially served will not utilize the center because their activity needs are not being met. Taietz (1976) warned program directors of the danger of neglecting the special efforts required to attract isolated and alienated elderly to the centers. Hanssen et al. (1978) added another cautionary note with the identification of another subgroup for whom activity programming is not always available:

> The senior center does not consistently accommodate those seniors with perceived physical limitations and those who are mildly depressed. This finding highlights a critical problem for senior centers. If they are to provide services beyond recreation, they must help those persons with greater perceived health problems and that have other limitations. (p. 198)

This early caution about services for "frail" elderly has continued to attract attention, as senior center directors note that more of their clients appear to be frail. Although 58% of the senior centers reported an increase in frail elderly in Krout's (1995) survey, this increase may represent not only the attendance of new individuals, but also the "aging in place" of longstanding members. Accurate tallying of the numbers of frail elderly receiving services at senior centers is difficult because of the lack of clear definition of the term "frail".

Many senior centers are beginning to make special efforts to serve elderly with special needs. These elderly may have serious chronic illnesses and physical impairments. It is clear, however, that resources, adequately trained staff, and attitudes towards the frail elderly are among the problems faced by centers interested in serving this important population of older persons (Krout, 1995). With increased emphasis in federal programs on the "frail elderly," we can expect these programs to expand.

The recreation-education component of center programming can be as varied as the community resources allow and as the participants' interests indicate. Common activities include arts and crafts, nature, science and outdoor life, drama, physical activity, music, dance, table games, special social activities, literary activities, excursions, hobby or special interest groupings, speakers, lectures, movies, forums, round tables, and community service projects. When center participants themselves identify their interests and plan the activities with expert assistance from staff, there is a greater chance of adequate participation and success.

Services

The services component of programming is the other essential ingredient for a successful senior center. What identifies the senior center as the community focal point for older people is the combination of both activity and service in one location. The availability of a lecture on horticulture, dental screening, or square dance lessons, along with Social Security advice at the same site and with the same friends, makes the senior center a unique community resource.

The services available through a senior center depend on the facilities, the resources, and the community supports available. These services can be provided directly by center staff, by agency staff assigned to the center, through satellite centers close to the agency, or by the agencies themselves rotating through the center.

Services likely to be available through senior centers fall into a number of categories (Cohen,1972).

1. Information, counseling, and referral, including general information, intake and registration, personal counseling, referral resource files, and special group education around special problems.

2. Housing and living arrangements and employment, including helping the older person locate appropriate housing situations, job referral and counseling programs, and job retraining.

3. Health programs, including screening clinics for a variety of health problems; pharmaceutical services; specialty services, such as dentistry, podiatry, hearing, and speech; and health education programs. These programs are most likely to be developed in conjunction with county health departments, doctors, nurses, extended-care facilities, hospitals, and outpatient clinics in the area.

4. Protective services, including preventive services such as planning for the appropriate use of funds or securing safe living arrangements; supportive services, to help enable the older person to be as self-sufficient as possible; and intervention services, including assistance in gaining access to such legal resources as commitment or guardianship.

5. Meals, such as those provided through the OAA nutrition program. The development of the nutrition program since 1973 has been the single biggest contributor to the development of senior centers. Since the nutrition program needed sites for the congregate meals and senior centers needed a meal program in order to continue adequate daily programming, the nutrition program has given the centers a much-needed resource.

6. Legal and income counseling, including helping determine eligibility for Supplemental Security Income (SSI) and the preparation of wills.

7. Friendly visiting as an outreach program, with the participants of the center providing the visiting and outreach services.

8. Homemaker assistance.

9. Telephone reassurance and buddy programs.

10. Handyman and fix-it programs.

11. Day-care services.

12. Transportation programs.

13. Nursing home resident activities within the senior center facility.

This list, developed in the 1970s, was still pertinent into the 1990s. The most common efforts reported by 424 centers were information and referral, transportation, and congregate meals (90%). Home-delivered meals were provided by 70% of the centers (Krout, 1995).

In the NCOA study, the majority of self-identified multipurpose centers were found to be offering at minimum educational, recreational, and either information and referral or counseling services. Many multipurpose centers were also providing health services and opportunities for volunteers. Specifically, the most frequently offered services were transportation to the center, arts and crafts, lectures, employment counseling, health screening, friendly visiting, and health counseling.

The programs garnering the greatest participation of elderly were meals, information and referral, and sedentary recreation. However, the activities that generated the most enthusiasm were tours and trips, particularly among women and African Americans. Some members joined the center in order to be eligible for the outings that were planned. Overall, participants indicated that their reasons for attending the centers were to meet others and for opportunities to use leisure time. Thus participants are able to select activities and programs based on individual preference and to participate in evaluations on how well the expectations are met (Leanse & Wagner, 1975).

It is clear that effective programming is essential for a senior center to fulfill its role as community focal point. Because senior center participants are more likely to attend by choice, or at least see their first coming to the center as motivated by choice rather than need, the importance of relevant programming determines the continued attendance of older community residents.

Programming Examples

Perhaps the best way to gain an overview of the multipurpose senior center is to examine some examples of centers that illustrate the wide range of programs that can be offered in these facilities.

The senior center in Franklin County, New York, is run under the auspices of the county's office on aging. Because the office serves a rural population, the primary service of the eight senior centers is transportation- 12- and 20-passenger vehicles provide 9,000 rides a year to the center, stores, and health facilities. In addition, the centers provide full-time nutrition, education, physical fitness, and craft programs. Assistance is also provided to seniors who are applying for special government programs. In the smaller communities in the county, senior citizen clubs meet monthly for social purposes. The clubs' membership links up with the senior centers for trips and other cooperative events.

The Waxter Center in Baltimore provides one of the most comprehensive services in the country. Built as a result of a $4 million bond issue, the center now has over 11,000 members. Housed in a large, specially designed three-story building, Waxter offers a range of activities including swimming, language classes, crafts, a library, lectures, and trips. Because a large number of separate rooms are available, 15 to 20 different activities can be carried out at the same time, giving each member a wide choice of individual or group settings. The center also operates an extensive health screening clinic, an adult day care program, and a special program to integrate nursing home patients with center members. Representatives from Social Security, SSI, Legal Aid, home care agencies, and other public agencies are at the center on a daily basis. The center, including the nutrition program, is open 7 days a week.

The Hudson Guild-Fulton Senior Center in New York City has a membership of 1,300, with 300 members present on any given day. An advisory committee helps to make decisions affecting the staffing operations of the center and to initiate programs that respond to their own interests and talents. The center views itself as a supermarket, with members selecting what they need from the center's offerings. The center's classes include crafts, exercise, drama, music, discussions, and languages. Tickets are available through the center to the wide range of concerts, theater, and opera offerings that are available in New York throughout the year.

The Hudson Guild-Fulton center provides assistance to its members for Medicaid, Medicare, Social Security, and other public-assistance problems. Personal and housing problems, as well as legal concerns, also receive attention from the center staff and volunteers. Clients are assisted in finding jobs and volunteer placements. Health-screening programs and a telephone reassurance program help to maintain the health of the elderly and keep them in contact with the center. A minibus is utilized to transport members to health-care appointments. The center also provides breakfast to about 30 seniors and lunch to an average of 200 older adults at the center and to 75 in their homes.

Although this description of senior centers concentrates on concrete services, the center can also be seen as having an important role in maintaining the self-esteem and integration of the older person in the society (Gelfand & Gelfand, 1982). Intergenerational programming can help to break down age segregation, and membership in the center can help foster identity of the older person with an organization at a time when their organizational affiliations are diminishing.

The center can also provide an opportunity for older individuals to develop new roles that may have been stymied by the demands of their daily work patterns. Perhaps most important of all is the opportunity that the center gives to older persons to develop friendships. These friendships may result from the general socializing that older persons engage in at the center. Indeed, there are indications that it is this opportunity for socializing, rather than specific programs, that attracts many older people initially to senior centers (Gelfand, Bechill,& Chester, 1991; Ralston, 1987). These opportunities to socialize may, in turn, lead to the enlargement of the older person's support network. The new members of the network may become confidants. In some centers, "quasi-formal" support groups have developed among members who are friends and keep tabs on important events in each other's lives. When some negative event occurs, such as the loss of a spouse or family member, they help by sending cards or visiting and gradually bringing the person back into center activities.

Senior centers can also provide support to family members, including members who are caregivers to older relatives. This support may be simply educational in nature, or it may take the form of groups that allow the caregivers to share feelings and problems. Viewing the center as not merely a service-delivery operation, but a facility that has the potential to meet some of the important emotional and social needs of the older person, can make a major difference in the attitudes and programming of the staff.

FACILITIES

Because senior centers can present an image that encourages older persons' participation in center programming, the choice of a facility has always been a very important part of senior center development. The fact that under the old Title V of the OAA monies were available only for the development of the center's physical plant underscores the importance of appropriate facilities:

> A senior center should be a place in the community which is attractive and makes older people feel that it is a place where they want to come. In addition, an attractive facility represents to the community that older people are valued by both the community and themselves. (U.S. Administration on Aging, 1977, p. VI-1)

In order to maximize opportunities for securing a wide range of clients, attempts are always made to locate a senior center in an area convenient to transportation. This location should also be in a neighborhood that is accessible to the target population of the center. Adequate parking facilities, outside activity spaces, and easy accessibility for the handicapped are also vital elements of the center's physical plan. The interior of the center should provide a variety of room sizes including private areas for counseling, a kitchen-dining area, and adequate space for staff and supplies.

A national study (Krout, 1990) indicates that three-quarters of senior centers are housed in separate facilities. Among centers that are combined with other types of settings, 33% are included as part of recreation/community centers; 20% are in multiservice agencies; 12% in churches; 7% in housing facilities/projects; and 6% in schools. An additional 20% are housed in a variety of other settings.

With the rising costs of building, rehabilitating, and renovating facilities, it is anticipated that development of adequate facilities could continue to be a barrier to expanding the senior center programs. Fortunately, in many communities, unused schools have been changed to senior centers. The recycling of buildings that had related purposes can help keep down costs.

FUNDING

Funding mechanisms for senior centers reflect the importance of integrating the center into the community. There is rarely a single source of support for all the activities that a center may wish to inaugurate. Instead, funding from a variety of sources is utilized to cover different components of the center's activities. The auspices under which the center is operated may thus be a crucial determinant of the sources of funds a center is able to tap, since the perspective various resource groups have of the center's sponsor will affect their willingness to make funds available for the senior center program.

A number of federal funding sources are available to centers including:

1. Title III of the OAA authorizes funds for multipurpose senior center construction, operation, nutrition services, and special programming. Title IV authorizes training and research funds as well as model projects. Title V of the OAA can fund senior community service employment programs through senior centers.

2. Block grants from the Department of Housing and Community Development can be utilized for developing, improving, and coordinating senior center activities and facilities.

3. As determined by the locality, General Revenue Sharing funds could be allocated to senior centers.

4. The volunteer programs of ACTION can provide additional personnel resources for the senior center.

5. If deemed a priority, a state may allocate funds from the Social Services block grant.

6. Funds from the Higher Education Act can assist centers in developing funding for educational activities and for the training of center staff to implement a variety of learning projects.

In addition to federal funds, state and local monies are also available. Centers have been funded through legislative appropriations in many states, and several centers have been financed through a bond issue, either city- or state-supported. Civic and religious organizations often make contributions to senior centers. Because the center is visible, contributions by these groups not only provide needed resources to the centers, but bring some visibility to the contributing organization. These groups can most easily donate labor, space, materials, and equipment for the center.

Private philanthropists and nonprofit groups also are likely to make contributions; and United Way, as well as local private foundations, can be a source of annual support. Finally, the center itself can generate some income from either membership dues, fund-raising projects, or the sale of center-generated products.

Most centers attempt to combine money from a variety of sources, with the primary source being Title III of the OAA. However, significant support has been made available by the Department of Labor, state and county funds, state and local revenue sharing, in-kind contributions, United Fund, religious organizations, foundations, membership fees, civic groups, and project income. Because in-kind contributions account for a substantial amount of support, center budgets are difficult to estimate. Free space, volunteers, and service agency personnel are all important, but are hard to quantify in dollar-and-cents terms.

The senior center has been seen by its advocates as the most likely candidate for the "focal point" of services outlined in the OAA. The centrality of the senior center as a service provider was underscored by its usage in the "channeling" demonstration to provide assessment and case management services for older persons (Mathematica Policy Research, 1986).

In order to be effective as a focal point, however, the senior center needs to maintain its identity as a place for all older individuals. Recent indications are that some older persons are beginning to view the senior center as a place exclusively for the frail elderly, but a majority of senior center directors questioned in Maryland (60%) stated that their participants begin to attend the center between the ages of 61 and 69 (Gelfand, Bechill, & Chester, 1989). Nationally, 41% of center participants are between the ages of 65 and 74, and 37% between 75 and 84. Smaller percentages are over 85 (10%) or between 55 and 64 (11%) (Krout, 1990). Unless senior centers are effective in attracting the "young-old" as participants, the median ages of the participants will continue to rise. Senior centers thus need to avoid being characterized as facilities with programs that exclusively focus on the frail elderly. The ability to maintain a position not only as a multiservice provider, but as a provider for all diverse groups of older persons, is a major challenge for senior centers.

REFERENCES

Cohen, M. (1972). *Senior centers: A focal point for delivery of services to older people*. Washington, DC: National Council on the Aging.

Fowler, T. (1974). *Alternatives to the single site center*. Washington, DC: National Council on the Aging.

Gelfand, D., Bechill, W., & Chester, R. (1989). *Maryland senior centers: Programs, services and linkages*. Baltimore: School of Social Work, Univ. of Maryland.

Gelfand, D., Bechill, W., & Chester, R. (1991). Core programs and services at senior centers. *Journal of Gerontological Social Work, 17*, 145–161.

Gelfand, D., & Gelfand, J. (1982). Senior centers and support networks. In D. Biegel & A. Naparstek (Eds.), *Community support systems and mental health* (pp. 162–174). New York: Springer Publishing Company.

Hanssen, A., Meima, N., Buckspan, L., Henderson, B., Helbig, T., & Zarit, S. (1978). Correlates of senior center participation. *Gerontologist, 18*, 193–199.

Kent, D. (1978, May–June). The how and why of senior centers. *Aging*, (281–282), 2–6.

Krout, J. (1988). The frequency, duration and stability of senior center attendance. *Journal of Gerontological Social Work, 13*, 3–19.

Krout, J. (1990). *The organization, operation and programming of senior centers in America: A seven year follow-up*. Fredonia, NY: (Unpublished.)

Krout, J. (1994). Changes in senior center participant characteristics during the 1980s. *Journal of Gerontological Social Work, 22*, 41–55.

Krout, J. (1995). Senior centers and services for the frail elderly. *Journal of Aging and Social Policy, 7*, 59–76.

Krout, J., Cutler, S., & Coward, R. (1990). Correlates of senior center participation: A national analysis. *The Gerontologist, 30*, 72–79.

Leanse, J., & Wagner. (1975). *Senior centers: A report of senior group programs in America*. Washington, DC: National Council on the Aging.

Maxwell, J. (1962). *Centers for older people*. Washington, DC: National Council on the Aging.

Mathematica Policy Research. (1986). *National Long-Term Care Channeling Demonstration: Final report*. Plainsboro, NJ: Author.

Miner, S., Logan, J., & Spitze, G. (1993). Predicting the frequency of senior center attendance. *The Gerontologist, 33*, 650–657.

National Council on the Aging. (1979). *Senior center standards: Guidelines for practice*. Washington, DC: Author.

Ralston, P. (1987). Senior center research: Policy from knowledge. In E. Borgatta & R. Montgomery, (Eds.), *Critical issues in aging policy: Linking research and values* (pp. 199–234). Newbury Park, CA: Sage.

Ralston, P. (1989, November). *Senior centers and minority elders: A review*. Paper presented at the Annual meeting of the Gerontological Society of America, Minneapolis, MN.

Ralston, P., & Griggs, M. (1985). Factors affecting utilization of senior centers: Race, sex, and socioeconomic differences. *Journal of Gerontological Social Work, 9*, 99–111.

Sabin, E. (1993), Frequency of senior center use: A preliminary test of two models of senior center participation. *Journal of Gerontological Social Work, 20,* 97–114.

Taietz, P. (1976). Two conceptual models of the senior center. *Journal of Gerontology, 31,* 219–222.

U.S. Administration on Aging. (1977). *Program development handbook for state and area agencies on multipurpose senior centers.* Washington, DC: U.S. Government Printing Office.

12

Housing

HOUSING CONDITIONS OF THE ELDERLY

Housing is a crucial aspect of the social environment. The type and quality of housing available to an older person has an impact on their general level of satisfaction, as well as on their ability to live in the community. Retired older persons also spend more time in their homes than younger, working individuals. A 1989 national survey found that 87% of older respondents want to remain in their own homes, even though two-thirds of them anticipate needing help with the maintenance of the outside of their house. Over half of the respondents also think they would need help in the future with heavy housework. Although 13% of these older people would like to move, a larger percentage (22%) saw a move as a future likelihood (American Association of Retired Persons, 1990).

Elders live in somewhat more modest dwellings, both in terms of size and quality, than do members of other American households. Elderly couples have the highest-income households, followed by older individuals living alone. The poorest is the multi-person household headed by a person 65 and over. Among the 17 million households headed by older persons, 75% owned their own homes (Newman, 1986). Although 80% of these homeowners have paid off their mortgages, many elderly find it difficult to maintain their homes. This is particularly true in rural areas. Data on housing conditions among older rural homeowners indicate that only 29% of farm homes and 46% of nonfarm homes had no deficiencies (Lee, 1986).

A few statistics help to clarify the housing situation of older persons:
Three-quarters of persons over the age of 65 own their own homes

* Home ownership is higher among individuals between ages 65 and 74 than among older age groups

- A substantial proportion of older households (20%) spend at least 30% of their income on housing. This figure compares with 10% of younger households
- Among older women 34% spend at least 30% of their income on housing, but only 23% of older men spend a comparable amount on their housing.
- In 1991, 35% of older homeowners were living in the same homes for at least 30 years.
- Households headed by older people are smaller than those the general household size: 1.6 individuals compared to 2.6 (Naifeh, 1993).

A 1992 survey by the American Association of Retired Persons of persons over the age of 55 found that 84% of the respondents wanted to stay in their current home and that only 6% were living in any form of housing developed for older adults (American Association of Retired Persons, n.d.). This 6% figure will probably grow as the older population continues to age and a greater variety of senior housing becomes available. Many older individuals with limited incomes have taken advantage of the subsidized housing made available through the Department of Housing and Urban Development or local state agencies. More affluent elderly have increasingly shown interest in retirement communities with specific age limits for residents or new continuing care ("life care") communities. This chapter discusses the major privately and publicly sponsored housing services available to the elderly.

History

The concept of federally supported housing began in the 1930s with the National Housing Act of 1934 and the United States Housing Act of 1937. The 1934 Act inaugurated the first home mortgage program—a restructuring of the private home financing system—under the Federal Housing Administration (FHA). Under the 1937 Act, the government offered subsidized housing to low-income families. Although the primary purpose of this latter legislation was to clear slums and increase employment, new housing resulted. Under the Housing Act of 1949, the national goal of "a decent home and suitable living environment for every American Family" was first stated. The act also included programs for urban renewal, increased funds for subsidized housing, and new programs for rural housing. During the 1950s, housing programs were more directed toward rehabilitation, relocation, and renewal.

Section 202 began under the Housing Act of 1959. The program provided low-cost loans to developers of private housing, and it was the forerunner of later mortgage subsidy programs. In the Housing Act of 1961, below-market interest rate mortgages were begun to assist rental housing for moderate-income families through section 221(d)(3). In 1965, two rent-subsidy programs were begun. In one program, residents would pay 25% of their income in privately owned housing units built with FHA financing. Under the Section 23 leasing program, the government would lease regular units for low-income families.

In 1968, Congress found that "the supply of the nation's housing was not increasing rapidly enough to meet the national goal of 1949" (U.S. Department of Housing and Urban Development, 1973). Congress then established a production schedule of 26 million housing units—6 million of these to be for low- and moderate-income families over the next 10 years. One of the programs of this act was Section 236, a program that provides a subsidy formula for rental housing. In 1969, the Brooke Amendment was passed, which limited the amount of rent that could be charged by local housing authorities to 25% of adjusted tenant income.

In September 1973, President Nixon halted all housing programs except the low-rent public-leasing program, in order that a thorough review could be accomplished of what was then viewed as a spendthrift and inadequate program (U.S. Department of Housing and Urban Development, 1973). Following a study, during which no new federally subsidized housing starts were approved, the Housing and Community Development Act was signed into law in August 1974. The act removed the suspension that had been placed on construction and required contracts annually of at least $150 million to help finance development or acquisition costs of low-income housing projects. Because most of the money was to be channeled through the new Section 8 program, which was authorized under this Act, funding was slow to begin. Administratively, at least 2 years elapsed before the Section 8 program was fully operational (U.S. Senate, Special Committee on Aging, 1975).

Public Housing

Although the term is often assumed to relate to all forms of subsidized housing, "public housing" was in fact the earliest means of providing adequate housing for low-income elderly. Public housing was established under the Housing Act of 1937. Funds for these complexes are appropriated by the Department of Housing and Urban Development (HUD). The 480,000 units now in existence are managed by local housing authorities who maintain the buildings and ensure that low-cost rentals are available to poor families. Rentals are set at 30% of the family's income. In addition HUD provides funds for maintenance of the buildings while other agencies may provide staff for special programs for older persons.

It is often difficult for older persons to live in public housing units, since many local housing authorities require that older residents who need supportive services arrange to have these needs met if they are to remain in the complex. A small percentage of housing authorities (10%) do not allow older persons who are not independent to live in the public housing complex.

Currently, 40% of public housing units are occupied by older people and many of these tenants have "aged in place." In recognition of the needs of this population, the National Affordable Housing Act of 1990 allows local housing authorities to charge HUD for the inception of "service coordinators" positions and for 15% of the cost of services to older tenants. These services may include meals, chore services, transportation, personal care, and health-related services. Approximately half of all public housing units are over 20 years old. The federal budget for FY 1992 provided enough money to build 7,500 public housing units. In recent years, the federal emphasis in the field of housing has shifted to other programs such as Section 8 and Section 202.

The Section 8 Existing Housing Program

Authorized under the Housing and Community Development Act of 1974, this program filled the void left by the 1973 moratorium. It provides no direct funding to the developer, but instead pays monthly rent, so that housing can be developed on the private market. As of 1992, of the 2 million units completed, 50% were occupied by older persons (Retsinas & Retsinas, 1992).

Section 8, or subsidized rent, is the rent for a unit in a development which is receiving federally subsidized Section 8 housing assistance payments. The Section 8 rent differs from the market rent in that it depends strictly on the amount of income of the tenant. Tenants pay 30% of their adjusted income for rent, with the Section 8 housing assistance payment making up the difference between tenant-paid rent and the full market rent. Tenants are now allowed to pay more than 30% of their income for rent if the public housing authority agrees that the rent is reasonable for both the unit and the family (U.S. Senate, Special Committee on Aging, 1991). The tenant could pay as little as $40 or $50 per month or nearly as high as the market rents, depending on the monthly adjusted income. Rents under Section 8 cannot exceed the fair market rent for the area as established by HUD. Rents are reviewed annually, and the tenants must move if 30% of their adjusted income meets the fair market rent for that particular housing project. Fair market rents are reviewed annually and take into account construction costs and maintenance fees for individual locations.

In order to qualify for Section 8 subsidies, the income of a family of four could not be above 80% of median income in their area of residence.

Congressional action between 1981 and 1984 reduced Section 8 eligibility to 50% of median income, thus making many families ineligible for Section 8 subsidies. Projects with Section 8 rental units are owned by private parties, profit and nonprofit, and by public housing agencies. Under Section 8, HUD has made 15– or 20–year contracts with private parties for the rental units, unless the project is owned by or financed with a loan or loan guarantee from a state or local housing agency, in which case HUD will guarantee the rental units for 40 years. Efforts have been made to increase the private guarantee time of 20 years because, in some situations, it is a disincentive for private parties to become involved in the program. Any type of financing may be used for the purchase or rehabilitation of a project which houses Section 8 rental units, including HUD-FHA mortgage insurance programs, conventional financing, or tax-exempt bonds.

Under Section 8, the owner handles the whole program and is responsible for leasing at least 30% of the subsidized units to very low-income families (families whose income is 50% or less of local median income). Under the Section 8 legislation, priority is given to projects with 20% of their units in Section 8 only to guarantee an income mix in the housing project. However, if the rental units are to be used for the elderly, there is no restriction on the number of Section 8 rental units per project.

The purpose of the Section 8 program is to develop rental housing for medium- and low-income families within the structure of the private housing market. Section 8 units can exist in houses, small apartment buildings, or any other location that has units to rent. Suburban, rural, and urban areas are equally eligible. However, HUD determines how many Section 8 rental units can be awarded to a given area in each state. Usually, applications far exceed the units available for the specific areas in question.

The Section 8 housing program had a slow beginning after it was authorized in 1974. In 1975, there were 200,000 applications, but only 30 new units actually materialized (U.S. House of Representatives, 1976). The cumbersome application and administrative procedures were blamed for the delay. In addition, because Section 8 was an entirely new program involving low-income families, the private financial community—the group that had to generate the construction monies—did not appear ready to fund the building of units which would house Section 8 families until the program had grown to become one of the key housing programs for the elderly. Section 8 covers only the actual rental units, but is most successful when combined with other housing construction and service programs. Concerns about cost appeared to create questions about the development of any large number of Section 8 units in the 1980s. By 1989, 46% of Section 8 housing was occupied by older persons. Between 1981 and 1987, funding for housing assistance dropped 67%. Section 8 rent subsidies are now available only for existing housing. Subsidies for new housing were eliminated in the Housing Act of 1983 (U.S. Senate, 1990).

In FY 1997, 1.1 million families were being assisted by the Section 8 program. A problem for the program, however, is the large number of original 15- or 20-year subsidies that had expired or were expiring by 1998. The federal government planned to renew many of these for short terms. Funding for Section 8 housing had also declined from $293 million in FY 1996 to $128 million in FY 1997.

As a possible alternative to the Section 8 Existing Housing Program, the Reagan Administration instituted housing vouchers. These vouchers allow individuals to find their own housing in the private sector. Funds for 33,000 certificates were appropriated in FY 1991. In the voucher program, the tenant also contributes 30% of their income to the rent. A payment standard based on fair market rents is determined for the local area. If the rent of the tenant's unit is less than the payment standard, the tenant's contribution is reduced by the difference. If the rent exceeds this payment standard, the tenant must make up the difference. There are no limits in the rent the tenant can pay under the housing voucher program (Leger & Kennedy, 1990). Housing vouchers have been authorized for only 5 years. By FY 1997, approximately 400,000 vouchers had been "reserved."

An evaluation of the experiences of a large number of enrollees indicates that the housing voucher program has been successful (Leger & Kennedy, 1990). Questions have been raised from the onset of the program as to whether enrollees will be able to find housing they can afford and landlords who will accept the vouchers. In areas with tight housing markets, these two factors could pose a major hurdle. The average success rate for finding housing was 65%. There were, however, three areas with lower success rates, and one area where the success rate was only 33%. The reasons for these differences could not be clarified. Overall, housing voucher recipients were slightly more successful in obtaining qualifying housing than were recipients in the existing housing certificate programs.

Over one-third of the recipients were able to stay in their existing apartments while obtaining vouchers. Housing voucher recipients who moved paid rents that were 6.7% higher than recipients in the certificate program. This difference may, in part, reflect "higher prices for higher quality units" (Leger & Kennedy, 1990, p. xii). Older persons had better success rates than younger age cohorts, and single-person older households had the highest success rate of any group. The success rate of older persons in the voucher program was somewhat higher than in the certificate program. There was a significant reduction in rent burden of elderly in the voucher program. The elderly were the only population group for which a significant difference was found.

The Section 202 Program

Authorized under the Housing Act of 1959, Section 202 provides federal loans at a set maximum interest rate directly to nonprofit sponsors. Rental housing can be provided for the elderly through new construction or rehabilitation of existing structures. The loans are repayable over a 40-year period. The property should include needed support services and can have such rooms as dining halls, community rooms, infirmaries, and other essential services. These supportive services are largely funded by funds from non-Housing and Urban Development sources. Many of the non-profit homes for the aged, such as Cathedral Residences in Jacksonville, Florida—a large housing complex which serves over 700 elderly—were partially constructed with money under Section 202.

The Section 202 program was very successful throughout the 1960s, but was phased out after that time in preference to Section 236, another federal loan program. However, Section 236 was frozen in 1973 when all federal housing programs were halted to allow for review. Section 202 was reinstated as part of the Housing and Community Development Act of 1974, but it did not return to full activity until the summer of 1975. Under the 1974 act, a $215 million borrowing level was approved for FY 1975, but it was not used until the following year. Regulations in 1976 reaffirmed the importance of the program in providing both construction and long-term financing for housing projects. By 1980, 734 projects had been approved and 247, containing 262,000 units, had actually been constructed (U.S. Senate, 1991). In fiscal 1997, $645 million was available for Section 202 programs.

Private nonprofit corporations and consumer cooperatives are eligible for Section 202 financing. Loans can carry the average market yield plus 1% during construction and .5% thereafter for administration and program losses. Housing developments under Section 202 cannot exceed 300 units. Section 8 participation is required, and approval of Section 202 loans is based on the feasibility of getting Section 8 financing. In other words, if the number of Section 8 units for a section of the state have already been obligated, Section 202 construction financing cannot be granted.

Section 202/8 allocations are made in accordance with Section 213, a fair share needs formula. The formula, which determines the number of eligible units for a given geographic area, is based on the following criteria:

1. The number of households with the head or spouse age 62 or older
2. The number of such households which lack one or more plumbing facilities
3. The number of such households with incomes less than the regionally adjusted poverty level

4. The prototype production costs for public housing units as adjusted by average cost factors within the loan region

The 1974 Housing Act also specified that 20–25% of funds for Section 202 housing must be awarded in rural areas. The residents of the housing must also reflect the racial population of the community. This provision was meant to ensure that minority elderly obtained housing. The projects are required to either have an adequate range of necessary services or to facilitate the access of residents to social services. The application process for Section 202/8 housing is extensive and consists of five stages. It usually takes 3 to 5 years from the time of idea to actual implementation, and approval is given only to those developers with a proven track record.

Although Section 202 projects continue to be built, the size of these projects has dropped substantially. Some of this reduction in size is related to the growth of 202 projects outside of central cities: 22% of the projects occupied after 1984 were built in areas with less than 10,000 residents, a figure that is in stark contrast to the 2.2% of the projects occupied before 1975. As in previous years, the largest proportion of projects are sponsored by religious groups (50%). Funds for Section 202 housing have not been increased, but instead declined from $830 million in 1996 to $645 million in 1997, with even more reduced funding expected in 1998 (U.S. Department of Housing and Urban Development, 1998).

Over the years, the residents of Section 202 housing reflect changes in the aging population. The average age of residents rose from 72 years in 1983 to 75 years in 1988. There was a 4:1 ratio of women to men, and 20% of the residents were from minority backgrounds. The managers of the projects reported an increased proportion of residents they would regard as frail. The highest percentage of the frail residents were in older projects, a reflection of these residents growing older in the 202 housing (U.S. House of Representatives, 1989).

Other Federal Housing Initiatives

Section 231 insures lenders against losses on mortgages for construction or rehabilitation of unsubsidized housing for the elderly. This program is available to both profit and nonprofit developers. By FY 1989, 67,000 units of housing for older persons were insured under this program. Although not specifically targeted for the elderly, Section 221(d)(3) and (4) play a larger role at present in insuring multifamily housing for the elderly. These two sections permit the inclusion of congregate programs in the developments they insure. One of the innovations of 221(d)(4) was Retirement Service Centers, which provide rentals at the market rate for older persons but also include congregate meals, housekeeping, and laundry services. Although the program had completed 128 projects providing almost 19,000 units by 1990, it was suspended by the Department of Housing and Urban Development. The decision to suspend this program was based on a default rate in excess of 35%.

Section 223(f) provides mortgage insurance for existing multifamily housing units for the elderly where the repair needs are not extensive; this program is available in connection with refinancing or purchase of a project (U.S. Senate, Special Committee on Aging, 1990). Section 236 authorizes interest-reduction payments on behalf of owners of rental housing projects designed for occupancy by lower-income families for the purpose of reducing rentals for such tenants. In recent years units built through 221(d)(3) and 236 financing have become unavailable to low-income tenants as landlords have prepaid their mortgages and raised the rents. The 1990 National Affordable Housing Act allowed landlords to sell the property. If a nonprofit group interested in purchasing the property cannot be found, the property can be sold. Older or disabled tenants, however, must be given 3 years to find another apartment. The displaced tenants will be given vouchers to subsidize their housing, and the former landlord will pay 50% of the moving costs (Retsinas & Retsinas, 1992).

The 1990 Housing Act also contains two important new initiatives. The HOME Investment Partnership provides block grants to localities with the expectation that most of these funds will be used for rental assistance, assistance to home buyers, or construction or rehabilitation of homes. The Home Ownership and Opportunity for People Everywhere (HOPE) reflects national support for an idea that originated with a public housing complex in Washington, DC. HOPE provides funds that allow public housing tenants who would not receive mortgages from banks to purchase their units. HOPE is oriented to first-time homeowners. In the Seattle-Tacoma area in 1996, 10 homes were purchased by the local housing authority and rehabilitated. Families with an average income of $25,000 were selected for low-cost mortgages and allowed to purchase these newly renovated dwellings.

State and Local Housing Programs

State and local housing agencies have become an important source of financing for the actual building or rehabilitation of housing units. These agencies provide mortgage money directly to developers through sale of notes and bonds. Construction financing may be provided through the sale of notes, and permanent loan funds are provided through the sale of long-term bonds. The bonds sell at an interest rate of 1–2% below that of conventional sources of real estate financing, allowing housing agencies to pass on the savings on the notes and bonds to developers in the form of lower interest rates, which result in lower rents and mortgage-carrying charges for market-rate tenants and home buyers.

The purpose of the housing agency programs is to attract private developers to the low- and moderate-income housing field with the aim of providing housing for a broad range of income levels. The programs usually place a limit on equity return to developers.

Services

The various HUD programs and state housing agencies support housing that ranges from public ownership and complete public financing to private financing, building, and renting, with federal insurance on the mortgage only. The upper-income limits allowed vary by program, with the most stringent limits being placed on the direct public housing and the least stringent limits on the mortgage insurance-only program.

As indicated earlier, nonprofit developers are free to design as much additional space as they wish, and are encouraged to add supportive services to the housing units financed under Section 202. However, because of the income limitations placed on those living in federally financed housing, the developer has to keep the rents within the fair market rates and within the rates that the limited-income residents can pay. This, in turn, places limits on the amount of additional support services which can be provided. For example, one high-rise for the elderly in Baltimore, financed under Section 202/8, has the entire top floor overlooking the city as a carpeted and draped multipurpose room. The cost of building as well as maintaining this large, well-equipped, and well-used room must be absorbed in the rental fees allowed for each individual apartment. With the rental ceilings being determined by the government, the room can be only marginally maintained.

Amenities built into the housing programs depend on finances available and on the cost of these amenities in relation to the cost of the overall building. The support from the community in maintaining additional housing facilities and regional preferences will also be determinants of a final design package. The potential resources that can be included in elderly housing are extensive, ranging from transportation, nutrition, and health-screening programs to craft rooms, groceries, and even small restaurants.

Elderly housing projects can thus be part of the larger service-delivery system of the community. Because federal housing funds are limited, services run under outside auspices may need to be incorporated into the housing units. Two excellent examples of a housing complex with integrated services are Worly Terrace, Columbus, and Glendale Terrace, Toledo,

Ohio. Geared to the elderly who are returning from mental hospitals and to low-income community residents—many of whom were losing their homes through urban renewal—these housing developments operate a unique series of integrated financing and service systems. While HUD paid for the basic construction of the units, the state of Ohio paid for the rooms not eligible under federal regulations (in this case, dining room, community building, clinic, and craft room); the local housing authorities manage the completed housing units.

Worly Terrace is located near public transportation, shops, and several churches. The complex has a six-story high-rise building with 106 living units; four one-story buildings with 120 units; and a centrally located community building. There are furnished and unfurnished quarters for as many as 270 residents, with apartments for single persons, couples, or two unrelated single persons to share an apartment. Available services include hot meals; beauty and barber services; preventive health services including health screening, services of a full-time registered nurse and licensed practical nurse, part-time physician, and podiatrist; social activities; and recreation (U.S. House of Representatives, 1976). The services available in publicly financed or insured housing depend on the developer, the sponsor, the interest of the residents, and the community resources available. Early planning and community support for the project enhances the chances for adequate support services.

Beginning in 1988, the Robert Wood Johnson Foundation and the Administration on Aging conducted a series of demonstration grants to ten state housing finance agencies. Using these funds, supportive services (primarily nonmedical in nature) were developed for older residents living in housing financed by these agencies.

Home Repair and Renovation

Many older homeowners find it necessary to seek alternative housing because of their inability to carry out the maintenance necessary to keep their home in good condition. They also may lack the funds to hire contractors to perform necessary repairs. As homeowners quickly learn, minor repairs that are delayed for a substantial period of time can easily become major costly repairs. In 1975, a report prepared by the state of Michigan commented:

> Many seniors reside in structures which are in desperate need of repair. Often a senior will relocate to a new structure when repair to his former living unit would have been more cost-efficient to the government. (Charter Township of Meridian, 1975, p. 4)

The Michigan investigators found that 40% of the single-family homes owned by the elderly in the state needed minor or major repairs. Home repair programs aimed primarily at low-income elderly have now been organized around the country. Many of these programs have dual purposes: (1) bringing substandard homes up to local code levels, and (2) providing supplemental income by hiring older persons to work on these projects.

In Evansville, Indiana, a major repair program for elderly residents was carried out in a number of neighborhoods. As in other geographic areas, the repair efforts were concentrated on functional aspects of the home including wiring, vermin control, replacement of broken window panes, and new plastering. The hope of the project coordinators was that instituting the repair program would produce a ripple effect, which would not only encourage the elderly to continue making their own repairs, but also encourage other neighborhood residents to undertake long-needed repairs. One of the reasons this ripple did not occur was because a majority of the elderly did not even tell their neighbors about the program. This silence was attributable to their ambivalent feelings about accepting aid. In order for the program to be more visible within the community, the evaluators argued that the repairs would have to be undertaken on a continuous basis, rather than bringing repairmen into the individual home for an intensive— but brief—period of time (Abshier, Davis, Jans, & Petranek, 1977).

Home repairs that are to be anything more than cosmetic are also costly. In Michigan, a Meridian Township program spent $6,500 per house to bring these homes up to code standards. As labor costs continue to increase, we can expect that this figure will apply to similar efforts around the country, although volunteer labor can reduce costs significantly. In one community, a neighborhood corporation provides regular home repair and renovation services for over 2,000 enrollees (McCleary, 1986). Older individuals comprise 60% of the households receiving Community Development Block Grant (CDBG) funds for home repairs (Weeden, Newcomer, & Byerts, 1986). In 1990 the Section 312 Rehabilitation Loan Program made loans for rehabilitation available to 1,250 individuals for important repairs to their homes. Among these loan recipients, approximately 22% were over 60 years old. Funding for these home repair programs can also be developed from a variety of possible sources including Title III of the OAA, the Social Services block grant, or local appropriations. In rural areas, low-interest home repair loans are available through the Farmers Home Administration Section 504 Program. Under the Department of Energy Weatherization Assistance Program, low-income elderly can also apply for funding to help them purchase energy-saving aids, such as storm windows or insulation.

Congregate and Assisted Housing

Housing for the elderly should respond to the wide variation in the needs of older persons. The growth in the interest and availability of assisted or congregate housing is a response to the need for housing among those elderly who cannot continue to maintain full independent living, and yet are not in need of some form of full-service institutional setting. The increase in need for this type of housing is related, at least in part, to increased average longevity, a phenomenon in which a greater proportion of the total population is over 75 years of age and has conditions that require some forms of care in addition to basic housing needs.

Service needs in housing programs often increase as the tenants age. Tenants who entered the housing program as healthy, independent persons find they need additional service supports with advancing age. New, unanticipated services are then required. Congregate housing is a housing environment which provides enough services to enable many impaired elderly to remain in a community-based residential situation. Lawton (1976) focuses more precisely on the services that might be available in such a congregate housing situation:

> Congregate refers to housing that offers a minimum service package that includes some on-site meals served in a common dining room, plus one or more of such services as on-site medical/nursing services, personal care, or housekeeping. (p. 239)

In contrast, assisted or "sheltered" housing as operated in many states offers a more extensive package of services with an emphasis on meals and personal care. Some states are instituting subsidized assisted housing in single-family homes. Assisted housing helps with personal needs, but is not a care facility. Individual residents remain responsible for their own care with support services available as needed. Assisted housing does not have ongoing health services.

The growth in congregate housing has come long after the availability of both independent-living housing situations and institutional settings. Congregate housing was authorized in 1970 in the congregate housing provision of the Housing and Urban Development Act. By 1990, almost $50 million had been appropriated for congregate services. These funds supported services for approximately 1,900 residents living in 60 projects. Between $5 and $6 million has been awarded in each recent fiscal year to support the congregate program.

Given the increasingly older population of the 202 units, it is not surprising that 28% of the projects are providing either congregate meals or housekeeping services for residents. More extensive services will also be required in Section 202 housing for residents. Under the 1990 National

Affordable Housing Act, a meal that meets daily nutritional requirements will be required. In addition, other services such as housekeeping, transportation, personal care, and chore services that meet the needs of the residents of the complex must be offered ("Conferences workout differences," 1990). As part of this increased emphasis on maintaining older persons in their community, a 5-year demonstration project was approved to combine Section 8 certificates and housing vouchers with supportive services such as meals, housekeeping, transportation, personal care, and health services. In FY 1997, $50 million was available for supportive services targeted at the elderly and disabled.

The idea of locating extensive services in 202 housing is not new. Projects in some communities include a variety of services operated and financed by state or local agencies. Operating funds can now be used to hire service coordinators. In Section 202 projects with Congregate Housing Services Programs, the salary for the services coordinator must be taken from operating funds rather than the congregate service budget. The service coordinator provides referrals, supports, and linkages for tenants with needs (Older Americans Report, 1990b). HUD allows service coordinators in housing projects.

Despite the need for congregate services in many housing facilities, caution has been recommended in their development. As Lawton (1976) points out,

> Maintenance of independent function is facilitated by an environment that demands active behavior from its inhabitants, and conversely, the presence of too easily accessible services will erode independence among those who are still relatively competent. (p. 240)

Whatever the validity of this belief, providing additional services does require additional money which cannot be fully recouped from fees charged the residents. Further, the provision of additional services could possibly duplicate other community resources available.

Foster Care

For many years, the concept of foster care has been familiar to those who work with children, but the service has been made available to the elderly only since the early 1970s. Currently, an estimated 60,000 state licensed adult foster care facilities are in operation (Advisory Panel on Alzheimer's Disease, 1996).

Foster care focuses on a population that cannot sustain full independence. It thus attempts to prolong independence and delay institutionalization. Foster care is a specialized form of sheltered housing whereby the client is placed in a new setting which has family supports. Although Newman and Sherman (1977) describe foster care as a system "for persons in need of care and protection in a substitute family setting for a planned period of time" (p. 436) a more recent survey of the literature has found at least six definitions of foster family care (Hudson, Dennis, Nutter, Galaway, & Richardson, 1994). These definitions differ in what they regard as a family and how many individuals fit into this family unit. It is fair to say, however, that in most foster care programs, the number of older persons per family unit is small, probably averaging not more than four. Louisiana defines adult foster care as "a private residence with the approved capacity to receive six or fewer adults who are aged, emotionally disturbed, developmentally disabled, or physically handicapped who require supervision on an ongoing basis but who do not require continuous nursing care" (State of Louisiana, 1997)

Foster care programs are generally administered by local departments of social services and have relied heavily on Title XX funds for operation. Strict income limitations were attached to the Title XX funding, which made moderate- or high-income elderly ineligible for foster care through Title XX funding. Although more limited, monies are also available through state departments of health or mental health and through the Veterans Administration. More liberal income policies are in effect when funds from these sources are being used. In some programs, the foster family is paid a percentage of the SSI check directly by the recipient of the foster care. In these cases, the foster family does not always break even on the costs.

Eligible homes are usually solicited through appeals to the general public. After eligibility is determined, the family is paid a fee, plus certain expenses, for the care of the older person in foster care.

One of the limitations to expanding the foster care program is in the recruitment of families. Foster care has been found to be especially effective for older discharged mental patients. The largest foster care program in the United States is run by the Veterans Administration. In a study of foster residences operated by five VA hospitals (Linn & Caffey, 1977), both younger and older patients were found to have improved after placement in foster care residences. Despite evidence that well-operated foster care is effective for older mental patients, it remains an "appropriate and underutilized resource" (p. 345).

An important test of the utility of foster care for individuals who would otherwise be placed in nursing homes has been conducted in Massachusetts and in Maryland since 1978. In this program, individuals being discharged from the hospital are assigned randomly either to foster care homes or to nursing home care in order to assess the relative social and cost effectiveness of these two service modalities. Caretakers are paid

$350–$500 per month. The cost of the Community Care program has been 32% below that of nursing-home care.

The participants in the program showed better or improved functioning on the Activities of Daily Living and better mental status scores than controls in nursing homes. The Community Care program participants also were more likely to achieve the nursing goals set for them. In contrast, nursing home residents were more involved in a variety of social activities and had higher life satisfaction scores at the end of 1 year (Oktay & Volland, 1987). A state-run foster care program in Massachusetts, Adult Family Care, matches older people with families in communities. As part of this effort, a Massachusetts Council for Adult Foster Care has been organized. As Oktay and Volland (1981) note, foster care cannot be used for all patients, some of whom are too hostile, demanding, or ill to be placed with a non-family caregiver. In some cases, patients or their families resist the idea of foster home care, either because it is new or the family feels that the care provided cannot be intensive enough to meet their relative's needs. Given the findings on social activities, it is also important to consider whether foster care results in social isolation of older persons in communities where social activities and transportation are not adequate.

Board and Care and Domiciliaries

Board and care homes are widely available, but there has been little information available about these facilities. Because there are no national regulations governing this level of care, each state has adopted its own terminology and regulations which govern the type of care given. Probably the best definition for this general level of care is contained in the Colorado regulations:

> An establishment operated and maintained to provide residential accommodation, personal services and social care to individuals who are not related to the licensee, and who, because of impaired capacity for self-care, elect or require protective living accommodations but who do not have an illness, injury, or disability for which regular medical care and 24-hour nursing services are required. (Glasscote et al., 1976, p. 58)

In summary, this level of care is primarily personal and custodial.

Regulations for board and care homes usually require that:

- Local and fire safety codes be met
- There be a full-time administrator responsible for the supervision of staff, residents, and safety
- Nursing personnel be on call most of the time
- There be facilities for occasional distribution of medication

The majority of board and care homes have no more than 10 residents. These homes usually provide assistance to the older person with the activities of daily living, supervision of medications, laundry and linens, cleaning services and protective supervision (Reisacher & Hornboster, 1995). As Reisacher and Hornboster make clear, board and care homes are neither nursing homes, congregate housing, nor shared housing or rooming houses. Although at least 30,000 licensed homes have been identified in studies (Hawes. Wildfire, & Lux, 1993; Lewin/ICF and James Bell Associates, 1990), there are estimates that an almost equal number of unlicensed homes exist (U.S. House of Representatives, 1989). The licensed homes provide over 600,000 beds (Advisory Committee on Alzheimer's Disease, 1996). As Lyon (1997) notes, board and care homes predominantly serve low-income older persons who have major functional impairments and cannot rely on family resources to provide care.

Residents of board and care homes are usually required to arrange for their own medical care and, in many instances, provide for their own social activities. In effect, this level of care provides a protected environment, meals, and some personal care services, but does not restrict or organize the activities of the residents. Many low-income board-and-care residents are able to pay for care through their SSI checks.

A study of board-and-care homes in Cleveland provides important information about the characteristics of these homes (Eckert, Lyon, & Namazi, 1990). Most of the 177 homes studied were private residences. The owners and operators were middle-aged or older women, two-thirds of whom had previously worked in a health care setting as aides or nurses. Residents were charged an average of $450 per month for their care, which included at least three meals a day, laundry service, and round-the-clock supervision. The residents of the homes had an average age of 77 and were predominantly female. The proportion of Black residents (15%) was higher than the representation of this group in the American population, and 16% of the residents had never married. The residents expressed positive feelings about the homes. The researchers warn against "overzealous" action that would regulate these types of living environments and reduce their ability to meet the needs of physically impaired and economically limited elderly. Reports to Congress about overmedication of board-and-care residents by untrained caregivers has prompted calls for further investigation of the quality of board-and-care homes.

Domiciliaries and homes for the aged are primarily nonprofit and often church-sponsored homes that provide personal care, but require that persons entering be healthy. These homes go well beyond the standards which are set by the various states in that they usually provide comprehensive activities, social services, and personal care programs. Many of the residents have private rooms, and rarely are there more than two people in each room. Residents can select activities that are offered and are free to come and go from the facility as desired. These facilities can be small, often accommodating as few as 50 residents, but in some cases are large enough to accommodate as many as 300. Attached to many of these homes for the aged are intermediate care or skilled care nursing units to provide appropriate medical treatment for those who need such care. Depending on the size of the facility, the home will either be able to continue to care for a resident that needs medical care on a regular basis, or will transfer that person to a regular skilled or intermediate care facility.

Retirement Communities

One of the more recent phenomena developing as a result of the large number of people who are retiring, particularly with good retirement incomes, is the retirement community. Retirement communities can range from small mobile home subdivisions to sizable communities like Youngstown and Sun City, Arizona. The latter had, in 1969, an estimated population of 37,000 (Anderson & Anderson, 1978). The communities can include apartments, semidetached houses, and units that can be purchased or rented. Beyond the living units themselves, varying forms of recreation and supportive services can be offered. The country's first development for senior citizens—Youngstown, Arizona—was founded in 1954 and incorporated as a retirement community in 1960.

Most retirement communities have age requirements as the key entrance requirement. In Sun Lakes, Arizona, only people over age 40 can purchase property, and no one under age 19 can be a permanent resident. The age limit for buying a home in Sun City is 50, and children of residents must be at least 18 years of age. Residents of any of the Rossmoor Leisure Worlds must be at least 52 years old, and the same age requirement holds for five retirement communities in New Jersey (Heintz, 1976).

The general characteristics of retirement communities include entrance requirements, complete community planning, and relatively low-cost housing coupled with high levels of amenity. The concept of low-cost housing, however, is not universal in retirement communities. The two-bedroom homes in retirement communities in southern New Jersey averaged around $60,000 in price in 1990 with a $150 monthly maintenance fee paid to the cooperative association.

In a study of five retirement communities in New Jersey, Heintz (1976) identified characteristics of people who elected to join such communities. She found that residents were primarily White, retired individuals with good incomes between the ages of 65 and 74. Families in retirement communities had the same household size as the national average, but there were more male-headed households (82.3%). The retirement community population was better educated and more likely to have worked in a high-status or highly skilled occupation. Even though the average age for entrance was only 52, 86% of the residents were actually retired. The satisfaction of residents with the retirement communities was expressed in the fact that there was an annual turnover rate of only 2–5%. Only 6% of the residents expressed a desire to move from the community.

The communities themselves devoted 80–95% of the acreage to housing, with the remaining land being used for recreation. The usual construction pattern is of single-family attached and detached houses in cul-de-sac arrangements, with the community focal point being the clubhouse.

One example of a successful retirement community is Leisure World in Laguna Hills, California. Begun in 1963, by spring 1977, it had nearly 12,000 residences and a population of 19,000.

> Leisure World was designed to provide security, quick accessibility to good health care, good nearby shopping, good transportation, excellent facilities for recreation and adult education and additional activities to ensure freedom from boredom. (Leisure World, 1977)

The importance of security in a retirement community is illustrated in the efforts Leisure World has made:

> Hundreds of Leisure World residents say one of the principal reasons they came to live in Leisure World is security. . . . The entire residential area is surrounded by about 8.5 miles of six-foot wall or fence. In some places the wall is topped by barbed wire. Entrance to the residential areas is only through one of eleven guarded gates. Cars of residents have a special symbol attached to the front bumper; all others are stopped for identification and for permission by a resident to pass through . . . a security force of 255 officers is backed up by full-time, armed officers who have specific police training. (Leisure World, 1977)

The facilities at Leisure World are extensive. Minibuses circulate over 11 routes, fare-free, carrying 88,000 passengers a month. There are five club-houses, concerts, movies, stage presentations, and 167 clubs and organizations. The enormous sports and recreational opportunities range from swimming pools and horseback riding to a variety of crafts facilities. All of the activities offered by Leisure World are free to residents except golf and horseback riding. Health facilities are available but on a fee-for-service basis. The success of Leisure World in Laguna Beach is evidenced by the fact that the houses are sold by lottery drawn from the extensive waiting list.

Despite potentially large purchase costs and monthly maintenance fees, retirement communities are growing in popularity, particularly because they offer security, recreation, good housing, and social opportunities with neighbors of a similar age. Researchers commenting on a survey of residents in a number of retirement communities note:

> Most persons living in a retirement community have weighed the advantages and disadvantages of this life style. The evidence gathered on thirty-six communities suggests that there is a high amount of satisfaction with their choice. Despite problems or uncertainties about land ownership these communities deliver the kind of environment that their residents desire. (Streib, LaGreca, & Folts, 1986, pp. 101–102)

Although the pattern may change as the residents age, many retirement communities do not provide extensive services for their residents. The CARES volunteer organization in Crestwood Village, New Jersey, provides transportation and free medical equipment to residents when needed.

"Continuing care retirement communities" or "life care communities" are more oriented to service provision for residents. These communities grew rapidly during the 1980s and guarantee to provide care for residents throughout the remaining years of their life, regardless of their physical condition. In many cases, residents pay a large entrance fee, ranging from $20,000 to $100,000, and a monthly charge based on the size of the apartment and number of individuals. In 1995, a survey of these communities found an average low entry fee of $59,000 for a one-bedroom unit to a high monthly entry fee of $86,000. An average low monthly fee for a one bedroom unit was $1,046 and a high average monthly fee was $1,400 (Scruggs, 1995). As in many life care communities, these monthly charges do not cover most nursing home costs. Some life care communities guarantee to return a specific percentage of the entrance fee to the individual's estate, while others retain the whole fee.

Because of the long-term care nature of the services guaranteed, financial demands on life care communities are extensive. Some life care communities have failed because of inadequate financial resources, and some have had to raise the monthly resident charges drastically to meet their operating costs. In response, states have begun to scrutinize the economic resources of proposed life care developers, and 30 states now regulate these communities. Life care communities based purely on rental payments are also now becoming available. In general, the resident population of life care communities tends to be over 75 years of age.

One example of a continuing care retirement community in Columbia, Maryland, offers two options. Under the first option, 90% of the entrance fee is refunded if the resident leaves or dies. In 1990, studio apartments cost $62,950, the least expensive one-bedroom apartment, $73,000, and two-bedroom apartments begin at $150,000. The second option offers lower entrance fees, but the amount refunded to the resident if he/she leaves or dies declines by 2% for each month the resident lives in the housing. Under this plan studios cost $54,000, one-bedroom apartments begin at $63,000, and two-bedroom apartments, $128,000. For individuals living in a studio, the monthly fee was $1100 in 1990 that covers one meal a day, utilities, housekeeping, linen, transportation, community activities, and building maintenance.. For a couple living in a one-bedroom apartment, the monthly fee was $1900. With the payment of the monthly fee, the resident is also entitled to lifetime nursing care services that include home health services and short- and long-term care in the community's Health Center. Non-nursing medical services must be paid for individually ("Continuing care retirement community," 1990).

By 1990 there were approximately 700 continuing care retirement communities with approximately 210,000 residents. Nationally, the entrance fees ranged from $30,000 to $100,000. Recently, in order to broaden the market for these communities, there has been a movement away from entrance fees to communities that only charge monthly fees; these are adjusted according to the service needs of the residents. Under this plan an individual who requires nursing care pays a higher monthly fee than other residents. As continuing care communities have grown in number, they have also begun to vary in what they offer. While some provide nursing care on the premises, others are linked to nursing homes, or guarantee a resident priority in obtaining a nursing home bed (Lewin, 1990). While these communities are expected to grow in number, the development by hotel chains and nursing home firms clearly targets an affluent segment of the older population.

Shared and Accessory Housing

One seemingly simple approach to meeting the housing needs of older people is the "matching" of individuals who have similar housing needs. While this may be a diverse group, including single younger individuals, this type of effort may enable older persons who require housing to find individuals with whom they can share homes. As housing costs continue to escalate and rental housing becomes scarcer, these types of matching efforts by local social services agencies have proliferated. A survey of 252 home sharing matches found a very positive feeling about home sharing among respondents. The home sharing reduced financial problems of the home sharers, and promoted greater feelings of safety and less loneliness (Bergman, 1994). Shared housing can run into problems with zoning regulations which may restrict housing in an area to "families." Individuals living in shared housing are now eligible for the Section 8 program.

Existing Housing Certificate Program

Accessory housing utilizes parts of single-family homes as separate apartments for older relatives. "Granny flats," or Elder Cottage Housing Opportunities (ECHO) units, have been adopted from Australia. These free-standing units are adjacent to existing single-family units, usually homes owned by children of the older individual living in the ECHO facility. Although ECHO units can be very cost-effective, they also raise zoning issues in many residential communities zoned exclusively for single family homes. ECHO housing units are now eligible for Section 202 financing.

Home Equity Programs

Many older people are "house rich and cash poor;" that is, they have a great deal of money invested in their homes. This is true of older persons at all income levels: 23% of elderly homeowners below the poverty line have over $50,000 equity in their homes (Fairbanks, 1990). Unfortunately, this money is not accessible unless the house is sold, a step that many older families do not want to undertake.

Many older people also find rising property taxes a difficult financial burden to bear. Legislation that limits property taxes for older people can be vital in allowing homeowners to stay in their houses. One such program is a "circuit breaker" that prevents property taxes from rising above a percentage of the older person's income ("threshold programs"). Sliding scale programs rebate a percentage of property taxes to older persons, the percentage being determined by the older person's income. Thirty states have instituted some form of this tax relief. In addition, 17 states allow property taxes to be deferred until the death of the older person or the sale of their property.

Home equity conversion is a more ambitious effort to make available the equity older people have in their homes. Since 1980 a variety of programs, most commonly referred to as "reverse mortgages", have become available. By 1994, they were being used by 10,000 older persons (Bary, 1994). In 1995, Fannie Mae (formerly the Federal National Mortgage Association) began to offer reverse mortgages. With a reverse mortgage, a homeowner can stay in their own home and use the funds they receive from a bank to cover other important expenses, including health care. The amount the homeowner receives is based on the equity in their home and their age. A 75-year-old individual with a home valued at $100,000 can receive a monthly payment of $363 (Romano, 1996). The loan is paid back when the homeowner dies or moves through the sale of the house.

High interest rates and fees charged by some banks have raised questions about the value of these reverse mortgages for many older homeowners.

These fees are substantially higher than those charged for conventional loans. The origination fee ("points") can range from 1–3% followed by closing costs of $1,700. In 1994, one lender in California was sued by homeowners incensed by its interest rates and fees (Bary, 1994). Individuals not planning to remain in their home for a long period after assuming a reverse mortgage can find this form of a loan very expensive. In Maryland, a 75-year-old homeowner obtained a reverse mortgage that provided $568 per month. If the homeowner left this property after two years, the homeowner would have paid 50.22% in order to receive $13,000 (Lohse, 1995). There are also potential problems with these reverse mortgages stemming from a depreciation in home values which could make it difficult to recoup the loan from the sale of the home.

A new innovation in the use of reverse mortgages was begun by Fannie Mae in 1997. The "Our Home Keeper for Home" program allows individuals over the age of 62 to use reverse mortgages to buy a home. Fannie Mae regards this program as an opportunity for older individuals to relocate in order to be nearer family members or to live in another area of the country. Another innovative program is the co-housing village in Berkeley, California (Stock, 1997). In this model, residents manage their community and share dinners a few times a week. In contrast to age-restricted retirement communities, the small Berkeley community is age-integrated. With no private lawns, the cottages and two-family townhouses ranged in price from $125,000 to $220,000. The variety of diverse housing programs available to older people can be expected to increase during the next decade.

REFERENCES

Abshier, G., Davis, Q., Jans, S., & Petranek, C. (1977). *Evaluation of the Cape-Smile home repair program*. Evansville, IN: Indiana State University.

Advisory Panel on Alzheimer's Disease (1996). *Alzheimer's Disease and related dementias: Report to Congress*. Washington, DC: U.S. Government Printing Office.

American Association of Retired Persons. (n.d.). *Understanding senior housing*. Washington, DC: Author.

American Association of Retired Persons. (1990). *Understanding senior housing for the 1990s*. Washington, DC: Author.

Anderson, W., & Anderson, N. (1978). The politics of age exclusion: The adults only movement in Arizona. *Gerontologist, 18*, 6–12.

Bary, A. (1994, July 4). Reversals of fortune. *Barrons*, 23–24.

Bergman, G. Shared housing: Not only for the rent.(1994). *Aging Today, 15*, 1, 4.

Charter Township of Meridian. (1975). *Home repair assistance for low income senior citizens*. Okemos, MI: Department of Development Control.

Continuing care retirement community opens in Columbia, MD. (1990). *Greater Washington Senior Beacon*. Washington, DC: Author.

Conferees work out differences on section 202 housing bill. (1990). *Old Americans Report, 14,* 375.

Eckert, K., Lyon, S., & Namazi, K. (1990). Congruence between residents and the environment in small board and care homes: An exploratory study. *Adult Residential Care Journal, 4,* 227–240.

Erikson, R., & Eckert, K. (1977). The elderly poor in downtown San Diego hotels. *Gerontologist, 17,* 440–446.

Fairbanks, J. (1990). Home equity conversion programs: A housing option for the "house-rich, cash-poor," elderly. *Clearinghouse, 23,* 481–487.

Glasscote, R., Biegel, A., Jr., Clark, E., Cox, B., Wiper, J. R., Gudeman, J. E., Gurel, L., Lewis, R. V., Miler, D. G., Raybin, J. B., Reifler, C., & Vito, E., Jr. (1976). *Old folks at homes.* Washington, DC: American Psychiatric Association and the Mental Health Association.

Hawes, C., Wildfire, J., & Lux, L. (1993). *National summary: The regulation of board and care homes: Results of a survey in the 50 states and the District of Columbia.* Washington, DC: American Association of Retired Persons.

Heintz, K. (1976). *Retirement communities, for adults only.* New Brunswick, NJ: Rutgers University Center for Urban Policy Research.

HUD allows service coordinators in certain elderly housing projects. (1990). *Old Americans Report, 14,* 432.

Hudson, J., Dennis, D. , Nutter, R., Galaway, G., & Richardson, B. (1994). Foster family care for elders. *Adult Residential Care Journal, 8,* 65–76.

King, G. (1976). Bugs, barrels and bush: Home repair in the Virgin Islands. *Aging, 263–264,* 8–11.

Lawton, M. (1976). The relative impact of congregate and traditional housing on elderly tenants. *Gerontologist, 16,* 237–242.

Lee, G. (1986). Rural issues in elderly housing. In R. Newcomer, M. Lawton, & T. Byerts (Eds.), *Housing an aging society* (pp. 33–41). New York: Van Nostrand Reinhold.

Leger, M., & Kennedy, S. (1990). *Final comprehensive report of the freestanding housing voucher demonstration: Vol. 1.* Washington, DC: U.S. Department of Housing and Urban Development.

Leisure World. (1977). (Brochure). Laguna Hills, CA: Leisure World.

Lewin, T. (1990, December 2). How needs, and market, for care have changed. *New York Times,* p. 36.

Lewin/ICF Inc. & James Bell Associates. (1990). *Descriptions of an supplemental information on board and care homes included in the update of the National Health Provider Inventory.* Washington, DC: U.S. Department of Health and Human Services.

Linn, M., & Caffey, E. (1977). Foster placement for the older psychiatric patient. *Journal of Gerontology, 32,* 340–345.

Lohse,D. (1995, November 24). Help for cash-poor, home-rich seniors at a price. *Wall Street Journal,* pp. C1, 15.

Lyon, S. (1997). Impact of regulation and financing on small board and care homes in Maryland. *Journal of Aging and Social Policy, 9,* 37–50.

McCleary, K. (1986). Minor repairs for older homeowners. *Aging, 352,* 2–5.

Naifeh, M. (1993). *Housing of the elderly: 1991.* Washington, DC: U.S. Bureau of the Census.

Newcomer, R., & Weeden, J. (1986). Perspectives on housing needs and the continuum of care. In R. Newcomer, M. Lawton, & T. Byerts (Eds.), *Housing an aging society* (pp. 3–9). New York: Van Nostrand Reinhold.

Newman, S. (1986). Demographic influences on the future housing demand of the elderly. In R. Newcomer, M. Lawton, & T. Byerts (Eds.), *Housing an aging society* (pp. 21–32). New York: Van Nostrand Reinhold.

Newman, S., & Sherman, S. (1977). A survey of caretakers in adult foster homes. *Gerontologist, 17,* 431–437.

Oktay, J., & Volland, P. (1981). Community care programs for the elderly. *Health and Social Work, 6,* 31–47.

Oktay, J., & Volland, P. (1987). Foster home care for the frail elderly as an alternative to nursing home care: An experimental evaluation. *American Journal of Public Health, 77,* 1505–1510.

Reisacher, S., & Hornbostel, J. (1995). *A home away from home.* Washington, DC: American Association of Retired Persons.

Retsinas, J., & Retsinas, N. (1992). Housing loophole may hurt elders. *Aging Today, 13,* 1, 2.

Romano, J. (1996, June 23). For reverse mortgages, a Fannie Mae imprimatur. *New York Times.*

Scruggs, D. (1995). *Dare to discover the future of continuing care retirement communities.* Washington, DC: American Association of Homes and Services to the Aging.

State of Louisiana. (1997). *Chapter 24-A: The Adult Foster Care Facility Licensing Act.* Baton Rouge, LA: Author.

Stock, R. (1997, December 18). Living independently in old age, without going it alone. *New York Times,* p. B10.

Streib, G., LaGreca., A. & Folts, W. (1986). Retirement communities: People, planning, prospects. In R. Newcomer, M. Lawton & T. Byerts (Eds.), *Housing an aging society* (pp. 94–103). New York: Van Nostrand Reinhold

U.S. Department of Housing and Urban Development. (1973). *Housing in the seventies.* Washington, DC: U.S. Government Printing Office.

U.S. Department of Housing and Urban Development. (1998). *Programs and Initiatives.* Available: www.huduser.org

U.S. House of Representatives, Select Committee on Aging. (1976). *Elderly Housing Overview: HUD's Inaction.* Washington, D.C.: U.S. Government Printing Office.

U.S. House of Representatives, Subcommittee on Health and Long-Term Care Policy.(1989). *Board and care homes in America: A national tragedy.* Washington, DC: U.S. Government Printing Office.

U.S. Senate, Special Committee on Aging. (1975). *HUD's response to the housing needs of senior citizens.* Washington, DC: U.S. Government Printing Office.

U.S. Senate, Special Committee on Aging. (1990). *Developments in Aging: 1989, Vol. 2.* Washington, DC: U.S. Government Printing Office.

U.S. Senate, Special Committee on Aging. (1991). *Developments in Aging: 1990: Vol. 1.* Washington, DC: U.S. Government Printing Office.

Weeden, J., Newcomer, R., & Byerts, T. (1986). Housing and shelter for frail and nonfrail elderly: Current options and future directions. In R. Newcomer, N. Lawton, & T. Byerts (Eds.), *Housing an aging society* (pp. 181–188). New York: Van Nostrand Reinhold.

13

In-Home Services

THE GROWTH OF IN-HOME SERVICES

Home care continues its development as a major program for the older American population and now accounts for 14% of Medicare expenditures. Despite this small number, in recent years home care has represented one of the fastest growing components in Medicare expenditures.

An individual's eligibility for home care depends on their degree of disability, but defining disability is difficult because of the various measurement standards that are used. The number of Activities of Daily Living that individuals cannot do without assistance is becoming more utilized as a disability standard. Stone and Murtaugh (1990) have estimated the size of the disabled elderly population eligible for home care using various criteria. One of these was the criterion of needing help with three or more ADLs for at least 12 months. By this standard, 4.1 million elderly, representing 15% of the elderly in the community, could be termed "disabled" and eligible for home care. With the most restrictive criteria, 400,000 older persons, representing 1.5% of the community-based elderly, could be termed disabled enough to need home care. In 1987, 5.6 million elderly living in the community had difficulty with at least one ADL or Instrumental Activity of Daily Living, or some problem that affected their ability to walk (Short & Leon, 1990).

The National Medical Expenditure Survey (Short & Leon, 1990) indicates that 36% of people classified as having functional difficulties received services. Not surprisingly, home care was the most commonly used service. A study of 426 older residents in Philadelphia, who report one or more ADL limitations, revealed 23.5% received in-home health care services (Axler, Kotranski, & Olsen, 1990). Those older individuals not receiving adequate

179

assistance may be forced to become part of an enlarged nursing home population.

In-home services are provided to individuals who live in their own home or apartment. The hope is that these services can

> through coordinated planning, evaluation and follow-up procedures, provide for medical, nursing, social and related services to selected persons . . . with a view toward shortening the length of hospital stay, speeding recovery, or preventing inappropriate institutionalization. (U.S. Senate, Special Committee on Aging, 1972, p. 25)

In-home services to the elderly are approximately evenly divided between health and welfare agencies, a phenomenon that has resulted from the parallel, but relatively independent, growth of social and health services to the homebound. Welfare agencies were the first to offer in-home services. In the early 1900s, private charitable family agencies provided homemakers to care for children whose mother was sick. During the 1930s, poor and unemployed women were hired as housekeepers for other poor persons who were in need of the service. By 1958, 145 agencies offered homemaker or home health aid services, of which one-half served adults (U.S. Administration on Aging, 1977).

After 1958, the number of agencies providing in-home services grew rapidly, with the percentage of public agencies comprising a larger portion each year until 1967. With the introduction of Medicare and Medicaid in the mid-1960s, the emphasis of service shifted from family and child care to serving the elderly. With this shift in recipient population came a shift in the type of care given, from home maintenance to personal care. The care of the sick, elderly person required an emphasis on personal care, and Medicare and Medicaid reimbursed only for the personal care aspects of in-home work.

The growth of agencies providing home health services has been remarkable. Medicare certified fewer than 2,000 home health agencies in 1967. Thirty years later, 10,000 agencies had Medicare certification and were providing assistance to 3.8 million of the current 38 million Medicare beneficiaries (Pear, 1997). The overwhelming proportion (83%) of this growth has been among for-profit agencies (U.S. General Accounting Office, 1996). In addition to these agencies, an estimated 3,700 to 6,000 agencies were providing services, although not certified by Medicare.

The diversity of services and service providers makes it difficult to guarantee the quality of in-home services. The 1992 OAA amendments required State Units on Aging to monitor the quality of in-home services. In addition, the amendments add a section to Title III that guarantees the rights of clients of in-home services. These rights include the right to be informed in advance about a service, participate in its planning, voice grievances about its delivery, be treated with respect, have records treated as confidential, and be informed of rights under the OAA [Section 314].

Health agencies—long established to provide health services in community and institutional settings—started to add home health aid services to their in-home services when reimbursements through Medicaid and Medicare became available. Skilled nursing care had been available through health agencies for some time before the new funding became available. With the availability of new funding, welfare agencies offering homemaker services and health agencies offering home health aid services began offering the same or similar basic services. Both personal and homemaking services are required to enable persons to remain in their own homes. Because of the overlapping of personal and homemaking services by both social and health agencies, a single person (home maker or home health aide) can provide both homemaking and personal care services. Unfortunately, some confusion still exists because some funds which pay for the services still retain the separate titles; i.e., Medicaid and Medicare reimburse home health aides, while Title XX reimburses homemaker services (U.S. Administration on Aging, 1977).

SERVICE PATTERNS

In-home services encompass several levels or types of services. However, the services and levels of services being given should be flexible and readily changed as the client's needs change. Because they are administered in the home of the client, in-home services are an extension of the individual's functioning. Because they are personalized to individual situations, there is a potential need to change the service components as persons respond to the services being given. Thus, coordination of services is an integral element of successful in-home services. A smoothly functioning network of services must be available to ensure that the individual receives exactly what is needed at the time it is needed. Strong links and easy accessibility among the services are essential to ensure cooperation for the benefit of the client. For example, Baltimore coordinates 10 in-home service agencies through a central intake system so that a client can be matched with the most appropriate services. As service needs change, the central intake system can continue to reassign the appropriate services.

Available in-home services can be grouped into three general categories, based on the level of intensity of service (U.S. Senate, Special Committee on Aging, 1972).

1. Intensive or skilled services

These services are ordered by a physician and provided under the supervision of a nurse. Skilled care is given to clients with such problems as cardiac difficulties, bone fractures, open wounds, diabetes, and terminal illnesses involving catheters and tube feedings. The services may require physician visits, regular visits by a nurse, and frequent physical and occupational therapy treatments. In addition, less technical services may be provided such as nutritional services, deliveries of drugs and medical supplies, home health equipment, transportation, and other diagnostic and therapeutic services which can be safely provided in the client's home.

The intensive or skilled service level usually involves a complex grouping of services. The services might not be needed for a long period of time, but modified amounts of these services would probably be part of client planning for an extended period of time. Coordination is particularly important for this level of in-home services because of the potential for change and probable number of different service components that could be needed.

2. Personal care or intermediate services

Clients eligible for personal care services are medically stable, but need assistance with certain activities of daily living, such as bathing, ambulation, prescribed exercises, and medications. These services can be given to persons who are convalescing from acute illnesses or to persons with temporary disabilities related to a chronic illness, or as part of a chronic illness. Personal or intermediate care services can be given independently or in conjunction with skilled care.

3. Homemaker-chore or basic services

These services involve light housekeeping, preparation of food, laundry services, and other maintenance activities that help sustain the client at home. In those circumstances where the clients can care for themselves but do not have the capacity to care for their personal environment, these basic services help sustain the home situation for them. Basic or chore services can be given in conjunction with both intermediate and skilled services and usually are given on an ongoing basis.

The key in-home service worker, particularly for both personal and homemaker-chore areas of service, is the homemaker-home health aide. Homemaker-home health aide services comprise the personal and homemaking services needed to enable persons who cannot perform basic tasks for themselves to remain in their own homes. The basic duties performed include cleaning, planning meals, shopping for food, preparing meals, doing the laundry, changing bed linens, bathing, giving bed baths, shampooing hair, helping the person move from the bed to a chair, checking the pulse rate, helping perform simple exercises, assisting with medications, teaching new skills, and providing emotional support. The homemaker-home health aide can perform primarily personal care services, homemaking services, or both, as the training usually involves skill development in both areas. Although the Department of Labor has rapid growth in the number of trained health aides, studies have already shown a shortage of home health aides. A possible effect of this shortage could be the hiring of minimally qualified individuals to provide these important services to older persons ("Study finds home health aids shortage likely," 1993).

Heavy house cleaning and simple home maintenance, such as painting and simple carpentry repairs, are usually performed by a person specifically employed for the purpose, and are not included in the home maker-home health aide functions. Special programs matching high school or college students with the chore needs of older persons have enabled this type of work to be done. Usually, the older person pays a minimum wage for the services, as such services are not covered under most funding programs.

An attempt to develop intensive services for seriously disabled older individuals without relocating them outside their own homes is exemplified by the Nursing Home Without Walls program. In New York State this program was begun in 1977 and designed to be an alternative to institutionalization (Cardillo, Horton, & Luther, 1988). Individuals accepted into the program are provided a wide range of services comparable to those offered in a nursing home. The services are available on a 24-hour, 7-day-a-week basis and are offered through hospitals, residential health care facilities, and certified home health agencies. An older person assessed as needing skilled nursing care is also evaluated to determine whether he or she has a suitable living environment at home for the nursing home without walls program. If the environment is physically suitable, a plan is prepared. The costs of the program's services are capped at 75% of the average annual cost for nursing home care, although exceptions are made to this formula. By 1988, 86 providers were providing care to 7,700 patients at approximately half the cost of nursing home placements.

A similar program is also in effect at the On Lok center in San Francisco. An evaluation of 16 community care demonstrations (including the New York and On Lok efforts) indicates a pattern of "higher life quality" for participants. The evaluators contend, however, that

> expanding publicly financed community care does not reduce aggregate costs, and it is likely to increase them—at least under the current long-term care service system which already provides some community care. (Kemper, Applebaum, & Harrigan, 1987, p. 96)

SERVICE AGENCIES

In-home services are provided by a variety of agencies which are usually based in the community and defined by the source of the funding and the service specialty:

An agency eligible to receive Medicare and Medicaid funds is a home health agency, a public or private agency which in addition to requirements for sound administration, adequate records, professional supervision, assessment and review, has as its primary function the provision of skilled nursing service and at least one additional therapeutic service. (U.S. Senate, Special Committee on Aging, 1972, p. 21)

The agency is thus defined by the type of service that it provides.

Home health agencies can be both hospital and community based, public, private nonprofit, or proprietary:

1. *Home care units of community hospitals.* These units have emerged as a part of the hospital program, primarily as a method of discharging patients as soon as appropriate. As a hospital affiliate, the patient can retain the same doctor and can move in and out of the hospital as needed for ongoing care. Hospital-based programs are particularly effective for terminally ill patients who can spend some time at home but who need a close affiliation with emergency health services. These home care units are staffed primarily with public health nurses and have on call the medical units from the hospital itself. These units provide primarily skilled-care services.

2. *Departments of social services.* Local departments of social services usually provide intermediate- and basic-level in-home services under their adult services units. Because their background is a welfare agency, these homemakers are more likely to be involved with household activities and to a lesser extent with personal care services.

3. *Private nonprofit community agencies.* Included in this group are such agencies as Associated Catholic Charities, Jewish Family and Children's Services, Family and Children's Services, and Visiting Nursing Associations. These types of agencies provide home-maker-home health aides, nurses, and other in-home service workers as part of larger community-related programs. Each agency usually selects which specific service area it will provide, such as personal care services only or nursing services, and incorporates them into the other agency services being given.

4. *Community health centers.* Community health centers can provide some in-home services as part of their community health services program. The in-home services are usually tied to those clients who are participating in the health center as an extension of services given.

5. *Proprietary agencies.* Proprietary agencies, such as Upjohn, provide in-home services to the homebound on a fee-for-service basis. The services are usually at the skilled level of care and provided for short periods of time.

Funding

The most difficult problem in the delivery of in-home services is that of funding. Because of current funding restrictions, the demand for services far exceeds the supply. Further, the demand is primarily for those types of services that are not readily reimbursable through the available funding sources. The community and institutional agencies which provide the services are available and prepared to deliver the services, if the repayment mechanism was available for reimbursement. The greatest unmet need for in-home services is for those with long-term disabilities and for the chronically ill whose conditions are not likely to improve quickly.

There are five basic ways for payment of in-home services. The first—client fees—is used by most agencies that provide in-home services. Voluntary agencies are more likely to offer sliding-scale fee schedules because they are usually supported in part through contributions from individuals, religious groups community groups, disease-related groups, or United Way fundraising organizations.

The second payment method—Medicare—is used by agencies which provide health-related services in situations when the client and the service meet Medicare eligibility requirements. In order to be eligible for Medicare reimbursement, the service must be given by a home health agency which has, as its primary function, the provision of skilled nursing service and at least one additional therapeutic service. The services that are reimbursable focus upon acute or short-term illnesses, not on chronic or custodial ones.

In addition, there are varying interpretations as to what is appropriate for reimbursement, interpretations that might be applied after the service has been given. Because of the potential unpredictability of Medicare reimbursements, agencies are often reluctant to give Medicare-reimbursed services other than those specifically defined as eligible services. This makes it difficult for clients to receive appropriate services for their situations. A survey of all 50 states indicated that 35 permit family caregivers to be paid for their assistance to an older person. The majority of these states utilize Medicaid funds for these payments (Linsk, Keigher, & Osterbusch, 1988).

Actual services provided under Medicare are restricted to home-bound patients (individuals unable to leave their home without the assistance of a person or a device such as a wheelchair or cane). Home care must be prescribed by the physician caring for the patient and the patient must require either intermittent skilled nursing care, physical therapy, or speech therapy (Leader, 1991). "Intermittent" care is defined as care provided at least once every 60 days, but once a patient meets Medicare eligibility, the services can be provided as long as they are medically necessary. As already noted, despite these restrictions, Medicare expenditures for home care continued to grow throughout the 1980s.

Reimbursable services under Medicare include part-time or intermittent nursing care (under the supervision of a registered nurse); physical, occupational, and speech therapy; medical supplies; home health aide services; and counseling for social or emotional problems. The important services missing from this list are crucial personal and home maintenance services. Medicare covered services have a maximum of 8 hours per day and 28 hours per week. A registered nurse for $20 to $60 per hour or a home aide for $7 to $15 per hour can mean an expense of $1,500 per week for a family attempting to maintain an impaired older person in the community (Alger, 1997)

Medicaid is the third payment method and is used by agencies which provide health-related services in situations when the client and the service meet Medicaid eligibility requirements. Unlike Medicare, in which every person age 65 and over is potentially eligible for the benefits, Medicaid is available only to those who meet strict income requirements. Although the actual income limit is determined within each state because Medicaid is partially financed by the states, the usual income limit is set to coincide with the SSI limit, plus whatever state aid for income is being given.

Home health care became a required service under Medicaid in 1970 and could be provided by the same agencies that are eligible for Medicare. Although the services provided under Medicaid vary among the states, Medicaid essentially covers nursing services, home health aide services, and medical supplies and equipment. Medicaid benefits do not require that skilled nursing care or therapy be given. The potentially eligible persons do not need prior hospitalization nor is there a limit on the number of visits.

Unlike Medicare, there is no requirement for prior hospitalization and no limit on the number of visits that can be provided under Medicaid. Medicaid also allows personal care and nonmedical services related to activities of daily living to be reimbursed. However, many states restrict the home health services they will cover under Medicaid. Few states actually reimburse personal care and nontechnical services. Thus, despite its potential as a funding source, the state limitations on covered services have meant fewer programs being offered to chronically ill elderly at home than Medicaid provisions allow (Oktay & Palley, 1981).

In 1985, $21 billion was allocated from federal and state coffers for home health care benefits under Medicaid (Nassif, 1987). Despite this impressive figure, the preponderance of Medicaid funds are still oriented to institutional care. It is thus clear that Medicare is more likely to pay for in-home services while Medicaid is used primarily for institutional care.

The former Title XX of the Social Security Act was a fourth source of funds for in-home services from public and private agencies. As already noted, Title XX monies were allocated on the basis of population to the state departments of social services. Unlike Medicare and Medicaid, the services were not reviewed on a service-by-service basis for reimbursement. Home-based services, such as homemaker, home health aide, home management, personal care, consumer education, and financial counseling, were eligible services under Title XX. These services could be ongoing and were not restricted to a limited amount per year. However, the program was limited by the income eligibility of the client and the amount of money available to the public and private agencies for personnel to provide the services. Despite the opportunities for funding of in-home services under Title XX, only limited amounts of funds have been addressed to the needs of older clients and home health.

The fifth payment source is Title III of the OAA, which provides monies for in-home services through the local Area Agencies on Aging. The funds are made available to provide services designed to assist older individuals in avoiding institutionalization, including preinstitution evaluation and screening and home health services, homemaker services, shopping services, escort services, reader services, letter-writing services, and other similar services designed to assist such individuals to continue living independently in a home environment.

The funds can provide for a variety of services by both public and private agencies for both the chronically and acutely ill. The only eligibility requirement is that the recipient be 60 or over. Although there is no income restriction on the services, efforts are made to make most of the services available to low-income elderly. The service limitation under Title III programs lies in the financial limits of the allocations themselves. Because eligible services are broadly defined under this act, efforts have been concentrated on using these funds and services for those people who are ineligible for services under the other funding programs—primarily those who were just over the scale for Title XX and those with chronic illnesses.

RELATED SERVICES

There has been a growth in the number and types of formal support systems for the homebound that complement in-home services, or even substitute for these services when regular contact and visiting are all that are needed. Two such programs, reassurance and friendly visiting, are most frequently available, primarily as adjunct programs within senior centers or agencies providing other programs and services to the elderly. Gatekeeper initiatives are unobtrusive, but valuable, mechanisms for monitoring the well-being of community-based elderly.

Reassurance and Gatekeeper Services

As the number of elderly maintaining independent residence in the community continues to increase, a method for ensuring their daily well-being becomes vital. In housing specifically designed for seniors, systems that require turning off a hall light outside the apartment each morning can be used to indicate that the resident has not suffered any mishap during the previous day.

For individuals living in other types of residences, telephone reassurance has been stressed as a means of maintaining daily contact with older individuals. The telephone reassurance systems can be traced to the efforts of Grace McClure during the 1960s. After attempting to contact an elderly friend for 8 successive days, Mrs. McClure made a personal check of the friend's apartment and found her on the floor after having suffered a stroke. Mrs. McClure's subsequent efforts in Michigan resulted in a telephone reassurance service and replication of this type of service in many parts of the country.

In the typical telephone reassurance service, the individual is called twice a day. If there is no answer, a policeman with a house key is dispatched to make a personal check. The individual must also inform the police when they are leaving their home in order to ensure that calls are not made when the house is vacant. In New York City, a private service provides two calls a day and includes information about television listings, news, and weather (Conait, 1969). Among publicly funded services a variety of volunteers have been used to do the telephoning, including residents of a nursing home in Nassau County, New York, and multiple sclerosis patients in other programs in New York State.

One possible side effect of these services is the friendships that can form between volunteer callers and clients. This potential for friendships is being built into some services that utilize a buddy system. This approach depends on a team of approximately 10 people who utilize a daily round robin of calling. If the chain is broken on any day, the individual unable to make contact with the next person reports the problem to a central office, and a personal visit is made to the home (Match, 1972).

If these services are well-run, they are important links for the aging. More affluent elderly are now able to enroll in a service that enables them to hook their home into a central office. Failure to punch a code on a specially designed machine will result in a checkup visit to the home. Under these systems, central offices can be alerted to emergencies by either push-button codes or, in some cases, voice activation of the system. Social service agencies as well as hospitals are now making these automated systems available under a variety of fee schedules. The key link in the machine-based or telephone-based reassurance service is the reliability of the staff responsible for checking on the elderly client who fails to utilize the designated code or answer the phone. Because of this problem, few services are relying totally on relatives because of their possible unavailability at crucial times.

"Gatekeepers" are individuals who have frequent contact with older persons and can alert agencies about serious problems. In rural areas, mail carriers are asked to alert a special office if they notice mail accumulating in an older person's mailbox (National Institute of Senior Centers, 1978). A customer representative for the utility company in Spokane, Washington, alerted Spokane Elder Services that a client had stopped paying her bills and appeared to be living in unsafe conditions. Other gatekeepers can include mail carriers, meter readers, bank tellers, clerks in stores, or pharmacists (Barnhill, 1997).

Visiting Services

Although they are now available in greater numbers, many cities have operated friendly visiting services for a long period of time. The visitors service in Chicago was begun in 1947.

Friendly visitors services utilize volunteers to visit elderly individuals who are homebound. Visitors may chat with the older persons, read to them, help them with correspondence, or play chess and board games.

While they are most often oriented to community-based elderly, a friendly visitor service was begun in Maryland in 1977 to provide companionship for nursing home residents who did not receive regular visits by family and friends. One friendly visiting service utilized members of a senior citizens club as visitors. Programs around the country rely on volunteers of all ages to reach elderly who might otherwise be isolated from social contacts.

Expansion of effective in-home services still hinges on funding mechanisms being instituted to make these services more reimbursable. Under the 1987 Older Americans Act amendments, a program of grants to individual states was authorized. The services that can be provided under this program to "frail" elderly are extensive. They include homemaker and home health aides as well as nonhealth services such as choice services, telephone reassurance, respite care in the home for family caretakers, and minimal physical modification of the home. In FY 1990, 88,000 older persons were served under this program. Over half of these clients were from low-income backgrounds. Even with their expansion, it is questionable whether in-home services from formal providers can substitute for emotional support from family and friends. In order to bolster the care-taking efforts of family and friends, Title III of the 1992 OAA amendments authorizes a program to offer training, technical assistance, and information to informal caregivers and frail older individuals (Part G).

REFERENCES

Alger, A. (1997, March 24). Nursing home or home nursing? *Forbes*, 160.

Axler, F., Kotranski, L., & Olsen, K. (1990, November). *Home care for the impaired elderly: Factors influencing use of and access to formal and informal health care*. Poster presentation at The Gerontological Society Annual Meeting, Boston, MA.

Barnhill, W. (1997). I was just passing by. *AARP Bulletin*, *38*, 2, 10.

Cardillo, A., Horton, R., & Luther, C. (1988). *Nursing Home Without Walls Program: A decade of quality care at home for NY's aged and disabled*. Albany: New York State Senate Health Committee.

Conait, M. (1969). *Guidelines for telephone reassurance services*. Ann Arbor, MI: Univ. of Michigan, Institute of Gerontology.

Kemper, P., Applebaum, R., & Harrigan, M. (1987). Community care demonstrations: What have we learned? *Health Care Financing Review*, *8*, 87–100.

Leader, S. (1991). *Medicare's home health benefit: Eligibility, utilization, and expenditures*. Washington, DC: Public Policy Institute, American Association of Retired Persons.

Linsk, N., Keigher, S., & Osterbusch, S. (1988). States' policies regarding paid family caregiving. *Gerontologist*, *28*, 204–212.

Match, S. (1972). *Establishing telephone reassurance services*. Washington, DC: National Council on the Aging.

Nassif, J. (1987). There's still no place like home. *Generations*, *11*, 5–8.

National Institute of Senior Centers. (1978). Senior center programming: Expanding services to the vulnerable elderly. *Senior Center Report*, *1*, 4–5.

Oktay, J., & Palley, H. (1981). A national family policy for the chronically ill elderly. In *The Social Welfare Forum, 1980* (pp. 104–120). New York: Columbia University Press.

Pear, R. (1997, September 16). Citing fraud in home care, Clinton halts new permits. *New York Times*, p. A15.

Short, P., & Leon, J. (1990). *Use of home and community services by persons age 65 and older with functional difficulties* (National Medical Expenditure Survey Research Findings 5, Agency for Health Care Policy and Research). Rockville, MD: Public Health Service.

Stone, R., & Murtaugh, C. (1990). The elderly population with chronic functional disability: Implications for home care eligibility. *The Gerontologist*, *30*, 491–502.

Study finds home health aide shortage likely. (1993). *Aging Today*, *14*, 7, 10.

U.S. Administration on Aging. (1977). *Human resources issues in the field of aging: Homemaker-home health aide services.* Washington, DC: U.S. Government Printing Office.

U.S. General Accounting Office. (1996). *Medicare: Home health utilization expands while program controls deteriorate.* Washington, DC: Author.

U.S. Senate, Special Committee on Aging. (1972). *Home health services in the United States.* Washington, DC: U.S. Government Printing Office.

14

Adult Day Care

THE ROOTS OF DAY CARE

Dependency and Aging

It is unfortunate that day-care services for the elderly often seem to resemble similar series for children. While the two programs may be similar in some aspects, services for the aged should not be based on viewing the elderly as childlike. As one advocate for adult day care urges:

> We object to the comparison to child care because it is inaccurate. We are not a place where people are left in safety as children are left, until someone is ready to "pick them up" again. Our services have an objective, and those who are consumers are not children. They are adults who may be limited for shorter or longer periods of time in their capacities for total self-care—but they are participants in their own care programs with everything that the term implies. (Lupu, cited in Trager, 1976, p. 6)

The common thread running through services for children and the elderly is that of dependency. Lupu argues, however, that dependency among the elderly and children stems from different sources. The elderly do not lack knowledge of "right from wrong," and have attained the skills necessary to conduct their everyday life. Dependency in the elderly usually stems from physical and mental impairments that make it difficult for them to continue to successfully accomplish routine tasks. These tasks may include "activities of daily living" such as dressing, bathing, using the bathroom, cooking, and self-feeding. The task of the day care center is to assist the individual in functioning as independently as possible given their physical and mental status.

192

A National Council on the Aging (NCOA) study defines day care as a

community based group program designed to meet the needs of functionally impaired adults through an individual plan of care. It is a structured,
comprehensive program that provides a variety of health, social, and
related support services in a protective setting during any part of a day but
less than 24 hour care. (Behrens, 1986, p. 5)

History of Day Care

Day care is one possible response to the need for families to have a daily
respite from caring for an impaired older person. Kaplan (1976, pp. 7–10)
has summarized the basic assumptions about day care as a belief in (1) "the
intrinsic worth of living within one's community;" (2) the merit in keeping
the family together; (3) the beneficial nature of allowing a person to continue independent living; and (4) independent living as beneficial in the
broader concept of social well-being for older persons and their families.

Day care for adults originated in Britain during the 1940s, when outpatient hospital centers for psychiatric patients were set up. These centers,
located in psychiatric hospitals, were designed to decrease the numbers of
individuals who would require admittance to inpatient units. By the late
1950s, the British had extended day care programs to include geriatric
patients; by 1969, 90 programs were already in operation.

In 1947, the first geriatric day hospital in the United States opened under
the auspices of the Menninger Clinic, and in 1949, a similar operation was
begun at Yale (McCuan, 1973). Bolstered by the increased interest and
funding for aging programs in the 1970s, day care programs have expanded
dramatically. In 1970, 15 day care centers were in existence. By 1996 more
than 3,000 were operating. Even with this dramatic increase, a federal
report estimates that more than 10,000 centers are needed to meet the
needs of American elderly (Advisory Panel on Alzheimer's Disease, 1996).

DAY CARE CLIENTS

Eligibility

Because of this short history, a variety of programs with varied focuses
now fall under the day care rubric. Federal guidelines have not yet been set
up to determine eligibility for federally funded day care programs. In 1974,
Congress authorized demonstration day care programs. In its guidelines for
these demonstration programs, HEW defined day care as a program "provided under health leadership in an ambulatory care setting for adults who

do not require 24-hour institutional care and yet, due to physical and/or mental impairment, are not capable of full-time independent living" (U.S. Health Resources Administration, 1974, p. 1).

An individual with physical and mental impairment is further defined under these guidelines as a "chronically ill or disabled adult whose illness or disability does not require 24-hour inpatient care but which in the absence of day-care service may precipitate admission to or prolonged stay in a hospital, nursing home or other long-term facility" (U.S. Health Resources Administration, 1974, p. 1). It is obvious that the major projected day care population is an at-risk group whose involvement in day-care programs may provide enough support to enable them to remain out of long-term care institutions. Among existing programs, day care is not often used for individuals discharged from nursing homes.

Present Users

In examining a number of day-care programs, Weissert (1975) commented on the participants: "Most are aged who need continuing support and will probably leave the adult day care program only to go into a nursing home or at death" (p. 14). The participants in Weissert's sample had between two and five diagnosed medical conditions. The same configuration of conditions was noted by Kaplan (1976) examining a day-care program in Ohio. Kaplan found that 75% of the participants had many of the same symptoms usually found among nursing home patients. As Gurian (1976) argues, day-care clients can thus potentially come from three major groups: (1) individuals enrolled in day hospital programs in mental hospitals which provide mental health treatment during the day; (2) nursing home patients; or (3) elderly living in their own homes or with their families. Interestingly, although the vast majority of elderly live independently, Weissert (1975) found that, on average, only 31% of the clients in the 10 programs studied by his researchers lived alone. Mahoney (1978) found that only 26% of the day-care clients in three Connecticut centers lived alone.

An Ohio study compared day-care users and impaired elderly. Day-care participants were more likely to be unmarried, living with other individuals, and in a physically more dependent position than impaired community elderly not involved with the day-care program (Barresi & McConnell, 1984). The need for day care may first be perceived by those who become caretakers as the elderly individual's physical or mental condition deteriorates. Referrals to day-care centers may come either from the families of elderly persons or from agencies or service providers who come into contact with the families and are aware of the centers. In contrast, the literature on nursing homes indicates that the majority of long-term residents have previously lived alone. It is therefore possible that day-care clients differ from nursing home residents in the degree to which economic, social, and psychological support is being provided by family members.

If individuals come into day-care programs from nursing homes, they will be those elderly whose conditions have improved and who are found not to be in need of the 24-hour nursing services offered by these homes. The day-care centers will be expected to provide a gamut of services necessary to maintain the participants near their present level of functioning.

Evaluating Benefit to Clients

The ambiguities that now exist in definitions of day care create an initial difficulty in evaluating the effectiveness of these programs. If day-care centers are maintenance-oriented, it still may be difficult to evaluate the centers that enroll large numbers of seriously impaired individuals. Deterioration, admission to nursing homes, or death are possible among these individuals, despite the extensive care a center may provide. A broken hip, myocardial infarction, or organic brain syndrome may occur at any point in the impaired elderly person's day, and these occurrences may be unaffected by attendance at a day-care center. While it is possible that the day services may delay the onset of these conditions or deterioration in existing conditions, the use of adult day care has not been shown to have an effect on the health or mental health outcomes of clients (Weissert et al., 1989).

Eligibility for day-care services as well as evaluation of the center's ability to meet its stated goals will be determined to a great extent by the range of services offered by the individual center. Thus the clients served and the criteria used for evaluation will differ between a center that is rehabilitation-oriented and has multiple medical services, a maintenance-oriented center with many different services (not all offered on-site), and a center that is socially oriented and has a minimum of medical services.

DAY CARE CENTER SERVICES

Program Outlines

The range of services that day-care centers currently provide to maintain impaired clients at their optimal level of functioning is clear: screening for physical conditions; medical care (usually by arrangement with an outside physician); nursing care; occupational, physical, and recreational therapy; social work; transportation; meals; personal care (e.g., assistance in going to the toilet); educational programs; crafts; and counseling. In contrast to senior centers, day-care services are not available on a drop-in basis. Clients are scheduled, usually on a minimal 2-day-per-week basis, but often on a full 5-day basis. While many clients are ambulatory, day-care centers endeavor to provide transportation and appropriately designed space to serve individuals confined to wheelchairs.

Most day-care centers are small, typically serving 15–25 clients a day. This size helps to prevent the development of an institutional atmosphere. Centers are located in settings ranging from schools, apartments, and churches to hospitals and nursing homes. A random sample of adult day care in five states (Brasher, Estes, & Stuart, 1995) found that 45% of the centers were free-standing.

Clients usually arrive at the center between 9 and 10 A.M. and may have coffee before becoming involved in an individual or group project. A period of exercise matching the client's capability may be held before lunch, followed by a rest period and another group or individual project. These projects range from crafts and reading to dances and discussions. At any point in the day, appropriate counseling, nursing care, and medical-social services may be provided. Activities are conducted in accordance with the individual plan of care developed for each client upon his or her acceptance into the program. Clients are transported back to their residence in the late afternoon (3–4 P.M.). This schedule would not apply to centers that run an extended-hours program in the morning and afternoon. As would be expected, the staff-client ratio necessary to provide the individualized attention described here is high, averaging around 1:5 or 1:7 at most centers. In order to maintain the client's relationship with the community, many centers make extensive use of volunteers and emphasize frequent outings, including picnics, shopping, and trips.

Program and Client Emphasis

The major disagreement among day-care advocates has revolved around the relative emphasis on particular services. This lack of consensus can be seen in the ambiguous guidelines for the 1974 HEW demonstration programs:

> The essential elements of day care programs are directed towards meeting the health maintenance and restorative needs of participants. However, there are socialization elements which by overcoming the isolation often associated with illness in the aged and disabled are considered vital for the purpose of fostering and maintaining the maximum possible state of health and well being. (U.S. Health Resources Administration, 1974)

The relegation of "socialization" programs to the second sentence of these guidelines reflects uncertainty as to the importance of these elements in the day-care program. Padula (1972) attempted to distinguish between "day hospital" programs, which are health-related and service the disabled or ill elderly, and "day care," as a social program for "frail, moderately handicapped or slightly confused older persons" (p. 8). A report by the NCOA (National Institute of Senior Centers, 1978) on adult day care distinguished between day care, in-home services, and senior centers: "Day care differs from in-home services in that the therapeutic care is given in a group setting, which reduces loneliness and social isolation of the impaired older person and facilitates the delivery of multiple services" (p. 3).

Unless federal or state guidelines clearly specify the outlines of day-care services, the components emphasized will partially depend on the affiliation or sponsorships of the centers. Day care centers sponsored by Area Agencies on Aging may have a greater degree of emphasis on social rather than health components, depending for their health services on linkages with medical and nursing schools. Programs such as the Mosholu-Montefiore program in New York place a heavy emphasis on health components because of their strong relationship to major hospital facilities and, in the case of this particular program, because it uses space provided by the hospital. The actual ratio of health to social services depends on the requirements of funding sources. Trager (1976) has succinctly summed up the problems that may result from viewing social and health components as distinct and separate day-care entities:

> The development of centers which set policies and objectives in the context of treatment and physical restoration may tend to exclude those in need of some, but not all of these services. For those who are considered candidates for supervision and socialization, there may be a tendency to ignore essential health related services. Facilities which are treatment oriented may also tend to take on institutional characteristics and to make a "patient" of the participant—an aspect of institutional care which often is counterproductive in terms of the objectives of treatment. On the other hand, major emphasis on a supervision-socialization policy excludes consideration of restoration and rehabilitation possibilities which may appear to be relatively limited but are of great importance to the participant and such facilities might take on the characteristics of current institutions which are "holding facilities" and ignore essential health needs. (p. 16)

A national study of day-care centers (Weissert et al., 1989) indicates a lessened tendency during the 1980s to view health and social services as separate entities. Three center models were found. Model I includes centers under the auspices of nursing homes or rehabilitation hospitals. Model II includes centers affiliated with general hospitals or social service agencies.

Model III centers are "special purpose" centers serving veterans, older persons with mental health problems or cerebral palsy, or the blind. Among these centers are some dedicated to older persons with Alzheimer's disease.

In Model I centers, the clients are a primarily "physically dependent, older, white population, most of whom do not suffer a mental disorder" (Weissert et al., 1989, p. 648). In Model II centers, the clients are

> predominantly unmarried females, more frequently racial minority populations, most of whom are under 85, typically not dependent or only minimally dependent in activities of daily living, but more than 40% of whom may suffer a mental disorder. (Weissert et al., 1989, p. 648)

Despite their physical problems, the day-care participants in Weissert's survey differed from nursing-home residents. Nursing-home residents are, on average, more than 4 years older than day-care participants, and twice as likely to be over age 85 and to be unmarried and functionally dependent. Model II participants, however, are more akin to community-based elderly than Model I participants. In all three models, a variety of services are offered. As expected, the centers under the auspices of nursing homes or rehabilitation hospitals (Model I) are more likely to have therapeutic or health-related programs than are Model II centers. Model II centers are more likely to offer social and supportive services. Despite these differences, Model II centers have enlarged the health services they offer since the 1970s.

In order to bring some coherence to adult day care, the National Adult Day Services Association, a unit of the National Council on the Aging, has developed a set of "Standards and Guidelines". These standards include specifications about varied levels of care that can be offered by day-care centers.

RESPITE SERVICES

Closely related to day care, respite services are strongly advocated, but receive only limited financial support. Although there are questions as to whether the target of respite is a caregiver or care receiver, respite services usually offer relief to individuals who provide intensive day-care for older relatives or even unrelated individuals. As usually defined, respite care is "planned" and "intermittent, short-term care" (Toner, 1993, p. 125). In addition to day care, other formal respite programs usually fall under the classification of "In-home sitter/companions" or "Overnight or short-term residential respite" (Toner, 1993, pp. 126–127).

A respite care program in Detroit, funded through the AAA, the Department of Social Services, and the United Way, offers 168 hours of respite per year or 3 hours a week for the caregiver (Durso, 1986). In 1987, this program was also made available on a fee-for-service option for higher-income individuals. A respite program in California is devoted to family caregivers of older people with chronic brain disorders (Griffin, 1985). This Family Survival Project included respite care as part of a full array of services for caregivers. In Oxon Hill, Maryland, the Crescent Cities Adult Medical Day Center provides respite care on Saturdays from 9 a.m. to 5 p.m. Caregivers must make reservations with the center on the Wednesday before but do not have to be regular users of the center or the respite program. At the Pennsylvania Medical Center in Philadelphia, the "HotelHospital" program provides 8–12 beds in a 12-bed unit for temporary residents (Hegeman, 1993). In Rochester, New York, St. John's Home provides two private skilled nursing facility rooms for respite stays of 1 to 6 weeks (Hegeman, 1993). Finally, INTERAC, a Phildelphia program, provides geriatric care in the older person's home. This care is available for a few hours or can be used for a few days (Hegeman, 1993).

FUNDING

As the discussion of funding sources in Chapter 2 indicates, services for the aging are now being kept afloat through funds obtained from a number of sources. This is exemplified by day care, where a variety of federal, local, and private funds are used. At the federal level, Medicaid plays a dominant role in funding adult day-care centers, but many centers also rely on fees paid by participants or their families. Support from fees or philanthropies was a primary source of income for the Model I centers described above. Day-care centers also obtain funding from the Social Services Block Grant as well as from Title III of the Older Americans Act.

In 1976, the Medical Services Administration issued guidelines designed to assist states in preparing regulations for reimbursable day-care centers. While the target population of these centers might not differ from the centers already described, the medical service requirement might be more extensive. Programs conducted by a hospital or programs that are recognized as "clinics under state laws" are eligible for Medicaid reimbursements. These reimbursements are authorized under the outpatient hospital provisions of Title XIX. Under the guidelines, the reimbursable medical services that day care centers might offer include:

1. Medical services supervised by a physician
2. Nursing services rendered by a professional nursing staff
3. Diagnostic services in addition to initial screening
4. Rehabilitation services including physical therapy, speech therapy, occupational therapy, and inhalation therapy
5. Pharmaceutical services

6. Podiatric services
7. Optometric services
8. Self-care services oriented toward the activities of daily living
9. Dental services
10. Social work services
11. Recreation therapy
12. Dietary services
13. Transportation services

Although existing centers may provide many of these services, provision of all of them is probably beyond the resources of many. The guidelines specify that the packages of services available for any individual must be a combination of some or all of the elements listed. All of these services might be available in a center, but it is expected that the most complex medical services would be found in day hospital settings, because of the close hospital-staff linkages. In all centers, the guidelines stress screening of clients by a multidisciplinary team and the development of an individualized treatment plan.

Based on the guidelines, each state has the responsibility to establish and approve a required package of services for reimbursable day-care and day hospital programs. Intense discussions have developed about the degree of medical supports that will be required by the state to qualify a center for reimbursement.

Under Title XX, many day-care centers were funded without the extensive medical services that may be required under Title XIX. Unfortunately, Social Services Block Grant (Title XX) funds were limited, and based on annual population figures for each state. Title XX funds are also allocated on the basis of public hearings and plans developed on a statewide level. Some states have not included day services for the elderly in their plans, while others have viewed block grant support only as seed money for programs. Programs that were instituted on the basis of Title XX allocations have now found that block grant funds are not always available to meet increasing inflationary costs, or even that states are cutting back individual program funding in order to distribute small amounts of money to a larger number of centers. In this way, the states hope to encourage a larger number of centers, but individual centers have had to scramble to meet the deficit imposed by the cuts in their funding.

COST-EFFECTIVENESS AND BENEFITS

Even before their social and psychological benefits have been determined, day-care centers have had to face the question of their costliness. Unfortunately, the cost-effectiveness studies fail to provide enough clarity to allow for a final determination of the financial question. Because of variations in services, costs may differ widely among centers. The NCOA study of 847 centers found that the expenditures averaged $27 per day. When subsidies from a variety of funding sources were included, day care expenditures rose to $31 per day. In 57% of the centers, fees charged to paying participants on a sliding scale ranged from $31 to $40 per day (Behrens, 1986). In some instances, costs borne by programs other than day-care centers are not included in these tallies. Space rental paid by other agencies is a major example. Weissert et al. (1989) found an average cost of $30 per day among day-care centers.

An additional cost factor that needs to be examined is the ability of day-care programs to provide the totality of services required by an elderly individual. In Connecticut, Mahoney (1978) found that 47% of the clients in three day-care centers also received assistance from other agencies. Clients who were receiving only day-care services were more likely to be living with their families and have fewer functional impairments. A final problem in cost computations for day care is that much of the presently available data are based on studies in centers performed soon after they had opened, when costs may have been higher than, or at least different from, what they would have been at a later point. It thus remains unclear whether a day-care center is more cost effective than a nursing home.

Holmes and Hudson (1975) have argued, however, that cost-effectiveness is not the appropriate question to be asked about the day-care approach. Rather, they propose a cost-benefit formula, in which the total benefits of participation in the day care program for the client, family, and community might be explored. These benefits can be related to Kaplan's (1976) basic assumptions about day care. Acceptance of these assumptions leads to a variety of questions which can be asked about day-care services:

1. Do day-care centers enable impaired elderly to maintain residence in the community?
2. Do day-care services improve or maintain their participants' level of physical or emotional functioning?
3. Do the centers increase the participants' independence on basic activities of daily living?
4. Do day-care services prevent or postpone institutionalization of participants?
5. Do day-care services improve or maintain the participants' interpersonal relationships with family and friends?
6. Do day-care services assist individual participants in reestablishing their desired lifestyles or increase their life satisfaction?
7. Do day-care services offer supports for family members involved in the care of an elderly individual?

These questions were examined by Weiler, Kim, and Pickard (1976) in a controlled study of a day-care center. Positive answers were found to a number of these questions. Most important, the researchers noted that the day-care participants were functioning at a lower level than the community control group when first examined in November, but at a higher level than the control group 5 months later. A similar result was obtained by Weissert, Wan, and Livieratos (1979) in a controlled study.

Day care has established itself as an important component of the continuum of services for the aged. With day-care programs available, the caregiver of an older person in the community has some alternatives to the often seemingly overwhelming burdens of care. The most appropriate model for day-care programs will probably remain an issue related to the availability of other services in the community, such as home care, and the characteristics of the older population for whom the day are center is targeted. With better staff-client ratios and more health programs, Model I centers may be better suited to participants with special or severe health needs. Model II centers may be more appropriate to individuals who require extensive social services.

One consequence of an increased emphasis on health-care services in adult day-care centers would be higher program costs (Weissert et al. 1991). This could create difficulties for smaller centers and possibly result in some centers being unable to meet state regulations. Centers oriented to serving Alzheimer's Disease patients will also be under scrutiny for their ability to meet the specialized needs of these older persons.

REFERENCES

Advisory Panel on Alzheimer's Disease. (1996). *Alzheimer's Disease and related dementias: Report to Congress.* Washington, DC: U.S. Government Printing Office.

Barresi, C., & McConnell, D. (1984, November). *Discriminators of adult day care participation among retired elderly.* Paper presented at the Gerontological Society of America Annual Meeting, San Antonio, TX.

Behrens, R. (1986). *Adult day care in America.* Washington, DC: National Council on the Aging.

Brasher, J., Estes, C., & Stuart, M. (1995). Adult day care: A fragmented system of policy and funding streams. *Journal of Aging and Social Policy, 7,* 17–38.

Durso, L. (1986). Respite care: Focus on caregiver needs. *Older American Reports, 10,* 5.

Griffin, K. (1985). Family Survival Project. *Generations, 10,* 57–58.

Gurian, B. (1976). Mental health model of day care. In E. Pfeiffer (Ed.), *Day care for older adults* (pp. 41–45). Durham, NC: Duke University Center for the Study of Aging and Human Development.

Hegeman, C. (1993). Models of institutional and community-based respite care. In L. Tepper & J. Toner (Eds.), *Respite care* (pp. 3–29). Philadelphia: The Charles Press.

Holmes, D., & Hudson, E. (1975). *Evaluation report of the Mosholu-Montefiore day care center for the elderly in the northwest Bronx*. New York: Community Research Applications.

Kaplan, J. (1976). Goals of day care. In E. Pfeiffer (Ed.), *Day care for older adults* (pp. 7–10). Durham, NC: Duke University Center for the Study of Aging and Human Development.

Mahoney, K. (1978). *Outside the day care center: Additional support for the frail elderly*. Hartford, CT: Connecticut Department of Aging.

McCuan, E. R. (1973). *An evaluation of a geriatric day care center as a parallel service to institutional care*. Baltimore: Levindale Geriatric Research Center.

National Institute of Senior Centers. (1978). Adult day care: An overview. *Senior Center Report, 1*, 3–8.

Padula, H. (1972). *Developing day care for older people*. Washington, DC: National Council on the Aging.

Toner J. (1993). Concepts of respite care: A gerontologiust's perspective. In L. Tepper & J. Toner (Eds.), *Respite care* (pp. 123–131). Philadelphia: The Charles Press.

Trager, B. (1976). *Adult day facilities for treatment, health care and related services*. Washington, DC: U.S. Government Printing Office.

U.S. Health Resources Administration, Division of Long-Term Care. (1974). *Guidelines and definitions for day care centers under PL. 92-603*. Washington, DC: U.S. Government Printing Office.

Weiler, P., Kim, P., & Pickard, L. (1976). Health care for elderly Americans: Evaluation of an adult day health care model. *Medical Care, 14*, 700–708.

Weissert, W. (1975). *Adult day care in the U.S.: Final Report*. Washington, DC: Trans Century Corporation.

Weissert, W., Elston, J., Bolda, E., Cready, L., Zelman, W., Sloane, P., Kalsbeek, W., Mutran, E., Rice, T., & Koch, G. (1989). Models of adult day care: Findings from a national survey. *The Gerontologist, 29*, 640–649.

Weissert, W., Elston, J., Musling, & Mutran, E. (1991). Adult day care regulation: Deja vu all over again? *Journal of Health Politics, Policies, and Law, 16*, 51–67.

Weissert, W., Wan, T., & Livieratos, B. (1979). *Effects and costs of day care and homemaker services for the chronically ill*. Hyattsville, MD: National Center for Health Services Research.

15

Long-Term Care Residences

NATURE AND HISTORY OF LONG-TERM CARE

Long-term care can be provided through in-home services or day care centers. In this chapter, however, the focus is on residential institutions for the elderly. The forms of care provided can range from assistance in dressing, bathing, and ambulating to sophisticated medical life-support systems. The uniqueness of long-term care facilities lies in their constraint on individual choice in everyday situations, since the person living in these settings must adjust to being removed from "normal" individual or family living patterns. Existing long-term care residences include chronic care hospitals, private and public nursing homes, homes for the aged, psychiatric hospitals, and Veterans Administration facilities. All of these facilities provide varied levels of care ranging from extended, skilled, and intermediate care to personal and boarding care. Long-term care facilities are run under a variety of auspices including public, private-nonprofit, or proprietary organizations.

History of Institutional Settings

The history of long-term care institutions in America began with the almshouses and the public poor houses of colonial America. When a family or individual could no longer care for the pauper, that person became the responsibility of the government. The disabled, aged, widowed, orphaned, "feeble-minded" and deranged, and victims of disasters were mixed together in almshouses, hospitals, workhouses, orphanages, and prisons. Officials made little distinction between poverty generated by physical disability and economic distress. Boarding out, or foster care programs, were not uncommon, although often harshly administered (Cohen, 1974).

204

Following the Revolutionary War, almshouses became increasingly popular, and in 1834, the Poor Law of England reaffirmed this approach. This philosophy of isolating the aged and infirm from society continued to be the predominant social policy throughout the 19th century.

Residents of almshouses were usually pressed into working for very low wages as a means of earning at least a meager salary. Any financing for the facilities was the responsibility of the towns and counties in which the facilities were located; all efforts at state or federal support were denied for three-quarters of a century. By the late 19th century, other resources were being located for some indigent populations, but the elderly were still relegated to the almshouses. In 1875, a New York State report noted:

> Care has been taken not to diminish the terrors of this last resort of poverty, the almshouse, because it has been deemed better that a few should test the minimum rate of which existence can be preserved than that many should find the almshouse so comfortable a home that they would brave the shame of pauperism to gain admission to it. (cited in Cohen, 1974, p. 14)

In the beginning of the 20th century, the rise of private foundations and philanthropy began to expand the types of institutional care available. In addition, by 1929, the Old Age Assistance Act began to offer an alternative to institutionalization in most states. In the 1930s, new welfare, loan, housing public works, and rent programs, as well as the Social Security Act (SSA), provided a new concept of income support for the aged.

In the early versions of the SSA, there were prohibitions against federal financial participation in the cost of any relief given in any kind of institutional setting. Later, this prohibition continued in relation to public facilities, because public institutions were considered a state responsibility (Cohen, 1974). The intent of the legislation was to encourage the elderly to live at home or with foster families. However, the actual effect was the displacement of people from public facilities—particularly to boarding homes. As these facilities began to add nurses to their staffs, the name "nursing home" emerged (Moss & Halmandaris, 1977). Individuals who could not afford to move to the boarding homes continued in the public homes at state expense (Drake, 1958).

Since the 1930s, the number of institutions providing long-term care has increased rapidly. In 1995, there were 16,700 nursing homes (excluding hospital-based facilities). Two-thirds of these homes were operated for profit, 55% were owned by large nursing home chains such as Beverly Enterprises or Manor Care. More than 1.5 million residents were living in nursing homes (National Center for Health Statistics, 1997).

Federal participation in the cost of assistance for indigent persons in private institutions was first authorized in 1953, but the ban on payment to public institutions continued. However, if states wanted to participate in the federal program, they were required to establish some standards for the institutions. Also, in the 1950s, several federal acts authorized monies through grants and loans for constructing and equipping long-term care institutions. The Hill-Burton Act, the Small Business Administration, and the National Housing Act provisions were the most prominent.

The passage of Title XVIII (Medicare) in 1965 and Title XIX (Medicaid) in 1967 opened new and major funding sources for long-term care institutions. With this legislation, service delivery requirements were reshaped and clarified. Prior to the enactment of Medicare and Medicaid, there was very little consistency among what were defined as institutions of long-term care. Nursing homes, homes for the aged, convalescent hospitals, and chronic care facilities were all defined separately by each state. The new funding sources set common definitions and basic national standards for service delivery in this important area and long-term care (Winston & Wilson, 1977).

Dunlop (1979), however, has argued that the growth in nursing-home beds was greater before passage of Medicaid than after. Indeed, Medicaid replaced earlier forms of medical assistance, and has enabled the continuation of nursing-home growth while developing a mechanism for enforcing nursing-home standards.

Extent of Long-Term Care Programs

Despite the extensive increase in the number of long-term care patients, only 5% of people aged 65 and over were residents in nursing homes in 1990. Importantly, this percentage is related to age: Although only 1% of individuals between the ages of 65 and 74 were living in nursing homes, this figure rises to 24% among individuals over the age of 85 (American Association of Retired Persons, 1996). As people get older, their chances of being in a nursing home increase. Murtaugh, Kemper and Spillane (1990) estimate that 43% of the individuals who are 65 in 1990 will spend some time in a nursing home during their lifetime. Among individuals living in nursing homes, approximately 24% will stay at least 1 year. These estimates are based on life expectancies as well as current usage patterns of nursing homes.

Not only has the number of beds increased, but the size of the homes has also, which reflects the change from family businesses to larger corporations. In 1963, the average nursing home had 39.9 beds, and this had increased to 84.7 beds by 1982 (Sirrocco, 1985). Despite this growth, nursing-home supply has not kept up with demand. An examination of national data on nursing homes reveals that over 6,500 of the 16,388 nursing homes had more than 100 beds. Nursing homes under government auspices had an average of 126 beds, nonprofit homes an average of 101 beds, and for-profit homes had an average of 87 beds (Sirrocco, 1988). Occupancy rates in nursing homes now average about 87%, a figure that creates problems for social workers and families seeking a nursing-home bed for an older person. Based on the current health profile and growth of older persons, it is estimated that 3.6 million people will need nursing home beds by the year 2018 (National Academy on Aging, 1997).

Long-Term Care Patients

There is an inverse relationship between age and nursing home residency. In 1995, 35% of nursing home residents were over the age of 85, and 90% were over the age of 65. There is only a small representation of minority elderly in nursing homes: 88% of nursing-home residents are White. As could be expected from life expectancy data, almost three-quarters (72%) of nursing home residents are women (National Centers for Health Statistics, 1997).

Importantly, more than 50% of nursing-home residents have no living close relatives, which may account for the fact that 60% receive no visitors. These figures indicate that one of the contributing factors to nursing-home admissions is the lack of family support that might enable the person to continue living in his or her own home.

Long-term care residences are increasingly being used for the care of very old patients, most of whom have some physical or mental impairment and many of whom have no close family on whom to rely. Long-term care residences are closer to being chronic disease hospitals for physically and mentally impaired elderly than care centers and homes for ambulatory aged who are not self-sufficient (Tobin & Lieberman, 1976). This change has occurred in part because there are community and quasi-institutional options for those who are reasonably self-sufficient. Because of the change in the residential population of nursing homes, the care has become increasingly more medical, rather than social and psychological. However,

> the loss of physical or psychological self-sufficiency does not automatically mean the loss of social needs; the consequences will indeed be dire if we retreat to warehousing these most needy elderly and do not make every effort to provide life-sustaining social as well as physical supports. (Tobin & Lieberman, 1976, p. 236)

TYPES OF LONG-TERM CARE RESIDENCES

There are many different types of long-term care facilities for the elderly. However, until the creation of national funding legislation in the mid-1960s, there were no national standards governing the types of care in any given facility. As a result of the Medicare and Medicaid legislation, extended-care facilities (ECFs), skilled nursing-home services, and intermediate-care facilities (ICFs) were identified and defined in terms of standards of care. Since that time, many of the long-term care institutions have adjusted their services to meet the outlined criteria in order to be eligible for reimbursements. Even so, both more extensive care (such as that provided in chronic-care hospitals) and less extensive care (such as that provided in "assisted living" residences) are still under regulation as defined by individual states and, therefore, are more difficult to define nationally.

Assisted Living Residence

"Assisted-living" residences are becoming increasingly popular among more affluent older persons and corporations. Hotel chains such as Marriott are investing heavily in the development of assisted living complexes, and a number of corporations have as their sole business the development and operation of assisted-living complexes.

Assisted living has been defined as

> a group residential program that is not licensed as a nursing home, that provides personal care to persons with needs for assistance in the activities of daily living and that can respond to unscheduled needs for assistance. (Kane & Wilson, 1993)

Assisted living can also been viewed as a service bridging the gap between living in the community and nursing homes or as an alternative to nursing homes ("Assisted living," 1993).

A 1993 study of assisting living facilities found residents with a median age of 83 years and a median daily rate of $33 for a single occupancy unit. These rates are considerably less than those of nursing homes. In 1996, assisted living was estimated to cost 25% less than skilled nursing care. The fees usually cover three meals a day and private or semi-private accommodations, and transportation to doctors and social activities within the complex (Nordheimer, 1996). Needed assistance from staff with ADLs increases the costs. As consultant Jim Hall remarked,

> There is a strong but invisible medical basis to the new forms of assisted living. . . . People have privacy and can lock their doors. Staff doesn't walk around in medical uniforms. Instead of a nursing station, there is a concierge desk. Families feel comfortable visiting there. (Nordheimer, 1996)

As assisted-living facilities increase in number, there is concern about the quality of care they provide. Regulations have been proposed that would prevent small hotels or board and care residences from calling themselves "assisted living." Medicaid is also being asked to provide waivers that would allow Medicaid funds to be used to subsidize assisted living for lower-income elderly (Nordheimer, 1996).

Extended-Care Facilities

Extended-Care Facilities (ECFs) are defined almost entirely in terms of Medicare reimbursement. In actual operation, they differ very little, if at all, from skilled nursing services:

> The extended care facility is a short-term convalescent care facility specifically arranged to take care of carefully selected patients coming from hospitals. . . It involves aspects of rehabilitation, social work, high-quality medical and nursing care, and supportive services—that is, those services usually associated with long-term care of high quality. (Cohen, 1974, p. 20)

Extended care is defined more in terms of the length of stay, origin of the patient, and rehabilitative potential than by the type of services that are actually given. Because Medicare defines eligibility for extended care so narrowly, there are very few ECF beds actually in use, and those beds that are available are usually in skilled nursing facilities. Currently, almost all long-term nursing-related care falls into the other two categories: skilled-nursing care and intermediate care.

Skilled-Nursing Facilities

Skilled-nursing facilities are required to provide certain services, including

> the emergency and ongoing services of a physician, nursing care, rehabilitative services, pharmaceutical services, dietetic services, laboratory and radiologic services, dental services, social services, and activity services (Glasscote et al., 1976, p. 34).

Some of these services must be a part of the facility itself, but rehabilitative, laboratory, radiological, social, and dental services may be provided by formal contractual agreement with outside resources.

There must be visits by attending physicians every 30 days of the first 90 days of a patient's stay. After that time, if justified, the visits can be reduced to every 60 days. A patient care plan should also be prepared and reviewed regularly, so that the patient is assured of receiving services that are needed, and so that changing conditions are being translated into appropriate care.

In 1986, a report of the National Institute of Medicine criticized the quality of care and life in nursing homes. The report stressed the need for greater federal involvement in the regulation of nursing-home operation. In 1987 new federal rules were passed in Congress that strengthened inspection of nursing homes accepting Medicare or Medicaid funds. Although the states can waive the rules in some cases, these homes must have a registered nurse on duty at least 8 hours each day and a licensed practical nurse on duty at all times. A social worker with a bachelor's degree in social work is required at all homes of over 120 beds. In addition, new training requirements for aides were instituted. Regular programs of activities, use and preparation of drugs, and physical facilities in relation to fire and safety codes are carefully delineated for skilled nursing facilities. In general, skilled-nursing facilities can be characterized as medical institutions that care for patients who are severely ill.

The most recent development in skilled-nursing home care is the growth of separate units within existing homes, or even separate nursing homes, for Alzheimer's Disease patients. These "special-care units" began in the 1980s. Fifteen percent of nursing homes now have special care units that provide 50,000 beds to older persons with Alzheimer's Disease or related disorders. These units vary in size, staff, auspices and programs. Although this diversity provides options for patients and their families it has made evaluation of the effectiveness of the program difficult. Studies now underway are attempting to answer many questions about special-care units, including what elements of these units make a difference in the functioning of residents, and which attempted interventions in the special-care units are most effective (Advisory Panel on Alzheimer's Disease, 1996).

Intermediate-Care Facilities

ICFs were defined in conjunction with the Medicaid legislation of the late 1960s. The definition evolved from the recognition that a large number of poor people were not ill enough to require full-time professional staff attention, but did need health supervision and access to various health and rehabilitative components (Glasscote et al., 1976). This level of care is defined only in terms of Medicaid reimbursement. Those patients who are paying privately pay a fee which is established by the nursing home, and are not involved in the definitions of levels of care.

Intermediate care can be provided not only in facilities that are set up for that purpose, but in skilled-care facilities, homes for the aged, hospitals, or personal-care homes. In other words, as with skilled care, the definition of intermediate care lies in the level of care provided, rather than in the facility providing that care.

Many regulations are the same as for skilled nursing facilities:

> Regulations for construction, sanitation, safety, and the handling of drugs are very similar. Theoretically and philosophically the difference is that the SNF is a "medical" institution and the ICF is a "health" institution. In the ICF, social and recreational policy is to be given near equal emphasis with medical policy. (Glasscote et al., 1976, p. 39)

In addition, there are lesser requirements for supervisory personnel. For example, on the day shift, nursing services must be supervised full-time by either a registered nurse or a licensed practical nurse. This is a less sophisticated nursing requirement than that of the skilled nursing facility.

The federal regulations for both skilled nursing facilities and ICFs leave room for interpretation, new regulations, and elaboration. This is important, because it allows the states who administer, supervise, and control the nursing home program to build an improved program based on their own particular needs and resources. It is also the states that set the criteria of who is eligible for which level of care. Potential patients who are eligible for Medicare must have their conditions reviewed by the locally designated authority to determine the appropriate level of care for each condition. The nursing home is then reimbursed for the designated level of care, with the intermediate level determination receiving less reimbursement than the skilled level. The levels of care must be separated, either by facility or by wings in a facility. Because of this requirement, if the condition of a patient already admitted to a nursing home should change to the extent that the required level of care changes, that patient will either be moved to another section of the nursing home or, in some cases, be moved to another facility. A private paying patient who becomes eligible for Medicaid after admission will, at that time, be evaluated and assigned a level of care that might or might not require a physical change.

In 1986, half of nursing homes were skilled nursing facilities. Representing the largest facilities, these homes account for almost 65% of certified and uncertified nursing home beds in the United States (Sirrocco, 1988).

Mental Hospitals

Mental hospitals continue to care for the elderly, but not in as significant numbers as before. Older persons now constitute 23% of the patients in state hospitals, but by 1983 older persons accounted for only 5.5% of admissions (Lebowitz, 1987). Many of the older patients are among the long-term hospital population. Large numbers of older individuals were transferred out of state mental hospitals following the passage of Medicare and Medicaid legislation. Many of these former state hospital patients instead became residents of nursing homes. The number of older patients in state hospitals has also been restricted by decisions in state and federal courts, which have made grounds for involuntary commitment to mental hospitals much more stringent.

Since 1989 the federal government has attempted to restrict the use of nursing homes as substitutes for mental hospitals. At present, nursing facilities may not admit anyone with mental illness or retardation to a nursing home unless they are first evaluated by the state to determine whether they need the services of a nursing home and active mental health treatment. Once admitted to a nursing home, the resident's condition must be reviewed annually to assess if he or she still need to be in the nursing home and need active mental health treatment. If the answer on these two criteria is negative, the resident must be discharged from the nursing home. Anyone who has resided in the nursing home for more than 30 months has the choice to stay in the facility or move to another setting. The state must also provide treatment for those individuals in the nursing home whose assessment indicates it is needed. Importantly, Alzheimer's Disease and dementia are not considered mental illnesses under Pre-Admission and Annual Resident Review. If this assessment and review process is enforced and substantial numbers of older persons are either kept out of nursing homes, hospitals, or are discharged, there may be problems related to finding appropriate placements for these individuals (Jones & Kamter, 1989).

FUNDING

The funding system of long-term care facilities has been a major influence on the development of types of facilities and care that are available. The two most important sources, in terms of shaping the long-term care industry, are Medicare and Medicaid. As indicated earlier, Medicare legislation, which was passed in 1965, authorized care in a long-term care institution for those patients who were hospitalized for at least 3 consecutive days, who needed skilled nursing care, and who were to be admitted to a Medicare-certified facility within 14 days of their discharge from the hospital. The patient had to be evaluated regularly and could stay in the long-term care facilities for no longer than 90 days under Medicare. This new funding source made ECFs very popular in the last half of the 1960s, as it was an excellent vehicle for shortening hospital stays.

In 1969, the rapidly rising costs for the program led to a change in the regulations. New administrative regulations required that participants in the program have rehabilitative potential. In addition, nursing care was defined in more narrow terms, which included only a very limited number of diagnoses and therapeutic situations. The effect of these new regulations was to virtually cut off Medicare as a vehicle for nursing-home care for the elderly (Moss & Halmandaris, 1977). Because many nursing homes were caught losing thousands of dollars in disallowed costs at the time the regulations changed, the number of nursing homes that even wanted to participate in the Medicare program dramatically decreased. However, the precedent of reimbursement for medical long-term care was set.

Legislation establishing Medicaid—a system of medical cost reimbursement for the poor—opened the greatest opportunity for funding nursing-home care. In 1995, Medicaid expenditures for long-term care amounted to $40.3 billion. The predominant expenditure ($36 billion) was for nuring homes. Out of a total of $77.9 billion being spent for nursing homes, 37% was paid for by older persons and their families (National Academy on Aging, 1997). Since Medicaid is a shared federal-state program, the federal government provides a basic set of requirements upon which the states build the program. The states determine their own definitions of "needy"; there is some flexibility from state to state as to who is eligible for Medicaid in long-term care institutions. States can include the categorically needy—those who are eligible for federally aided financial assistance—and the medically needy—those whose incomes are sufficient for daily living expenses, but are not enough to pay for medical expenses. Because of the nature of this definition, persons who might not be eligible while in the community could be eligible for Medicaid if entering a long-term care residence. Often, the residential Medicaid eligibility factors for long-term care residences relate more to personal assets than monthly income, and so once the assets are liquidated, a person entering a nursing home can become eligible for Medicaid reimbursements.

Formerly, to achieve eligibility, a married couple had to "spend down" almost all of their assets. One result was that the spouse who remained living in the community was reduced to impoverished conditions. Under the "spousal impoverishment" provisions of Medicaid, the spouse remaining in the community is now allowed to retain a maximum of up to one-half of the couple's assets and a minimum of $15,348 (in 1996). The states are allowed to raise this minimum. Raising the minimum to $20,000, for example, allows couples with assets of $20,000–$40,000 to preserve all of these funds for the use of the spouse living in the community. This new minimum would have no effect on couples with assets of $40,000 or more. By 1991, some states had raised the minimum to the maximum, a change that allows the older couple to preserve a good portion of their assets. The maximum in 1996 was $76,740. The couple's house can be transferred to the community-based spouse without penalty. Other possible transferees include minor, blind, or disabled children living in the house or sons or daughters who lived in the home for 2 years as a caregiver prior to the institutionalization of the nursing-home resident. Patients can also enter a home as private paying patients, and as their assets diminish, they become eligible for Medicaid.

Extensive publicity has been generated about potential abuses of Medicaid reimbursements. As Moss and Halmandaris (1977) point out, conflicts between profits and quality of care are likely when services become a money-making operation. The conflicts will be greatest in firms that operate a number of homes, since they may attempt to maximize their profits by lowering the costs they incur at any one particular home. State regulatory agencies, understanding the financial incentives of the nursing-home industry, promulgate reimbursement regulations that are designed to encourage quality care and limit profits. There have been variations in the success of these regulations.

Under the Medicaid program, nursing homes are reimbursed in relation to their costs. All costs must be included in the reimbursement fee, and the patient is not to be charged extra for services given. The states must set their reimbursement rates to allow the nursing homes to operate efficiently and meet quality standards. In setting their cost rates, the states are also expected to take into account the special situation of nursing homes that predominantly serve low-income individuals. Medicare also uses a cost-related system for reimbursement, but allows a prospective reimbursement for some types of nursing homes.

All patients in nursing homes under Medicaid are eligible for at least $30 a month in spending money for anything the patient wants, including cigarettes, haircuts, clothes, and magazines. This spending money is in exchange for the fact that any income the patient is receiving, such as Social Security, is to be paid to the home and subtracted from the amount of the Medicaid reimbursement. For those patients who can personally handle the money, the program is successful. However, for those patients who cannot manage their own resources, there has been potential for abuse in the use of the money, since it can come under the supervision of the nursing-home administration.

Private Payments

As already noted, a significant percentage of nursing-home payments come directly from the patients or their families. A patient may have significant assets and enter the institution as a private paying patient. At a cost of $30,000 to $50,000 per year, payments for nursing home care can quickly deplete all of a resident's assets. Between 1986 and 1990, 54% of all individuals admitted to nursing homes during that period were forced to rely on Medicaid reimbursements to pay for their care. The percentage is higher among residents who remain in nursing homes longer than a year (Rivlin &

Weiner, 1988). Unlike reimbursements under Medicaid, the home can charge the patient for extra services which may be required for care. For example, extra padding, extra toileting time, and extra time for feeding could all result in extra charges. Private paying patients usually cannot predict the exact costs of the home, and have no recourse if they object to the prices charged except to find another nursing home.

Much of the care which is provided under board-and-care, personal-care, and domiciliary-care homes is paid directly by the residents of the facilities. SSI and Social Security checks are turned over to the facility in exchange for personal care services that are rendered.

Long-term care insurance that covers skilled nursing home and in-home care is now offered through a number of private insurers. The number and purchasers of these policies increased dramatically during the last part of the 1980s. Although only 17 companies offered long-term care insurance before 1985, this number had grown to 130 by 1991. By 1995 these policies had been purchased by 3.4 million people (Moon & Mulvey, 1995). There have been strong criticisms of many of the policies offered because their benefits are inadequate and they do not adjust for inflation. Without an inflation clause, the policy may continue to reimburse $100 per day for nursing-home care in 1990 and the same $100 per day in 2020, when nursing-home costs may have risen substantially. Many policies have also contained clauses excluding individuals with preexisting conditions.

The policies allow the individual to choose a nursing-home benefit, usually $100 or $200 a day. For nursing-home care, the whole benefit is paid. For home health care, adult day care, and homemaker services such as meal preparation, laundry, and shopping, one-half of the daily benefit is paid. Some policies will also pay for respite care, including a stay by the patient in a custodial care facility or a visit from a companion who serves as substitute caregiver. An assessment that the individual had a preexisting condition 6 months before enrolling in the plan could delay payment of benefits for 6 months. The individual must demonstrate that he or she is unable to perform two of the Activities of Daily Living before becoming eligible for benefits. According to the Health Insurance Association of America, the cost of a long-term care policy for a healthy 65-year-old individual is about $3,000 per year (Brooks, 1996).

Long-term care insurance remains a new, important, but basically untested approach to long-term care. The expensive payments may deter many 65-year-old persons from enrolling. A 1990 study indicates that 84% of older people between the ages of 65 and 79 could not afford the policies then offered by nine insurance companies (National Council on the Aging, 1990). Even lower costs of approximately $1500 per year may seem high to the 55-year-old who cannot envision the future need for this type of benefit. The benefits for home care may also not be sufficient to meet the needs of severely impaired elderly who do not have relatives or friends nearby to supplement the care provided by a home health aide or nurse. Despite these problems, it is expected that the number of long-term care policies in force will continue to grow.

A combination of public and private long-term insurance may become more prevalent in future decades. A plan adopted in New York and a number of other states allows individuals who purchase long-term care insurance to keep a dollar in assets for each dollar of insurance they purchase. This proviso reduces the assets that must be spent to qualify for Medicaid. The equity of this type of plan for older people of different incomes has been contested as well as its ability to adequately pay for nursing-home care (estimated at $62,000 per year in New York) (Freudenheim, 1992).

State and Local Funding

State funding, which covers about one-half of the Medicaid reimbursement (it varies slightly from state to state), reimburses the board and care, personal-care, and domiciliary-care facilities when personal income is inadequate to cover the allowed daily reimbursement rate. It also covers the costs of individual care in mental hospitals, and in these settings the total cost of patient care is paid. One of the reasons for the increase in the number of elderly who are being transferred to nursing homes and personal-care facilities from state hospitals is the states' desire to develop a situation where the federal government is paying at least part of the cost of caring for the elderly.

Long-term care facilities provide an excellent example of how the funding mechanisms have shaped the types of services and the amount of service available for the elderly. In addition, long-term care is unique in that the majority of care is being provided by profitmaking organizations, a factor that both influences and is influenced by the funding available for this particular type of service. Whatever the source, the cost of nursing-home care is striking.

PERSONNEL AND PROGRAMMING

Staffing Patterns

Staffing patterns of long-term care residences are closely related to reimbursement rates. Homes attempt to meet state regulations regarding personnel while at the same time keeping costs in line with reimbursement allowances, including profit. Unfortunately, the end result is generally an inadequate and poorly trained staff. Aides and orderlies perform between

80% and 90% of all nursing care actually given patients. Most aides and orderlies receive no training for their jobs, and high turnover rates among these important personnel remain a problem. One important reason for the lack of trained and committed staff is the salary, which is usually at or just above minimum wage. This is a disincentive to produce a commitment to the job, to seek additional training, or even to stay on the job for any length of time beyond that of getting enough experience to get another, perhaps better-paying, job. However, any job training beyond the minimal in-service programs required by the homes would raise the demands for higher wages, which in turn would reflect directly on the Medicaid reimbursement figures. Community colleges are beginning to offer special training for aides, which in certain situations could help provide stability to staffing patterns.

The number of staff (including aides) actually on the floor of a nursing home influences the quality and amount of care given. The stated minimum requirement, which varies from state to state, usually says that a certain amount (2 to 3 hours) of nursing care is required per patient per day. However, when this is translated to personnel, it could be actual on-floor nursing care, or on-floor care except for lunches and breaks, absences, and vacations. For the latter, the actual on-floor care is half an hour below that required. The interpretation affects the care, the cost, the reimbursement rate, and the profit margin. Some states have been reluctant to interpret such regulations precisely until they can generate a Medicaid reimbursement rate that can pay for actual staffing requirements.

In addition to the basic nursing and support staff, homes are required to have access to certain types of professional staff. The extent to which the home actually hires the professional person required, as opposed to responding to the need through contractual agreements, affects the quality of care in the home. For example, actually hiring a social worker, a dietician, an occupational therapist, and a full-time physician brings more services to the home than using these people a few hours a week on a contract basis. The size of the home, the relationship of the individual home to a larger organizational structure (the individual hired by a chain of homes can work in two or three facilities), and the type of reimbursement mechanism all influence the extent to which the home actually hires the additional personnel required.

Programming and Advocacy

Beyond having an activity director whose responsibility is to provide some activity for patients, state regulations do not stipulate the types of programming for nursing homes. The result is that there is a tremendous variety of programmed activities available in long-term care institutions. Some homes make only the minimum number of programs available, while others establish links with the community to ensure that those programs most appropriate to the patients' needs are presented.

Sensory training, reality orientation, and remotivation are essential components of nursing-home programing. Reorientation of the patient to the larger world, heightening the patient's sensory sensitivity, and reestablishing earlier interests all help to improve the patients' daily functioning. As in other major services, the range of activities that may be well received by patients runs the gamut from picnics, dance, theater, and crafts to movies and guest speakers. Some nursing homes have links with senior centers, adult day care centers, and nutrition programs in order to provide ways of getting patients into other settings and of bringing community people into the nursing homes. Volunteer organizations from the community also provide special services for patients in many community nursing homes.

Programming that has a purpose and recreates the interests and talents of the patients is the most successful. Many patients have little opportunity to share their experiences and even themselves with others when they enter a nursing home. Programming can create these opportunities if it is seen by the patient as being meaningful. In a study by Dudley and Hillery (1977), long-term care institutions had the highest scores on alienation and high scores on deprivation of freedom when compared to several other types of residential organizations. The level of alienation in part results from the practice of placing restrictions on the resident's ability to make decisions. Programming on a voluntary basis, with a variety of activities from which the patients may choose and which, from time to time, they suggest, can have the effect of reducing the sense of alienation that comes with the institutional process.

Families can also be built into the programming for the home. As Miller and Beer (1977) point out, familial friendships are the most meaningful and the most enduring of all preexisting resident relationships. There are no substitutes for positive family relationships. However, if a patient has only minimal family ties, the nursing home can create an atmosphere of the extended family through its programming by bringing in volunteers and using other patients, when appropriate.

Two advocacy programs in recent years have focused on the special needs of patients in long-term care settings, particularly nursing homes, and on how to get those needs vocalized in a way which produces a response. One, the patients' rights movement, began in the early 1970s when several states passed patients' rights legislation in response to the belief that the personal rights and liberties of patients were being lost with the institutional process (Wilson, 1978). In 1974, the federal government developed regulations which established a set of patients' rights for patients in skilled and intermediate care facilities. These rights, which relate to individual liberties and dignities, are readily displayed, explained to the patients, and assigned to nursing-home personnel for enforcement. Some of the rights covered in the regulations include being informed of the services available in the facility, being informed of one's medical condition and the plan of treatment, being encouraged and assisted throughout the stay in the nursing home, being able to manage personal financial affairs, being free from mental and physical abuse, being assured of confidential treatment of personal and medical records, being able to retain use of personal clothing and possessions as space permits, and being assured privacy for visits by one's spouse. Unfortunately, there are conditional clauses that make enforcement difficult, and the only disciplinary tool available is decertification of the facility, a recourse that is too severe for individual violations. Despite the difficulties of enforcement, the federal government, working through the states, has made a firm commitment to enforce patients' rights.

The second advocacy program created to respond to specific needs of patients is the ombudsman program, which is designed to examine complaints by patients and, through investigations, give patients a voice in determining their own individual circumstances. Begun in 1972, five ombudsman programs were funded nationally as models of the ways that the program could be most effective. Two more programs were added in 1973. Today, most ombudsman programs are affiliated with the State Units on Aging and work through the Area Agencies on Aging. They still retain the objective of being the focal point for complaints regarding nursing-home care, but they also act as a nursing-home referral service, an organizer of friendly visiting programs, and a center for educating patients and the community on the rights of nursing-home patients (U.S. Administration on Aging, 1977).

In recent years, the role of the ombudsman has been strengthened through both federal and state legislation. The nursing home reforms place an emphasis on the nursing-home resident knowing about the ombudsman program. In New Jersey the state ombudsman is permitted to investigate complaints and hold hearings as well as subpoena individuals and records. In the District of Columbia the ombudsman serves as "resident's representative" and can file petitions for receivership, as well as complaints for civil damages and actions against the District (Schuster, 1989).

Despite these legislative enactments, representatives of ombudsman programs still encounter a number of difficulties. A survey by the National Association of State Long-Term Care Ombudsman Programs indicated funding problems that restrict the availability of ombudsman services and their ability to respond to complaints. In addition, the survey found a wide range in the frequency of services. Only 16% of the states in the survey report that an ombudsman pays more than one visit a month to nursing homes and the frequency of visits is even lower in board-and-care homes.

In these facilities, over 50% of the states reported no visits by the ombudsman. Overall, ombudsmen investigated 154,000 complaints in fiscal 1990
("Ombudsman provisions," 1990; "AOA release FY 19-00 data," 1992).

Title VII of the 1992 OAA amendments defines the functions and duties of
the ombudsman more extensively than in the 1987 amendments. The functions range from investigation of complaints to informing residents of long-
term care facilities about means of obtaining services and ensuring that the
residents obtain these services. The duties are similar to the functions, but
also include review and comment on proposed laws and regulations that
may affect residents; facilitation of public access to review of these laws
and regulations; and support for the development of resident and family
councils in long-term care residences.

QUALITY IN LONG-TERM CARE RESIDENCES

How well the long-term-care residence is carrying out its mandate, meeting
requirements, and providing the level of care agreed to under its contract
with the funding sources is evaluated through the inspection system. The
federal government provides the regulative substructure on which the
states build specific codes for operation. The states then divide the inspection responsibilities between local fire and safety agencies. The result is a
series of inspections of the homes for different purposes, which are, at
times, in conflict with one another.

The two biggest problems with the current inspection systems are:

1. inspections are primarily to evaluate the physical plant rather than to
evaluate the actual quality of care; because actual quality of care is very difficult to measure, long lists of physical requirements become the substitute;
and

2. there is essentially no weapon for noncompliance except revoking the
license to operate—a very difficult step, in many cases inappropriate to the
situation, both because the need for nursing-home beds is so acute and
because shutting down a home and moving patients is traumatic; hence, a
state or local enforcement body will not usually impose such a step until
after years of flagrant abuse.

Basically, most states have four components to their inspection systems:
(1) sanitation and environment, (2) meals, (3) fire safety, and (4) patient
care. This means that there is a visit by a sanitarian, a dietician, a professional review team, and a fire inspector (Moss & Halmandaris, 1977). In
most states, at least two of the inspections are to be unannounced,
although this is not always the case. Until the inspection system develops

better organized procedures and more effective ways of measuring the actual quality of care, this system will not be the best answer to improving the care in long-term care residences.

In 1987, a comprehensive set of nursing home reform amendments was passed, which went into effect in October, 1990. Under the amendments, skilled-nursing facilities and intermediate-care facilities are termed "nursing facilities" and are held to a single standard of care. Within each of these facilities, a comprehensive assessment of residents must be undertaken at admission, when the residents' physical or mental condition changes, and at least on an annual basis. These assessments form the basis of a care plan designed to help the residents maintain or attain the highest level of physical, mental, and psychosocial functioning possible given their condition.

Each facility must have a licensed nurse on duty at all times. A registered nurse must be on duty during at least one shift per day. The nurse aides who work at the nursing facilities must complete a 75-hour training course within 4 months of being hired. A physician must visit the home every 30 days during the first 3 months of a resident's stay and thereafter every 90 days. The amendments allow the visits to be conducted by a physician's assistant or nurse practitioner if they are supervised by a physician. A full-time social worker must also be employed in all nursing facilities over 120 beds in size.

All of the above changes are an effort to ensure quality of care in nursing facilities. In addition, the facilities must maintain a Quality Assessment and Assurance Committee which can identify the issues that need to be assessed and implement action designed to correct deficiencies. The facility must also offer an activities program and rehabilitative services. An independent consultant must be utilized to monitor all psychopharmacologic drugs. The amendments also include a clear statement of residents' rights in the home (National Citizen's Coalition for Nursing Home Reform, n.d.).

REFERENCES

Advisory Panel on Alzheimer's Disease. (1996). *Alzheimer's Disease and related dementias: Report to Congress.* Washington, DC: U.S. Government Printing Office.

American Association of Retired Persons. (1996). *A profile of older Americans.* Washington, DC: Author

AoA releases FY '90 data on Title III State programs. (1992). *Older American Reports, 16,* 156.

Assisted living continues to be hot issue, AAHA says. (1993). *Older American Reports, 17,* 259.

Brooks, A. (1996, August 15). Pitfalls in home-care insurance for the elderly. *New York Times,* p. B4.

Cohen, E. (1974). An overview of long-term care facilities. In E. Brody, (Ed.), *A social work guide for long-term care facilities* (pp. 11–26). Rockville, MD: National Institute of Mental Health.

Drake, J. (1958). *The aged in American society.* New York: Ronald.

Dudley, C., & Hillery, G. (1977). Freedom and alienation in homes for the aged. *Gerontologist, 17,* 140–145.

Dunlop, B. (1979). *The growth of nursing home care.* Lexington, MA: Lexington Books.

Freudenheim, M. (1992, May 3). Medicaid plan promotes nursing-home insurance. *New York Times,* p. 1, 20

Glasscote, R., Biegel, A., Jr., Clark, E., Cox, B., Wiper, J. R., Gudeman, J. E., Gurel, L., Lewis, R. V., Miler, D. G., Raybin, J. B., Reifler, C., & Vito, E., Jr. (1976). *Old folks at homes.* Washington, DC: American Psychiatric Association and the Mental Health Association.

Haber, P. (1987). Nursing homes. In G. Maddox (Ed.), *The encyclopedia of aging* (pp. 489–492). New York: Springer Publishing Company.

Jones, E., & Kamter, A. (1989). Advocating for freedom: The community placement of elders from state psychiatric hospitals. *Clearinghouse Review, 44,* 444–449.

Kane, R. & Wilson, B. (1993). *Assisted living in the United States: A new paradigm for residential care for frail elderly persons?* Washington, DC: Author.

Lebowitz, B. (1987). Mental health services. In G. Maddox (Ed.), *The encyclopedia of aging* (pp. 440–442). New York: Springer Publishing Company.

Miller, D., & Beer, S. (1977). Patterns of friendship among patients in a nursing home setting. *Gerontologist, 17,* 269–275.

Moon, M. & Mulvey, J. (1995). *Entitlements and the elderly: Protecting promises, recognizing realities.* Washington, DC: Urban Institute Press.

Moss, F., & Halmandaris, V. (1977). *Too old, too sick, too bad.* Germantown, MD: Aspen Systems Group.

Murtaugh, C., Kemper, P., & Spillane, B. (1990). The risk of nursing home use in later life. *Medical Care, 28,* 952–962.

National Academy on Aging.(1997). *Facts on long-term care.* Washington, DC: Author.

National Center for Health Statistics. (1997). *An overview of nursing homes and their current residents: Data from the 1995 National Nursing Home Survey.* Hyattsville, MD: Author.

National Citizen's Coalition for Nursing Home Reform. (n.d.). *A brief summary of selected key provisions of the Nursing Home Reform Amendments of OBRA '87.* Washington, DC: Author.

National Council on the Aging. (1990). LTC insurance out-of-reach. *Networks, 2,* 5.

National Institute of Medicine. (1986). *Improving the quality of care in nursing homes.* Washington, DC: Author.

Nordheimer, J. (1996, June 10). A mature housing market: Growing business of not-quite-nursing-home care. *New York Times,* pp. C1, 4.

Ombudsman provisions need clarification during OAA reauthorization, Congress told. (1990). *Older American Reports, 14,* 263–264.

Rivlin, A., & Weiner, J. (1988). *Caring for the disabled elderly: Who will pay?* Washington, DC: The Brookings Institution.

Schuster, M. (1989). Legal support to the long-term care ombudsman program: A practical guide. *Clearinghouse Review, 44,* 418–421.

Sirrocco, A. (1985). *An overview of the 1982 National Master Facility Inventory Survey of Nursing and Related Care Homes.* Hyattsville, MD: National Center for Health Statistics.

Sirrocco, A. (1988). *Nursing and related care homes as reported from the 1986 Inventory of Long-Term Care Places.* Hyattsville, MD: National Center for Health Statistics.

Tobin, S., & Lieberman, M. (1976). *Last home for the aged.* San Francisco: Jossey-Bass.

U.S. Administration on Aging. (1977). *Nursing home ombudsman program: A fact sheet and program directory.* Washington, DC: U.S. Government Printing Office.

Wilson, S. (1978). Nursing home patients' rights: Are they enforceable. *Gerontologist, 18,* 255–261.

Winston, W., & Wilson, A. (1977). *Ethical consideration in long-term care.* St. Petersburg, FL: Eckerd College Gerontology Center.

16

Challenges for the Aging Network

The 1980s were a time of growth and change in the field of aging. The number of programs and services grew so rapidly that criticism began to be heard about the "aging enterprise"(Estes, 1979). As is true of any health and social welfare endeavor, rapid growth produces critical discussion of the effectiveness of the efforts or the ability to maintain these endeavors over a long period. This has happened to programs developed through the aging network as it has in other social service and entitlement programs. There are, however, a number of differences that need to be noted.

CHANGES IN LIFE STAGES

Many social welfare programs maintain a social problem orientation: i.e., a problem exists and efforts need to be developed that target and reduce the negative effects of this problem. As has been argued vociferously over the past 30 years, aging is not a problem. It is a natural process that unfortunately was not allowed to take place in many societies. Mortality rates among infants and young children prevented individuals from reaching later stages of life. These later stages can be very positive or negative in their impact. What is clear, however, is that increasing numbers of individuals in developing and developed societies will encounter the later stages of life In developed societies such as the United States, these later stages may take on profiles that were not even contemplated at the turn of the century. This can be seen by a brief examination of the possible life course of Americans in the 21st century.

For many Americans, school has become an extended period of life. Where high school was an educational endpoint for most individuals in

1950, high school is increasingly seen as a terminal degree that restricts employment opportunities unless followed by a college education. Even a bachelor's degree, however, is now seen as an entry level for many professions. Increasingly, graduate education is required for advancement in fields that include business, law, academia, the health professions, and social welfare. With this emphasis, it is not surprising to find many individuals remaining in school until they are 25.

After this long period of education, individuals enter into their years of employment. Until the 1980's, it was assumed that retirement occurred at age 65. This expectation is no longer correct, since the proportion of workers retiring at earlier ages continues to increase. Many workers are now retiring as early as age 55, often encouraged by "buy-outs" from companies interested in replacing higher-paid, older workers with lower-paid new employees. The old phrase of "30 years and out" may thus still be true for many workers.

Having retired at age 55, the retired worker may now enter a period of retirement that lasts 30 years. This estimate is based on the life expectancy of individuals reaching the age of 65. In 1995, women could expect to live an additional 19 years on average, and men an additional 16 years (American Association of Retired Persons, 1996). The possibility thus now exists that the longest period of a person's life may be that time when they no longer face work responsibilities. How to utilize this extended period beyond "killing time" is one of the challenges that will face many older Americans. As the life stage of school expands at one end of the life cycle and retirement at the other, programs and services will have an important role to play in meeting this new opportunity and challenge.

POPULATION GROWTH

A social problems approach to aging cannot confront the implications of the growth of the older population. This growth means that the society has been able to mitigate many of the basic negative conditions related to poor environment and health that make it impossible for many people to enjoy their later years. That these positive changes can also be reversed is indicated by the substantial reduction in life expectancy that has occurred in Russia in recent years.

The growth of the older population, particularly the old-old (over the age of 85), is expected to continue, and could even increase if any breakthroughs are made in reductions in mortality resulting from cancer or heart disease. The challenge for programs and services is twofold: 1) to enable older people to maintain their health and social functioning and engage in activities that they find rewarding; and 2) to enable people to enter their later years with adequate financial resources.

The first challenge is one to which all service providers probably subscribe. The second challenge is more difficult. Even if this forms one of their goals, services targeted at older people can only hope to remedy or alleviate problems encountered by people at younger ages. These problems may be the result of a whole set of inadequate services available in the community. They may also result from major structural issues such as restricted job opportunities, discrimination, or inadequate educational systems. Statistics such as the high proportion of high school dropouts among Latino students have negative implications for the health and economic status of future Latino cohorts of elderly.

INCREASING DIVERSITY

The United States of the 1960s was a country of White descendants of European stock, with a substantial population of Black residents with African roots; a population of Native Americans whose numbers had been depleted through almost two centuries of warfare and impoverishment; a population of Latino residents whose roots could often be traced to periods before the annexation of the Southwest into the United States, and a small population of Asians, predominantly from Japanese and Chinese backgrounds.

The United States of the year 2000 is considerably different than the United States of 1960. The Latino population is rapidly growing through immigration and through a high birth rate. By 2010 or 2015, Latinos will be the largest minority population in the United States. Latinos stem from a variety of countries in Latin and South America with a diversity of cultural backgrounds and beliefs. The African American population continues to grow, but not as rapidly as the Latino.

The Asian population is also growing rapidly, and is very visible in its concentration in a number of urban areas. This population growth spurred on by immigration reform of 1965 and the end of the Vietnam War now includes not only substantial numbers of Chinese and Japanese individuals but also Vietnamese, Cambodians, Laotians, Filipinos, Indians, and Koreans. Political conditions in countries such as Haiti have also promoted immigration to the United States, political problems in other areas of the world, including Eastern Europe and Hong Kong, promise to continue the United States' role as the destination of choice of individuals suffering economic or political problems.

For some Americans, the changed political composition of the country appears threatening to basic values as well as economic opportunities. For others, it presents a new challenge: how to utilize the vitality of new cultural infusions into a country whose cultural institutions reflect a variety of European influences. Whatever our views on diversity may be, the backgrounds of future cohorts of elderly will be much more varied than they have been in earlier times. Some of the seniors who will be being served in coming decades arrived in the United States as adults of various ages. Others arrived as children. Some will speak English fluently, others will have only a minimal fluency in this new language. Some will have strong connections to family members in this country. Others will have lost family members through immigration to the United States. The aging network faces the difficult of developing the variety of programs effectively targeted at the needs and desires of all of these groups.

CHANGING COHORTS

In many locations, senior-center or adult day-care programs have settled into a pattern based on the background of current cohorts of older persons. At the same time, senior centers have also noted that their participants are "aging-in-place" and that they are attracting fewer numbers of younger participants than in the past. Some activities such as trips appear to attract younger participants, but other activities, including crafts and recreational activities, appear to have less appeal, particularly to men.

The problem of attracting new participants to a number of current programs and services will probably increase as the 21st century progresses. Many "baby boomers" born after the end of World War II have substantially more education and more financial resources than their predecessors. Their pensions and savings allows them to undertake a variety of activities, and their educational background makes them more demanding about the programs they find worthwhile. The aging network faces the challenge of developing the programs and services that will be attractive to the baby boomers and the cohorts of older people that will follow them. The success of initiatives such as ElderHostel indicates that many alternatives are available.

CHANGING HEALTH CARE

The fee-for-service health care system that served generations of Americans is rapidly disappearing. As Americans became accustomed to health insurance as a component of their employment, employers began to find health care an increasing part of their costs. It also appeared that older employees and retirees accounted for a larger percentage of health care costs. With the growth of new health technology and increased doctor and hospital fees, the traditional approach to health care began to shift dramatically in the 1980s.

Rather than hospitals being paid according to how long a patient stayed in the hospital, the new system paid fixed rates based on the patient's diagnosis. Health maintenance organizations and a variety of other arrangements have encouraged the growth of plans where physicians are on salary arrangements, or are provided a fixed amount for each patient they serve ("capitation"). With encouragement from the federal Health Care Finance Administration, health maintenance organizations have been encouraged to recruit older persons as members.

The overall impact of these and other changes in the health care system is not yet clear. There have been complaints about restrictions on needed health care by some older persons. There have also been complaints that health maintenance organizations are only interested in recruiting healthy older people who will not utilize many services, while leaving other older persons to the Medicare program. The challenge for the aging network will be to ensure that programs such as information and assistance and ombudsmen assist older people in their efforts to receive the health care they need.

CHANGING PUBLIC IMAGES

In the 1960s and 1970s, requests for funding of aging programs and services received sympathetic responses in Washington and in state legislatures. During the 1980s, the responses became less positive. For the first time, older Americans were seen as well-off individuals, an "interest" group intent on preserving programs that were only of benefit to them. As the numbers of younger workers continued to decline and the number of older individuals and retirees increased, attacks on Social Security and Medicare grew. Fears about the economy and federal deficits also promoted a view that changes in these programs had to be undertaken.

For the Medicare program, this meant cutting back expenditures by reducing reimbursements to physicians or hospitals and possibly requiring more affluent older individuals to pay higher Medicare deductibles or Part B premiums. For Social Security, this meant proposals to again raise the age of eligibility for full benefits.

Funding aging programs and services also became low priority in Congress. While the Older Americans Act reauthorization of 1992 ended in 1995, a new reauthorization had still not been signed into law by the end of 1997. Part of the delay may have stemmed from disputes about particular components of the Act, particularly the older employment section. It was clear, however, that reauthorization of programs and services for older persons was less important to Congress than finding mechanisms to ensure that these efforts did not become more costly to the federal budget.

LONG-TERM SERVICES

Whatever the changes in public perception of the aged, it is evident that services for this population must be long-term in nature rather than oriented to short-term crises. In a senior center, long-term services means the planning of programs for members who will attend the center for many years. The same is true of adult day care centers oriented to very frail older individuals. Long-term educational programs must be offered in a framework that emphasizes continued intellectual growth rather than discrete one-time short courses.

The most pressing, and the most costly, initiatives in the next few decades will be for long-term care intended to assist the severely impaired older person, including patients with Alzheimer's Disease. Nursing homes, home care, and adult day care are the most widely discussed elements in these efforts. Private long-term care insurance that pays for home care services and nursing homes is an important innovation, but its current high cost limits its appeal to many older persons. The quandary facing the aging network is how to develop financing mechanisms that balance payments by older individuals and their families with assistance from government programs. This need is clearly seen by providers of adult day care programs who are concerned about becoming eligible for Medicare reimbursement, particularly as the population targeted for this service changes:

> We certainly need more adult day programs. . . . We all know of areas in our communities that have no program, or are underserved, But, be aware. The field has changed, and continues to change. Fifteen years ago, the population we were serving was not as medically needy. Today the folks we serve are much more physically frail. (Schull, 1997, p. 3)

INNOVATION AND THE AGING NETWORK

The role of the public aging network in long-term care and in the provision of programs and services to older people is more in question now than it has ever been since the passage of the Older Americans Act in 1965. As Hudson and Kingson (1991) reaffirm, there can be no question that the intent of the Older Americans Act was to serve all older persons, regardless of their situation. Over time, as the economic situation of the older population has improved, it has seemed more important to stress the needs of economically needy, socially needy, and impaired older persons.

To some extent, the growth of provisions in the OAA is a positive reflection of the growth of the field of aging and groups concerned about specific issues. It is questionable, however, whether one major piece of legislation based on the administrative structure of State Units on Aging and Area Agencies on Aging can effectively embody all of these concerns. There are arguments that AAAs should become coordinators of all community programs and services. In the American social welfare structure, coordination is a difficult task because of the myriad of administrative arrangements that exist to provide services at state and local levels. Many of the most crucial programs and services for the aged are not under the control of the Administration on Aging. These include transportation, housing, education, and health care. Because the American social welfare structure is organized along these functional lines (e.g., transportation), an agency concerned with a specific population group (e.g., the aged) has difficulty pulling together the resources and overcoming the "turf" issues that will enable it to mount effective methods. In the 1960s, the federal Office of Economic Opportunity, organized to coordinate programs for the poor, encountered the same obstacles. Even if it were possible to implement, coordination of programs and services for older people by the AAA would not necessarily reduce costs for long-term care, delay nursing home placement, or lead to positive changes in functioning among older people (Fortinsky, 1991).

The expansion of the field of aging has also brought many new groups into the service provision arena. Hospitals, concerned about reduced numbers of inpatients, are promoting outpatient and in-home services. Private firms have begun to develop products specifically geared to older people, and the housing industry has grown very interested in the potential retirement and life-care community markets. Voluntary agencies now provide services similar to those offered through public agencies. Employers are beginning to offer elder-care programs for employees. Private case managers have developed a network around the country to serve families who can afford these services; private adult day care programs have also begun to appear in some locales. The public sector, which involves State Units on Aging and Area Agencies on Aging, is now only one element in an enlarged service delivery complex concerned about older people (Quirk, 1991).

The failure of federal funding to grow has made it difficult for AoA to maintain its past programs at an adequate level. Area Agencies on Aging increasingly chafe at federal guidelines about their programs since, for many, less than half of their current budget stems from federal funds (Fortinsky, 1991).

One possible source of revenue is cost-sharing. The question of whether sharing the costs of the programs with consumers is the appropriate mechanism for financing efforts of AAAs and State Units on Aging is a major point for debate. A second method of increasing income is for public agencies to offer services to corporations. Many Area Agencies on Aging are currently involved in the development of elder care services in the workplace. These services include education, caregiver consultation, and case management. In Massachusetts, one AAA offers elder care for the Stride Rite Corporation, the General Accounting Office, and General Equipment Corporation.

The model for these initiatives has been Public-Private Partnerships (PPP) in which AAAs cooperate with profit-making organizations to provide services to older persons (Boich & Hyde, 1990). While these PPPs may allow AAAs to expand their programs and services, they also raise questions that need to be confronted. Among these questions are whether the involvement of AAAs in these new partnerships will not siphon off their interest in other non-income generating activities. There is also the possibility that in their endeavor to develop these income producing partnerships, the AAAs will lose sight of the low-income and minority elderly who cannot afford these new services or who are located in less accessible communities. The 1992 OAA amendments require all AAAs to disclose the PPPs in which they are engaged and to demonstrate that rather than diluting the quality of the services they provide, these partnerships will enhance the quality of the services. The AAA must also provide assurances that the partnership does not result in employees of the private organization receiving preferential treatment.

Cost-sharing and Private-Public Partnerships do not resolve the issue of future directions for the public aging network and, in particular, the role of the Older Americans Act. Alternatives to the approach currently embodied in the latest amendments of the Older Americans Act are possible. This approach would narrow the Act's focus to a few priority services that are targeted at frail and impaired older persons and low-income elderly. While this approach would clarify the intent of the Act, it would certainly negate its universal emphasis and, over time, perhaps result in means-testing for eligibility.

A change in direction for the aging network cannot be made without extensive discussion and evaluation of the effectiveness of programs operated through the aging network. Unfortunately, evaluation of these programs is weak, partly due to a lack of standards. Rather than the effects of a program on any number of criteria, reports by AAAs, the state, and the AoA stress numbers of participants, numbers of meals served, or numbers of older workers placed in jobs. Kutza (1991) views these "failures to be self-critical" (p. 67) as weakening the aging network. The reluctance to be self-critical, however, also reflects the maturity of the aging network, and the self-protective desire of agencies to ensure their continued funding and existence. Full-scale valid evaluations of aging network programs now confront an aging network less concerned about innovation than survival, particularly in a period of economic uncertainty. The dilemma of increased demands, but limited resources, may force an intensive reexamination of the effectiveness of programs, the simplification of access to important programs and services, and the development of programs designed to deal with some of the most difficult remaining problems, such as long-term care.

These goals cannot be accomplished in a framework which views programs and services for the aged as separate from those for other populations. Social welfare advocates must unite in a framework that sees the needs of children, the aged, minority populations, and other groups as interrelated rather than competitive. A failure to bridge seeming differences in needs will mean continued competition for social welfare dollars—a competition that will eventually defeat the best intents of all advocacy groups.

REFERENCES

American Association of Retired Persons. (1996). *A profile of older Americans.* Washington, DC: Author.

Boich, L., & Hyde, J. (1990). Public policy and public-private partnerships. *Minority Aging Exchange, 3,* 1–3.

Estes, C. (1979). *The aging enterprise.* San Francisco: Jossey-Bass.

Fortinsky, R. (1991). Coordinated, comprehensive community care and the Older Americans Act. *Generations, 15,* 39–42.

Hudson, R., & Kingson, E. (1991). Inclusive and fair: The case for universality in social programs. *Generations, 15,* 51–56.

Kutza, E. (1991). The Older Americans Act of 2000: What should it be? *Generations, 15,* 65–68.

Quirk, D. (1991). The aging network: An agenda for the nineties and beyond. *Generations, 15,* 23–26.

Schull, P. (1997) Adult day services: Future directions: From a national perspective. *Respite Report, Special Issue: Adult Day Services: 10 Years in 2 Days,* Summer. Wake Forest, N.C.: Bowman Gray School of Medicine.

Appendix: National Nonprofit Resources Groups in Aging

Administration on Aging (AoA), Office of Human Development, U.S. Department of Health and Human Services, Washington, D.C. 20402; (202)245-0213.

Coordinates programs, services, and research to help older Americans. Administers and authorizes funds for major programs. Operates National Clearinghouse on Aging, which collects, stores, and disseminates information about the elderly. Responds to all inquiries from the general public. State agencies and local Area Agencies on Aging offer consultation, grant application assistance, program information, and help to individuals.

AoA is the major starting point for all program information. As advocate for the elderly, AoA is committed to coordinated action of all federal agencies with programs and services involving older people and to the development of comprehensive information and referral programs. If you cannot locate your area agency in the phone directory, contact the mayor or local executive's office.

Publications: *Aging,* monthly magazine updating national, state, and local resources, legislation, and agency news.

Other: *AoA Fact Sheets,* technical assistance documents, and other materials to meet the needs of the aged, general public, planners, and gerontologists. Publication list available.

ACTION, 806 Connecticut Avenue, N.W., Washington, D.C. 20525; (800) 424-8580.

Federal volunteer agency administering Peace Corps, VISTA, and Older American Volunteer Programs: SCORE, which draws on the skills of retired business people; Foster Grandparents, volunteers who work with children on a one-to-one basis; Retired Senior Volunteers Program (RSVP), retirees who volunteer service to helping organizations; and Senior Companions, older people who serve older people with special needs.

Grants made available by 10 federal regional and 47 state offices to private nonprofit or public community organizations on cost-sharing basis. For information on site sponsorship or volunteer participation, call tollfree number, local office on aging, or local RSVP program office.

Food & Nutrition Service (FNS), U.S. Department of Agriculture, Washington, D.C. 20036; (202) 447-8371.

Coordinates federal food stamp programs. Information available here or more directly from food stamp offices in most major cities. Six regional FNS offices: San Francisco, Dallas, Chicago, Atlanta, Princeton, Waltham; may provide consultation or speakers in areas of nutrition or food management. Surplus food for use by nonprofit, tax-exempt, residential institutions may be available from FNS; contact regional of fices.

Editor's note: While food distribution for congregate dining programs may be coordinated by this office, the Nutrition Program for the Elderly is directed by AoA, and inquiries should be addressed to AoA or its area agencies. Meals delivered to homebound elderly as part of this program may be paid for with food stamps; contact food stamp offices for information.

Publications: *Cooking for Two*, large-print recipe book; U.S. Government Printing Office, PA-1043, $1.25.

American Association of Retired Persons/National Retired Teachers Association (AARP/NRTA), 601 E St., N.W., Washington, D.C., 20049; (202) 434-2277.

National organization of older Americans with 2,000 local chapters. Services include legislative representation at the federal and state levels; mail-order pharmacy service for prescription medicine and other health needs; a well-developed preretirement education training program, Action for Independent Maturity (AIM); continuing education at the Institute of Lifetime Learning and its extensions; the Church Relations Office, which explores ways to expand services to older congregants; a travel service and insurance plan. Programs designed for chapter involvement: Health Education, Driver Improvement, Crime Prevention, Consumer Information, Senior Community Service Aides Project, and Widowhood Project.

Publications: *Modern Maturity*, bimonthly magazine of general interest and information for retired people; *News Bulletin*, practical monthly magazine; Better Retirement Series, individual booklets written for the older person: *Consumer, Food, Health, HobbK Home, Job, Legal, Moving, Pet, Safety, Anti-Crime, and Psychology Guide*, single copies free.

Other: Booklets geared to retirement preparation and the older person to parallel the various program activities; *Dynamic Maturity*, AIM magazine for the preretirement year.

American Society on Aging, 833 Market St., Suite 512, San Francisco, CA. 94103; (415) 882-2910. The ASA provides a national forum for the discussion of major programmatic and policy issues in aging for practitioners and academics. Society based projects (e.g., Aging in the Neighborhood), conferences and publications are supported by a national membership.

Publications: *Aging Today, Generations* (quarterly journal).

Asociacion Nacional Por Personas Mayores (National Association for Spanish Speaking Elderly), 3875 Wilshire Boulevard, Suite 1401, Los Angeles, California 90010; (213) 487-1922.

The Asociacion Nacional serves all segments of the Hispanic older population. Administers a five-state employment program for low-income persons 55 and over, a national needs assessment of the Hispanic elderly, and technical assistance to local regional and national organizations serving Hispanic elderly. National and local conferences on Hispanic elderly.

Publications: Newsletters and legislative bulletin for members.

Gerontological Society, 1275 K Street, N.W., Washington, D.C. 20005; (202) 842-1275.

Promotes scientific study of aging and application of research findings. Four areas of education stressed at annual meeting: biology; clinical medicine; behavioral and social sciences; social planning, research, and practice.

Publications: *Journals of Gerontology*, bimonthly journal of original scientific research (emphasis on data analysis, methodology); *Gerontologist*, bimonthly journal of applied research (interpretive).

Gray Panthers, 311 South Juniper Street, Philadelphia, Pennsylvania 19104; (215) 505-6555.

Eschews special interest focus; advocates change that will benefit people of all ages. Nationally, monitors issues of social justice and joins coalition groups speaking out on issues of health care, consumer fraud, nursing home reform, public transportation. Some 32 units in 18 states engage in community social action and legislative lobbying. Speakers bureau. Assists local groups to organize.

Publications: *Network: Age and Youth in Action, Health Watch, Media Watch Guide.*

National Asian Pacific Center on Aging, 1511 Third Ave. Suite 914, Seattle, WA. 98101; (206) 624-1221. An advocacy organization, the NAPCA develops demonstration programs and ongoing direct service programs. NAPCA also identifies community-based resources for the Asian/Pacific Island elderly and disseminates information through the nation via resources directories and a fax-on-demand system.

Publications: *Pacific Asian Affairs; National Directory of Community Services to the Pacific/Asian Elderly; Directory of Pacific/Asian Media Services.*

National Association of Area Agencies on Aging, 1112 16th St., N.W., Suite 100, Washington, D.C. 20036; (202) 296-8130.

National Association of State Units on Aging, 2033 K St., N.W., Suite 304, Washington, D.C. 20006; (202) 785-0707.

National Caucus on the Black Aged, 1424 K Street, N.W., Suite 500, Washington, D.C., 20005; (202) 637-8400.

Advocates attention and programs for the Black aged. Recommends public policies responsive to the needs of the older Black American. Conducts research, curriculum development in the area of Black aging, training of Black professionals in gerontology, training of Black elderly to assume leadership roles in services to Black aged, and aids in participation of minority social organizations and businesses in service delivery to the elderly. Also conducts employment program for rural Black elderly and operates elderly housing. National and local conferences on black aged.

Publications: Newsletters, job bank publications; reports on health, research, curriculum, and theoretical and policy perspectives on Black aged.

The National Center for Citizen Involvement, 1111 N. 19th St., Arlington, VA 22209; (703) 276-0542.

Advocate for voluntary action. Prime source of information on successful programs involving volunteers; files on over 5,000 projects are updated regularly. Strengthens voluntary action movement through leadership education in training volunteers and volunteer administrators; consultations and materials in the areas of public relations, fund development, community resources assessment, information systems development. Community impact through 31 state offices and local Voluntary Action Centers.

Publications: *Voluntary Action News*, bimonthly magazine for volunteers or organizations—includes program profiles, legislative updates, and book reviews—$4.00; *Voluntary Action Leadership*, quarterly forum for volunteers leaders and administrators, free.

National Council on the Aging (NCOA), 409 Third St., S.W., Second Floor, Washington, D.C. 20024;(202)479-1200.

Professional organization providing training, consultation, and technical assistance, under contract, to public and private agencies working with older people. Maintains Center for Public Policy, which monitors legislation, research department, and extensive library containing books, journals, pamphlets, and local project reports. Library is open to public. Special projects include the National Voluntary Organizations (NVOILA) and Generations United.

National Institute of Industrial Gerontology provides analysis and information in the areas of age, employment policies, job design, and retirement. National Institute of Senior Centers (NISC) guides local center personnel in operations, community coordination, and upgrading services.

Publications: Free membership periodicals include: *Perspectives on Aging*, bimonthly magazine of general interest; *Current Literature on Aging*, quarterly summary of recent publications with brief annotations; *Senior Center Report*, NISC's monthly newsletter containing news of successful center programs, new resources; NVOILA Newsletter, irregular newsletter of voluntary groups concerned with the provision of alternatives to institutional care.

Other: NCOA actively publishes in areas of interest to those working with or planning services for the elderly. Current publications list available.

National Council of Senior Citizens (NCSC), 925 15th Street, N.W., Washington, D.C. 20005; (202) 347-8800.

Information service to strengthen grassroots-oriented social and legislative action program. Prepares Congressional testimony on critical issues such as Medicare, age discrimination, improved housing, health care, and pension reform. Membership open to individuals of all ages and to senior clubs and groups. Nonprofit services include a mail-order drug program, health insurance, and travel service.

Publications: *Senior Citizens News*, monthly legislative newspaper for members.

National Hispanic Council on Aging, 2713 Ontario Rd., N.W., Washington, D.C. 20009; (202) 745-2521. The NHCoA is a membership-based organization that promotes the well-being of the Hispanic elderly through demonstration projects, research, policy analysis, training, development of educational and informational resources. The NHCoA provides an opportunity to the Hispanic elderly to use the resources of an organized effort to promote and facilitate the process of self help and mutual help to find resolution to their many problems.

Publications: Newsletters: *Noticias, Noticias en Espanol and Alliance.*

National Indian Council on Aging, P.O. Box 2088, Albuquerque, New Mexico 87103; (506) 242-9305.

The overall purpose of the council is to bring about improved comprehensive services to the Indian and Alaskan Native elderly. Membership consists of 40 Indian and Alaskan Native individuals, of whom 12 constitute the board of directors. The council encourages legislative action, communication, and cooperation with service provider agencies, dissemination of information to the Indian communities, and supportive resources; and, when necessary, it intercedes with appropriate agencies to provide access to resources.

Publications: *National Indian Council on Aging NEWS,* $2.00

Other: Reports: *Tribal Nursing Homes and State Regulations; and American Indian Elderly: A National Profile* (1981).

Index

AAAs. *See* Area agencies on aging (AAAs)
AARP (American Association of
  Retired Persons), 234–235
  pharmacy program of, 73
Abuse, of older adults, 107–109
Accessibility, of transportation
  systems, 85
ACTION, 233–234
Activities of daily living (ADLs), 5
Activities therapy, in long-term care
  facilities, 217–218
ADLs (activities of daily living), 5
Administration on Aging, *See* AoA
Adult day care, 192–202
  benefits of, 200–202
    evaluation of, 195
  cost-effectiveness of, 200–202
  definition of, 193
  eligibility for, 193–194
  funding of, 199–200
  history of, 193
  services of, 195–198
    debate on, 196–198
    respite, 198–199
    scope of, 195–196
  users of, 194–195
  vs. child day care, 192–193
Adult Health Development Clinic, 72
Advocacy, in long-term care facilities,
  218–220
Age, median, ethnicity and, 4
Age discrimination, legislation on, 112
Aging
  and dependency, 192–193
  without adequate income, 29–34
"Aging in place," 7

Aging programs, funding for, 20–24, 21t
  block grants, 21–24
  geographic, 20–21
Aging services network
  challenges to, 224–232
    changes in life stages as, 224–225
    changing health care system as,
      227–228
    changing image of older adults as,
      228–229
    increased diversity as, 226–227
    need for long-term services as,
      229–232
    population growth as, 225–226
  structure of, 24f
Alcohol/Drug Abuse and Mental Health
  block grant, 22
Almshouses, 204–205
Alzheimer's disease, special care units
  for, 210
American Association of Retired
  Persons (AARP), 234–235
  pharmacy program of, 73
Americans, older. *See* Older Americans
American Society on Aging, 235
AoA (Administration on Aging), 233
  budget of, 21
  and 800 number, 65
  and elder abuse, 107
  formation of, 12
  and nutrition, 123, 125–127, 128–129,
    132
  role of, 13-14
  and transportation, 84, 86
Area agencies on aging (AAAs)
  challenges of, 229–232

Area agencies on aging *(continued)*
  day care centers sponsored by, 197
  integration of mental health services
      into, 79–80
  legal services of, 101
  ombudsman programs of, 219–220
  service plans of, 14–15
Asociacion Nacional Por Personas
      Mayores, 235
Assisted living facilities, 166–167
  long-term care in, 208–209

Benjamin Rose Institute, protective
      services project at, 102–103
Block grants, 21–24
  and mental health services, 79–80
"Blow the Whistle on Crime" program, 96
Boarding homes, 169–171
Building Ties program, 80

Case management, 136–137
Categorical programs, 11
Child day care, *vs.* adult day care,
      192–193
Cliff vesting, 40
Clinics, geriatric, 70–71
Co-housing, 176
Community agencies, nonprofit, home
      care services of, 184
Community colleges, programs for
      older adults, 119–120
Community Development block grant, 23
Community health centers, home care
      services of, 184
Community mental health centers,
      73–75
  older Americans in, 78–79
Community programs, grants for, Title
      III, 14–17
Community service advocates, 100
Community service employment pro-
      grams, 18
Community Services block grant, 23
Community Support Program, of
      National Institute of Mental
      Health, 76
Competency, 106

Confidence schemes, 94
Congregate housing, 166–167
Congregate meal programs, 124–129
  funding for, 16
  history of, 124–125
  operation of, 125–127
  in senior centers, 146
Consumer fraud, 94
Continuing care communities, 173–174
Cost-sharing, of Older Americans Act
      services, 12, 230–231
Counseling
  about employment, 113
  peer
    in mental health prevention
        programs, 75
    for widows/widowers, 79
Crime
  concern about, 91–92
  and confidence schemes, 94
  consequences of, 92
  patterns of, 92, 93t
  victims of, assistance for, 96–98
  vulnerability to, 92–94
Crime prevention
  educational programs for, 95–96
  security systems for, 96

Day care, adult, 192–202. *See also* Adult
      day care
Deinstitutionalization, 75–76
Dental care, programs for, 72
Dependency, aging and, 192–193
Diagnostic Related Groups (DRGs), 50
Dietary programs. *See* Nutrition
      programs
Disability, risks of, 45–49
Disability benefits, Social Security,
      45–47
Disability insurance, temporary, 48–49
Discrimination, based on age,
      legislation on, 112
Diversity, as challenge to aging services
      network, 226–227
Domiciliary care, 169–171
DRGs (Diagnostic Related Groups), 50
Drugs, payment for, programs for, 72–73

Early retirement, and Social Security
benefits, 33
Earnings test, for Social Security
income, 34
Eating, and socializing, 127–128
ECFs (extended care facilities)
long-term care in, 209
Medicare coverage in, 52
ECHO (Elder Cottage Housing
Opportunities), 175
Educational programs, 119–121
for crime prevention, 95–96
in senior centers, 144–145
Educational status, of older
Americans, 8
Elder abuse, 107–109
ElderCare Locator, 65
Elder Cottage Housing Opportunities
(ECHO), 175
Elder-Ed program, 73
ElderHostel, 120–121
Elderly persons. *See* Older Americans
Elderly Protection Program, 108–109
Elder Support Network, of Jewish
Family and Children's Services,
137
Emergency guardianship, 105
Employers, sick leave programs of,
47–48
Employment
counseling about, 113
legislation on, 111–112
Employment programs, 112–116
Employment status, of older
Americans, 8–9
Entrance fees, for life care communities,
173–174
Ethnicity
and coverage by pension plans, 42
and life expectancy, 3–4
and living arrangements, 6, 6t
and median age, 4
and use of senior centers, 141–142
Exercise programs, 71–72
Extended care facilities (ECFs)
long-term care in, 209
Medicare coverage in, 52

Fannie Mae reverse mortgages, 176
Foster care, 167–169
Foster Grandparents Program, 117
Frail elderly, in senior centers, 145
Franklin County, New York senior
center, programs of, 147
Fraud, consumer, 94
Friendly visitor services, 189–190
Functional status, chronic conditions
affecting, 5

Gatekeeper services, in-home, 188–189
Gateway I program, 66
Gateway II program, 136åGender, and
life expectancy, 3–4
General assistance programs, 39
Geographic areas, funding by, 20–21
Geriatric Assessment and Continuity of
Care Outpatient Clinic, at VA
Hospital in Baltimore, 71
Geriatric clinics, 70–71
Geriatric Evaluation Services, 105
Glendale Terrace, 163–164
Graded vesting, 40
Grandparents, foster, 117
"Granny flats," 175
Grants
block. *See* Block grants
for Native Americans, 18–19
Title III, 14–17
Gray Panthers, 235–236
Green Thumb program, 115
Group homes, for mentally ill persons, 76
Guardianship, 103–109
consequences of, 104–105
elder abuse and, 108
emergency, 105
Geriatric Evaluation Services for, 105

Health care, roadblocks to, 69
Health care programs, 70–73
geriatric clinics, 70–71
in senior centers, 146
Health care system, changing, 227–228
Health insurance
history of, 48
private, 56–58

Health maintenance organizations
      (HMOs), and Medicare, 53–54
Health promotion programs, 71
Health status, of older Americans, 5
HMOs. *See* Health maintenance
      organizations (HMOs)
Home care. *See* In-home services
Home-delivered meals, 129–132
Home equity programs, 175–176
Home health agencies, 184–187
HOME Investment Partnership, 162
Homemaker services, 182–183
Home Ownership and Opportunity for
      People Everywhere (HOPE), 162
Home repair programs, 164–165
Home-sharing, 174
HOPE (Home Ownership and
      Opportunity for People
      Everywhere), 162
Hospitals, home care departments of, 184
Hotlines, for legal assistance, 99–100
Housing, 6t, 6–7, 154–176
   assisted living, 166–167
   board and care, 169–171
   congregate, 166–167
   domiciliary, 169–171
   foster care, 167–169
   history of, 155–156
   home equity programs for, 175–176
   home repair programs, 164–165
   local programs for, 162–163
   public, 156–159
   quality of, 154–155
   retirement, 171–174
   Section 8, 157–159
   Section 202, 160–161
   shared, 174
   state programs for, 162–163
   vouchers for, 159
Housing Act, 155–156
Housing and Urban Development
      (HUD), Section 8 program of,
      157–159
HUD (Housing and Urban
      Development), Section 8 program
      of, 157–159
Hudson Guild-Fulton Senior Center, 148

IADLs (instrumental activities of daily
      living), 5
Illness, risks of, 45–49
Impoverishment, spousal, long-term
      care and, regulations concerning,
      213
Incapacity, criteria for, 104–105
Income
   inadequate, 29–34
      risks of, 45–49
      unemployment and, 42–44
   minimum adequacy standard for, 30
   of older Americans, 8–9
   taxable, for Social Security, 31
Income maintenance programs, 27–58.
      See also Social Security program
   categories of, 27
   fragmentation of, 27
   for veterans, 31–32
Individual Retirement Accounts (IRAs),
      41
Inflation, and Social Security income, 36
Information and assistance programs,
      61–67
   access to, 65–66
   evaluation of, 65
   funding of, 67
   as gateway, 66
   goals of, 61
   history of, 62
   importance of, 67
   operation of, 62–63
   scope of, 63–64
   standardization of, 64
   types of, 64–66
In-home services, 179–190
   agencies providing, 180, 184–187
   coordination of, 181
   eligibility for, 179
   friendly visitor, 189–190
   funding of, 185–187
   gatekeeper, 188–189
   goals of, 180
   growth of, 179–181
   homemaker, 182–183
   intermediate care, 182
   personal care, 182

quality assurance for, 180–181
skilled, 182
telephone reassurance, 188–189
types of, 181–183
Inspection, of long-term care facilities,
220–221
Instrumental activities of daily living
(IADLs), 5
Insurance, health. *See* Health insurance
Insurance and Public Benefits program,
of Older Americans Act, 41
Interagency Task force on Crime
Against the elderly, 95–96
Intergenerational programs, 118–119
Intermediate care, in-home, 182
Intermediate care facilities, 210–211
IRAs (Individual Retirement
Accounts), 41

Jewish Family and Children's Services,
Elder Support Network of, 137

Legal services, 98–101
Legislation, 11–24. *See also* Older
Americans Act; Social Security
Act
on age discrimination, 112
on elder abuse, 108
on employment, 111–112
on home-delivered meals, 130
on private pension plans, 40
on retirement age, 111–112
on senior centers, 140–141
Leisure World, 172
Life care communities, 173–174
Life expectancy
ethnicity and, 3–4
gender and, 3–4
Life stages, changes in, 224–225
Living arrangements, of older
Americans, 6t, 6–7
Long-term care
in assisted living facilities, 208–209
in extended care facilities, 209
federal regulation of, 211
funding of, 212–216
local, 216

by long-term care insurance,
215–216
by Medicaid, 56, 213–214
private, 214–215
state, 216
history of, 204–207
increasing need for, as challenge
to aging services network,
229–232
in intermediate care facilities,
210–211
ombudsman programs for, 101,
219–220
patients in, characteristics of, 207
in psychiatric hospitals, 211–212
scope of, 206–207
in skilled nursing facilities,
209–210
and spousal impoverishment,
regulations concerning, 213
types of, 207–212
Long-term care facilities
advocacy in, 218–220
mental health programs in, 77–78
placement in, *vs.* foster care, 169
programming in, 217–218
quality assurance in, 220–221
staffing patterns in, 216–217
Long-term care insurance, 215–216
Long-term care ombudsman program,
101
LSC (Legal Services Corporation),
98–101

Mass transit, 84–85
Meals
congregate, 124–129. *See also*
Congregate meal programs
home-delivered, 129–132
Median age, ethnicity and, 4
Medicaid, 54–56
funding of day care services by,
199–200
funding of home care services by,
185–186
funding of long-term care by, 56,
213–214

Medical Assistance, 54–56
Medically needy, as qualification for
    Medicaid, 55
Medicare, 51–54
    financing of, 50
    health maintenance organizations
        and, 53–54
    Part A, 51–52
    Part B, 52–54
    payment for home care services by,
        185–186
    payment of physicians' charges by, 53
    premiums of, payment by Medicaid,
        55
Medications, payment for, programs
    for, 72–73
Medigap policies, 57
Mental health programs, 73–76
    block grants and, 79–80
    community, 73–75
    in nursing homes, 77–78
    older Americans in, 77–79
    preventive, 75
Mental hospitals, long-term care in,
    211–212
Minority population, older, growth of,
    4–5
Mortgage assistance programs, 162
Mortgages, reverse, 175–176
Multipurpose senior centers, 139–151.
    See also Senior centers

National Affordable Housing Act,
    166–167
National Asian Pacific Center on Aging,
    236
National Caucus on the Black Aged, 236
National Center for Citizen
    Involvement, 236–237
National Council of Senior Citizens, 237
National Council on the Aging, 237
National Hispanic Council on Aging, 238
National Housing Act, 155
National Indian Council on Aging, 238
National Institute of Mental Health,
    Community Support Program
    of, 76

National Long-Term Care demonstration
    project, 66
National Medical Expenditure Survey,
    on in-home services, 179
National Senior Citizens Law Center
    (NSCLC), 99
National Study on Food Consumption
    and Dietary Level, 124
Native Americans, grants for, 18–19
Needs, social, for aging services, 20–21
Non-English-speaking older Americans,
    services for, 15–16
Nonprofit community agencies, home
    care services of, 184
Nonprofit groups, list of, 233–238
Northwest Victim Services, 95
NSCLC (National Senior Citizens Law
    Center), 99
Nursing homes. *See* Long-term care
    facilities
Nursing Home Without Walls, 183
Nutrition, and socializing, 127–128
Nutrition programs, 123–132
    of ACTION, 234
    congregate, 124–129
    funding of, 128–129
    goals of, 123–124
    home-delivered, 129–132
    identification of other needs by, 128
    provided by Older Americans Act, 16

OAA. *See* Older Americans Act (OAA)
Old-age benefits, of Social Security
    program, 31–34
Old Age Pension, 29
Older Americans
    abuse of, 107–109
    changing image of, as challenge to
        aging services network, 228–229
    cultural backgrounds of, 7
    educational status of, 8
    employment status of, 8–9
    health status of, 5
    income of, 8–9
    living arrangements of, 6t, 6–7. *See
        also* Housing
    in mental health system, 77–79

minority population in, growth of, 4–5
non-English-speaking, services for, 15–16
Older Americans Act (OAA), 11, 12–19
and Administration on Aging, 13–14
appropriations for, 21t
employment provisions of, 113–116
funding for elder abuse services, 107
Insurance and Public Benefits program of, 41
nutrition programs of, 16, 123–132. *See also* Nutrition programs
objectives of, 12–13
provisions for vulnerable older adults by, 19
purpose of, 12
and purpose of senior centers, 16–17
reauthorization of, 228
services of
cost-sharing of, 11–12, 230–231
supportive, 15–16
target population of, 13
Title I of, 12–13
Title II of, 13–14
Title III of, 14–17, 140, 150–151
Title IV of, 17–18
Title V of, 18, 140
Title VI of, 18–19
Title VII of, 19
Older population, size of, 3–5
Ombudsman programs, 101, 219–220
On Lok Center, 183–184
Organized labor, unemployment benefits of, 44

PACE (Program of All-Inclusive Care for Elders), 54
Paralegal assistance, 100–101
Paratransit systems, 86–87
Part A Medicare, 51–52
Part B Medicare, 52–54
PATCH (Psychogeriatric Assessment, Treatment, and Teaching program), 80
Peer counseling
in mental health prevention

programs, 75
for widows/widowers, 79
Pensions, private, 30, 39–42
Personal care, 182
Pharmacy programs, of American Association of Retired Persons, 73
Physicians, charges of, Medicare payment of, 53
Population
growth of, 225–226
increased diversity of, 226–227
older. *See also* Older Americans
size of, 3–5
PPPs (Public–Private Partnerships), 231
Prevent-care exercise program, 72
Prevention programs, mental health, 75
Program of All-Inclusive Care for Elders (PACE), 54
Property, and Medicaid payment for long-term care, 56
Proprietary agencies, home care services of, 185
Protective services, 101–103
changes in, 106–107
in senior centers, 146
Psychiatric care, in nursing homes, 77–78
Psychiatric hospitals
long-term care in, 211–212
patients discharged from, 77
Psychogeriatric Assessment, Treatment, and Teaching program (PATCH), 80
Public assistance programs, 39
Public housing, 156–159
Public–Private Partnerships (PPPs), 231
Public transportation. *See* Transportation systems
Public Works Development and Investment Act, and funding for senior centers, 141

Quality assurance
for in-home services, 180–181
in long-term care facilities, 220–221

Race, and life expectancy, 3–4
Reassurance programs, 188–189
Recreational programs, in senior
    centers, 144–145
Rehabilitation, vocational, and Social
    Security disability benefits, 47
Rehabilitation Loan Program, Section
    312, 165
Rent, Section 8, 157
Research, funding for, 17–18
Respite services, of adult day care,
    198–199
Retired Senior Volunteer Program
    (RSVP), 116–117
Retirement
    age at, legislation on, 111–112
    early, and Social Security benefits, 33
    prolonged, 225
    vs. unemployment, 42–44
Retirement communities, 171–174
Retirement Service Centers, 161–162
Reverse mortgages, 175–176
RSVP (Retired Senior Volunteer
    Program), 116–117

SCORE (Service Corps of Retired
    Executives), 118–119
Screening programs, 71
SCSEP (Senior Community Service
    Employment Program), 114–115
Section 8 housing, 157–159
Section 202 housing program, 160–161
Section 231 housing, 161–162
Section 312 Rehabilitation Loan
    Program, 165
Security, in retirement communities, 172
Security systems, for crime prevention, 96
Senior centers, 139–151
    characteristics of, 144
    classification of, 143
    definition of, 139
    facilities for, 149–150
    frail elderly in, 145
    funding of, 150–151åhistory of,
        139–140
    legislation on, 140–141
    models for, 142–144
    programming in, 144–149
        educational, 144–145

examples of, 147–149
    recreational, 144–145
    purpose of, Older Americans Act
        and, 16–17
    services of, 145–147
    users of, 141–142
Senior Community Service
    Employment Program (SCSEP),
    114–115
Senior Companion Program, 117–118
Service Corps of Retired Executives
    (SCORE), 118–119
Service plans, of area agencies on
    aging, 14–15
Shared housing, 174
Shared ride programs, 87
Short-term disability insurance, 48–49
Sick leave, 47–48
Skilled care, in-home, 182
Skilled nursing facilities, 209–210
Social agency model, for senior centers,
    142–144
Social health maintenance
    organizations, 54
Socializing, eating and, 127–128
Social need, for aging services,
    definition of, 20–21
Social Security Act, Title XX of, 22–23
    funding for adult day care by, 200
    funding for home care by, 187
    funding for senior centers by, 141
Social Security program
    disability benefits of, 45–47
    financing of, 34–36
    income benefits from, 30
    income from
        adjustment of, 32
        early retirement and, 33
        earnings test for, 34
        inflation and, 36
        for spouses, 33–34
    old-age benefits of, 31–34
    survivors' benefits of, 36–37
    trust fund for, 35
Social services, departments of, home
    care services of, 184
Social Services block grant, 22–23
Special care units, for Alzheimer's
    disease, 210

Spousal impoverishment, long-term care and, regulations concerning, 213
Spouses, Social Security income for, 33–34
SSI (Supplemental Security Income), 37–39
State Outreach Counseling and Assistance Program, 19
State programs
  for funding of long-term care, 216
  general assistance, 39
  grants for, Title III, 14–17
Supplemental Medical Insurance, 52–54
Supplemental Security Income (SSI), 37–39
Supportive services, provided by Older Americans Act, 15–16
Survivors' benefits, of Social Security program, 36–37
Syracuse University, geriatric clinic at, 70

Taxable income, for Social Security, 31
Taxes, for Social Security income, 35
Taxicabs, transportation programs using, 87–88
Teaching–Learning Communities, 118–119
Telephone reassurance programs, 188–189
Title I, of Older Americans Act, 12–13
Title II, of Older Americans Act, 13–14
Title III, of Older Americans Act, 14–17, 140, 150–151
Title IV, of Older Americans Act, 17–18
Title V, of Older Americans Act, 18, 140
Title VI, of Older Americans Act, 18–19
Title VII, of Older Americans Act, 19
Title IX, of Older Americans Act, 113–114
Title XX, of Social Security Act, 22–23
  and funding for home care, 187
  and funding for senior centers, 141
  and funding of adult day care, 200
Training, funding for, 17–18
Transportation systems
  coordination of, 88
  financing of, 85–86
  future trends in, 88–89

lack of, 82
mass, 84–85
models of, 83–84
options for, 83
Triage program, 136

UMTA (Urban Mass Transportation Act), 84
Unemployment, vs. retirement, 42–44
Unemployment compensation
  extension of, 43
  in organized labor, 44
Unions, unemployment benefits of, 44
United States Housing Act, 155
Universities, programs for older adults, 120
Urban Mass Transportation Act (UMTA), 84

Vesting, of private pension plans, 40
Veterans, income benefits for, 31–32
Veterans Administration, foster care program of, 168
Veterans Administration Hospital, in Baltimore, Geriatric Assessment and Continuity of Care Outpatient Clinic, 71
Victim assistance programs, 96–98
Victims of Crime Act, 97
Visiting services, 189–190
Vocational rehabilitation, and Social Security disability benefits, 47
Voluntary organization model, for senior centers, 142–144
Volunteer programs, 116–119
Vouchers, for housing, 159
Vulnerable older adults, provisions for, of Older Americans Act, 19

Waxter Center, programs of, 148
Welfare agencies, in-home services of, 180
Widows/widowers
  peer counseling programs for, 79
  Social Security income for, 36–37
Worcester State Hospital, geriatric clinic at, 70
Worker's Compensation, 48
Worly Terrace, 163–164

Springer Publishing Company

A Secure Old Age
Approaches to Long-Term Care Financing

Kathleen H. Wilber, PhD, **Edward L. Schneider**, MD, and **Donna Polisar**, MA, MED

In this book, leading researchers in long-term care address the central policy questions confronting long-term care financing reform and advance the debate on how to fund long-term care services. The book offers an overview of the challenges that confront individuals, families, and societies facing worldwide demographic changes. It also presents proposals for improving the financing of long-term care. The final section provides a critique of the proposed models and addresses the policy and political context for future reform.

Contents:

- Population Aging: Consequences of Long-Term Care Financing
- Long-Term Care Financing: Challenges and Choices Confronting Decision Makers
- Private Insurance in Search of Market
- Public-Private Partnership: State Strategies for Sharing the Long-Term Care Funding Risk
- The Social HMO: Flexible Models for Enhance, Finance, and Integrate Services
- A "Three-Legged Stool" for Financing Long-Term Care
- The Good, the Bad, and the Ugly: Comparing Models of Long-Term Care Financing
- Cross-Cultural Comparison of Long-Term Care Practices: Modifications to Financing and Delivery Approaches in Seven Countries
- Policy and Political Context of Financing Long-Term Care

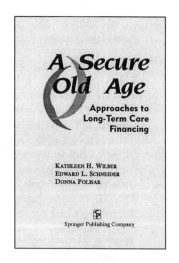

1997 208pp 0-8261-9431-1 hardcover

536 Broadway, New York, NY 10012-3955 • (212) 431-4370 • Fax (212) 941-7842

S *Springer Publishing Company*

Aging and Ethnicity
Knowledge and Services
Donald E. Gelfand, PhD

This volume contributes to the understanding of the process of aging among the ethnic elderly. Social issues associated with aging and ethnicity are addressed, and the author provides theories on aging and information on services available to ethnic elders.

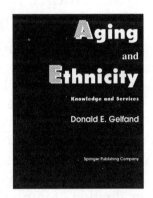

"This volume is organized to fill two existing gaps: 1) a lack of strong theoretical direction in the literature on ethnicity and aging; 2) a lack of material oriented to the service delivery issues that emerge from the characteristics and needs of the ethnic aged."

—from the Introduction

Contents:
- Ethnicity, Gerontological Theory and Research
- Ethnicity, Immigration and the Ethnic Aged
- Ethnic Aged in the United States
- Security and the Ethnic Elderly
- Family and Church as Sources of Assistance
- Reaching and Meeting the Ethnic Aged's Needs
- Programs, Services and the Ethnic Aged
- Paradigms, Assumptions and Assessments

1993   440pp   0-8261-7420-5   hard

536 Broadway, New York, NY 10012-3955 • (212) 431-4370 • Fax (212) 941-7842

𝕊 *Springer Publishing Company*

New Ways to Care for Older People

Building Systems Based on Evidence

Evan Calkins, MD, **Chad Boult,** MD, MPH
Edward H. Wagner, MD, MPH, **James T. Pacala,** MD, MS

The editors systematically examine successful interventions and those which fail to improve health outcomes among the full range of older people – from triathletes to those near the end of life. Focusing primarily on the person, rather than on the facilities or professionals providing care, the editors describe optimal systems of care. This book is a valuable reference for all health service administrators, medical directors, health providers, researchers, and policy makers concerned with the design and evaluation of improved systems of health.

Contents: Preface, *T.F. Williams* • Foreword, *R.L. Kane*

Section I. When the Older Person is Healthy and Independent • Prevention of Frailty, *D.M. Buchner* • Prevention of Disease, *J.T. Pacala*

Section II. When the Older Person is Chronically Ill or at Risk • Care of Older People with Chronic Illness, *E.H. Wagner* • Care of Older People at Risk, *C. Boult*

Section III. When the Older Person is Acutely Ill • Care of Acute Illness in the Home, *B. Leff and J.R. Burton* • Emergency Care, *C.J. Michalakes et al.* • Care of Older People in the Hospital, *E. Calkins and B.J. Naughton* • Subacute Care, *T. von Sternberg et al.* • Rehabilitation, *A.M. Kramer* • Care of Older People Who are Dying, *R.M. McCann*

Section IV. When the Older Person is Disabled • Overview of Community-Based Long-Term Care, *A.B. Ford* • Community-Based Long-Term Care, *W.G. Weissert and S.C. Hedrick* • Comprehensive Care of People with Alzheimer's Disease, *D. Johnston and B.V. Reifler* • Long-Term Care in the Nursing Home, *D.B. Reuben and J.F. Schnelle*

Section V. Concluding Observations • Integrating Quality Assurance Across Sites of Care, *E.A. Coleman and R.W. Besdine* • Integrating Care, *C. Boult and J.T. Pacala* • The Role of the Older Person in Managing Illness, *M. Von Korff and E.H. Wagner* • Medicare and Managed Care, *H.S. Luft* • Necessary Changes in the Infrastructure of Health Systems, *G. Halvorson*

1998   272pp (est.)   0-8261-1220-X   hardcover

536 Broadway, New York, NY 10012-3955 • (212) 431-4370 • Fax (212) 941-7842

Springer Publishing Company

Guardianship of the Elderly
Psychiatric and Judicial Aspects

George H. Zimny, PhD
George T. Grossberg, MD
Foreword **Jessie A. Goldner**

This book provides a basic explanation of guardianship of elderly persons and the process by which it takes place. Through contributions by geriatric psychiatrists, psychologists, attorneys, and judges, this volume provides a basic understanding of what can occur before, during, and after guardianship.This concise volume reviews all aspects of the guardianship process and provides new insights to insure that the future development of guardianship is in a direction that makes it as humane and effective as possible. This book is a valuable guide to students and members of disciplines and organizations involved with the care of elderly persons including: social work, gerontology, law, medicine, psychology, nursing, and finance.

Contents:

Part I. Introduction • Guardianship of the Elderly, *G.H. Zimny* and G.T. Grossberg • Legal Basis of Guardianship *M.B. Kapp*

Part II. Psychiatric Aspects • Assessing Competency in the Elderly, *F.M. Baker* • Psychiatric Disorders Affecting Competency, *D.P. Hay, K.K. Hay, G.E. Fagala*

Part III. Judicial Aspects • Judicial Process in Guardianship Proceedings, *J.N. Kirkendall* • The Courts, *F.C. Benton* • Judicial Decisions in Guardianship Cases, *James Brock* • Guardianship and Abuse of Dependent Adults, *I.H. Grant* and *M.J. Quinn* • Monitoring of Guardianship, *S.B. Hurme*

Part IV. Research • Empirical Research on Guardianship, *G.H. Zimny*

1998   155pp   0-8261-1176-9   softcover

536 Broadway, New York, NY 10012-3955 • (212) 431-4370 • Fax (212) 941-7842

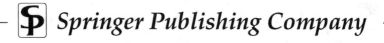
Springer Publishing Company

Societal Mechanisms for Maintaining Competence in Old Age

Sherry L. Willis, PhD
K. Warner Schaie, PhD
Mark Hayward, PhD

In this volume, renowned researchers examine how societal mechanisms and social support systems enable individuals to continue leading independent lives within their communities.

The chapters address topics that contribute to maintaining competence in old age, including: the concept of active life expectancy; psychological issues; social relationships; housing design; and institutional care. As a special feature, each chapter is followed by two insightful commentaries from experts in neighboring disciplines.

Contributors include Toni Antonucci, Margret Baltes, Eileen Crimmins, Victor Regnier, Timothy Salthouse, Fredric Wolinsky, among others. This volume is of primary interest to academics, researchers, and graduate students of social gerontology.

Contents:

What Can We Learn About Competence at the Older Ages from Active Life Expectancy?, *E.M. Crimmins and M.D. Hayward* • Psychological Issues Related to Competence, *T.A. Salthouse* • Does Being Placed in a Nursing Home Make You Sicker and More Likely to Die?, *F.D. Wolinsky, T.E. Stump, C.M. Callahan* • Long-Term Care Institutions and the Maintenance of Competence: A Dialectic Between Compensation and Overcompensation, *M.M. Baltes and A.L. Horgas* • Social Support and the Maintenance of Competence, *T.C. Antonucci and H. Akiyama* • The Physical Environment and Maintenance of Competence, *V. Regnier*

1997 304pp 0-8261-9690-X hardcover

536 Broadway, New York, NY 10012-3955 • (212) 431-4370 • Fax (212) 941-7842